SAMURAI BATTLES

JAPAN'S WARRIOR LORDS IN
700 YEARS OF CONFLICT

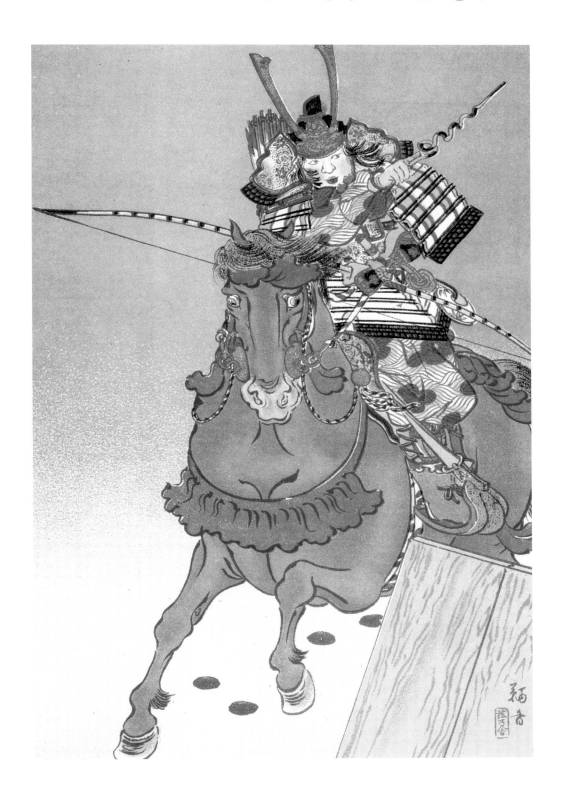

SAMURAI BATTLES

JAPAN'S WARRIOR LORDS IN
700 YEARS OF CONFLICT

MICHAEL SHARPE

First published in 2009 by

CHARTWELL BOOKS, INC.
A Division of
BOOK SALES, INC.
114 Northfield Avenue
Edison, New Jersey 08837

ISBN 13: 978-0-7858-2379-7
ISBN 10: 0-7858-2379-4

Project manager: Ray Bonds
Designer: Mark Tennent
Maps: Mark Franklin

Printed and bound in China

Page 1: Minamoto Yoritomo was the founder and first *shogun* of the Kamakura *Shogunate*. He had Imperial blood from his father and Fujiwara noble blood from his mother. *(The Art Archive)*

Pages 2-3: Takeda Shingen defends himself with his *Gumpai-wichiwa* (fan) when attacked by Uesuji Kenshin during the Fourth Battle of Kawakanajima. *(via Clive Sinclair)*

Right: Torii Mototada on horseback with his retinue. *(British Museum/Jo St Mart)*

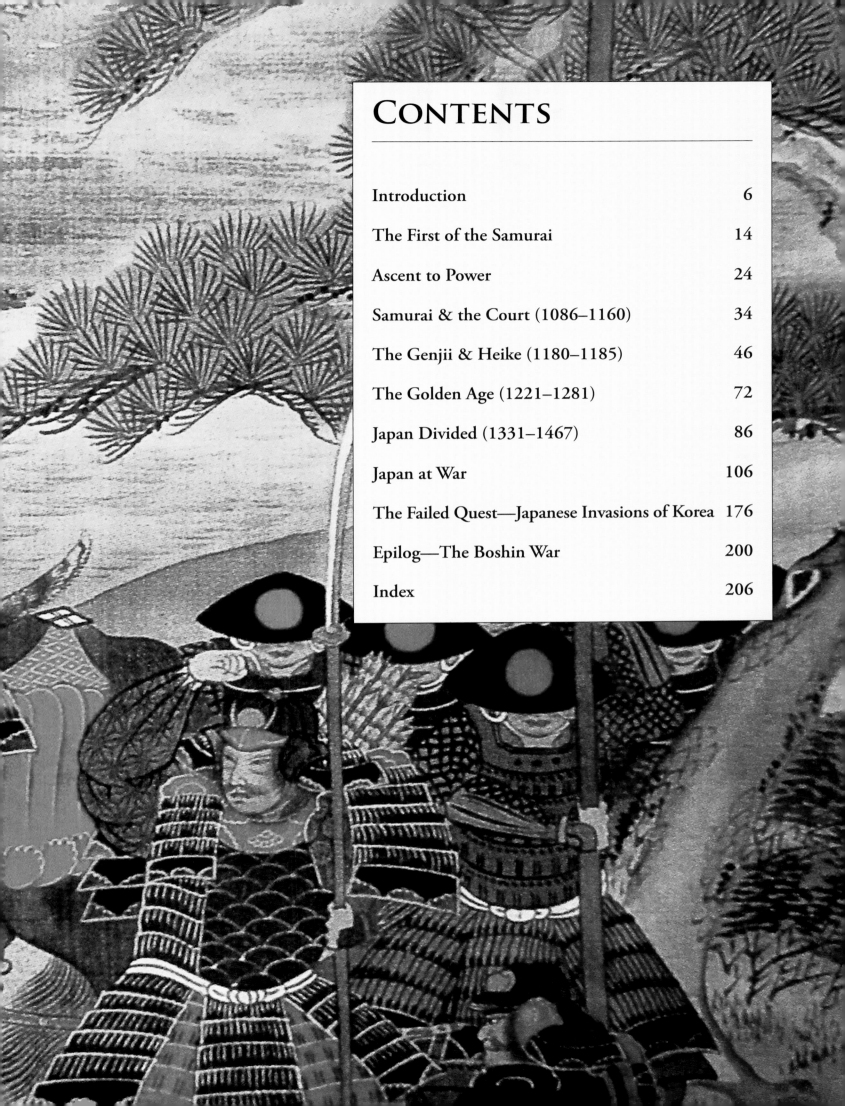

CONTENTS

INTRODUCTION

Japanese history and culture continue to have a strong draw on the popular imagination, fueled in no small part by Japan's comparatively recent isolationist stance and enigmatic character. It is conspicuous that so much of the literature about Japan concerns the unique class of men we know as the *samurai*. In some ways it is puzzling that, for a country that has such cultural richness, so much attention should focus on the *samurai*. The fascination is perhaps best explained by an examination of cross-cultural traditions that herald the virtues of the warrior. The *samurai*, it seems, embody many of the virtues we venerate. In Japan, too, the *samurai* are revered and lauded as heroes of a bygone age of chivalry that many Japanese uphold with deep regard.

Below: Saigo Takamori (1827–1877), Japanese leader in the Meiji Period, carries out *seppuku* (ritual suicide). *(The Art Archive/Private Collection/Laurie Platt Winfrey)*

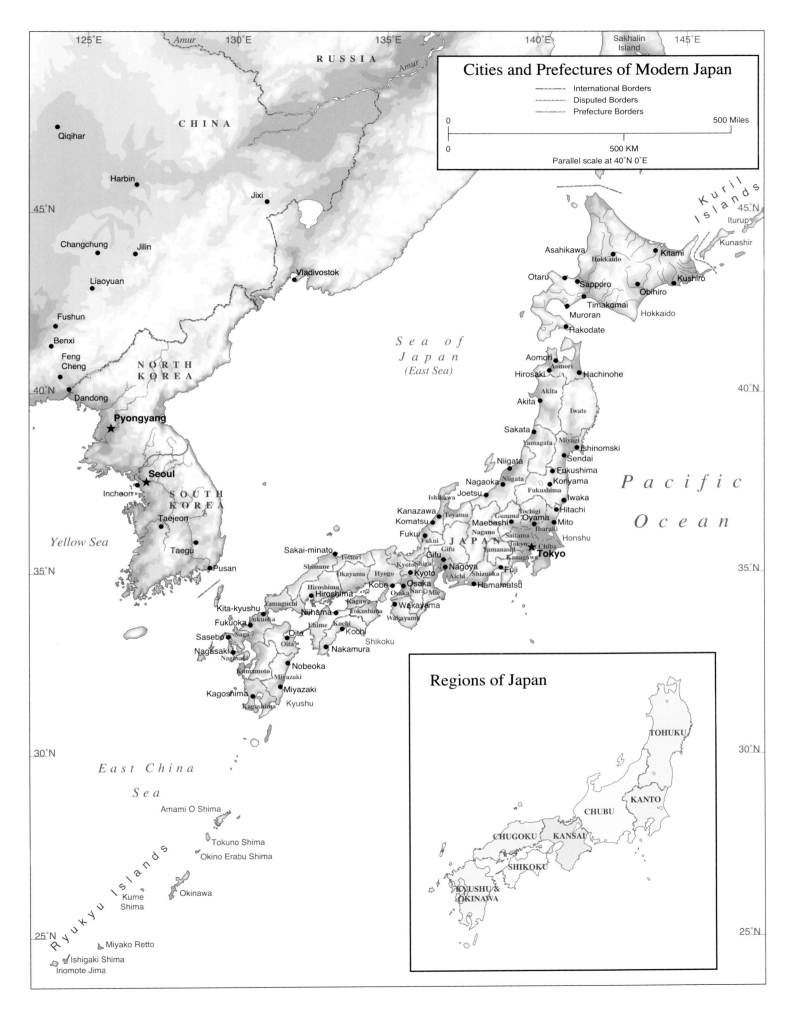

Cities and Prefectures of Modern Japan

International Borders
Disputed Borders
Prefecture Borders

0   500 Miles

0   500 KM
Parallel scale at 40°N 0°E

RUSSIA

Amur

CHINA

Qiqihar

Harbin

Jixi

Changchung   Jilin

Liaoyuan

Vladivostok

Fushun

Benxi

Feng
Cheng

Dandong

NORTH
KOREA

Pyongyang

Seoul

Incheon

SOUTH
KOREA

Taejeon

Yellow Sea

Taegu

Pusan

Sakai-minato

Kita-kyushu

Fukuoka

Sasebo

Nagasaki

Kumamoto

Kagoshima

Nobeoka

Miyazaki

Kyushu

East China

Sea

Amami O Shima

Tokuno Shima

Okino Erabu Shima

Ryukyu Islands

Kume
Shima

Okinawa

Miyako Retto

Ishigaki Shima
Iriomote Jima

*Sea of
Japan
(East Sea)*

Asahikawa   Hokkaido   Kitami

Otaru   Sapporo   Obihiro   Kushiro

Timakomai
Muroran   Hokkaido

Hakodate

Aomori   Aomori   Hachinohe
Hirosaki

Akita   Akita   Iwate

Sakata   Yamagata   Miyagi   Ishinomski

Niigata   Sendai

Nagaoka   Niigata   Fukushima
Koriyama

Joetsu   Fukushima   Iwaka

Ishikawa   Hitachi

Kanazawa   Toyama   Tochigi   Oyama   Mito
Komatsu   Gumma   Ibaraki

Maebashi

Fukui   Nagano   Saitama   Honshu
Fukui   JAPAN   Tokyo
Gifu   Gifu   Yamanashi   Kanagawa   Tokyo

Tottori   Shiga   Nagoya   Chiba
Shimane   Kyoto   Shizuoka   Fuji
Okayama   Hyogo   Kyoto   Aichi   Hamamatsu
Osaka
Hiroshima   Kobe   Nara   Mie
Hiroshima   Osaka
Yamaguchi   Kagawa   Wakayama
Nihama   Tokushima   Wakayama

Ehime   Kochi
Oita   Kochi
Saga   Oita   Shikoku
Nagasaki   Nakamura

Miyazaki
Miyazaki
Kagoshima

Pacific

Ocean

Tokyo

*Sakhalin
Island*

*Kuril
Islands*

Iturup

Kunashir

Regions of Japan

TOHUKU

CHUBU   KANTO

CHUGOKU   KANSAI

SHIKOKU

KYUSHU &
OKINAWA

7

The art and practice of warfare was a fundament of the *samurai*, and was regarded with a zeal that cannot be overestimated. One of the tenets of the *samurai* ethical code (*bushido*), which was very roughly outlined in the mid-Heian Period (795–1198), is the absolute requirement to die a "good death" with one's honor intact. This could be achieved in two ways, through *seppuku* (ritual suicide) at one's own hand, or else on the battlefield. Either was preferable to defeat, a fate far worse than dishonor. The battles the *samurai* fought thus take on an additional, dramatic significance, aside from the historical. This quote from the feted Asakura general and military theorist Asakura Norikage (Soteki) draws this into sharp focus:

> ***"The warrior doesn't care if he's called a beast or a dog; the main thing is winning."***

Beginning in the early days of modern Japanese history, in this book we trace the rise and fall of the warrior class over the space of a millennium, from the days of the birth of the Japanese nation through centuries of feudalism[1] to the establishment of the Western model of democracy in the late 19th century.

Glossary

ashigaru	foot soldiers
ashigaru-taisho	*samurai* placed in command of a contingent of *shogunate*
bakufu	shogunate; rule of the shogun; Japanese military rule
bakyu-jutsu	art of mounted archery
betto	chief administrator
bo-jutsu	fighting with staves
boshin	Restoration War (1868)
budo	the "way" of combat
bushi	warrior; name given to all warriors who made up families with a warrior tradition
bushido	"way" of the warrior; code of honor and social behavior, which succeeded the unwritten code of the "way" of the bow and the horse
chokuto	straight sword used in Japan's early history
daijo daijin	chancellor
daimyo	feudal lord, who maintained numbers of *samurai* in his service
daisho	a *samurai's* two swords: (long) *katana*; (short) *wakizashi*
do	chest protector
domaru	type of armor that wraps round torso and fastens at the side
ebira	quiver
Genpei kassen	Genpei (sometimes Gempei) wars of 1180–85 between Taira and Minamoto clans
Gosannen kassen	Later Three Years War— fighting in the 1080s in Mutsu province
go-tairo	council of five elders
han	domain
Heian Period	era when Japan's capital was located in Kyoto (782–1184)
Heiji no ran	Heiji rebellion; Heiji Incident (1160)
Hogen no ran	Hogen rebellion; Hogen Incident (1155)
Ikko-ikki	Buddhist rebellions against *samurai* lords during 15th and 16th centuries
insei system	Mainly seen in the 11th and 12th centuries, this system saw a retired emperor exert influence; also known as cloistered rule
jidai	age or period (eg *sengoku jidai*, Warring States Period)
kabuto	helmet
haishaku	attendant at a *seppuku*
Kamakura Period	when the capital was in Kamakura (1185–1332); also known as the "golden age" of the Japanese sword
kampaku	first secretary and regent who assists an adult emperor

At he core of this book are the battles fought by these warriors during a period of over a thousand years. Although the major focus is on conflicts between the 12th and 17th centuries, the initial chapters cover the history and conflict of pre-12th century Japan, before the time that the *samurai* are traditionally said to have "emerged"[2] as a distinct class within Japanese society. During this timeframe there were many hundreds of battles—far more, unfortunately, than could be reasonably included here. However, it is hoped that some sense of the matter is provided, and that the omissions do not detract from the reader's enjoyment. It is highly recommended that readers conduct further inquiry through any of the extensive references provided in the footnotes to the text.

Before examining the Japanese warrior class, the spread of their influence, and the battles themselves in more detail, a word on the so-called archaic (pre-7th century) period of Japanese history.

Prior to the first century AD there appear to be no written records[3] of the peoples that inhabited the group of islands that we now call Japan. There is general accord that, in around 30,000BC, the first inhabitants probably crossed the land bridges that once existed between Korea and Kyushu in the south and between Siberia and Hokkaido in

kanrei	*shogun*'s deputy
kassen	wars
keiko	one of the types of armor worn during Kofun era, with laces used to secure scales
ken	ancient, two-edged sword made before 9th century
kendo	"way" of the sword, developed from the earliest times by *bushi*
kokushi	provincial overlord
komaku	protective shield for an individual archer
koto	swords made before Edo Period
kutsu	shoes
kyu-jutsu	the art of archery
kyuba no michi	"way" of the horse and bow
mempo	face armor
Momoyaa Period	(1573–1599, when *samurai* bega wearing daisho
moshi-yari	spear
Muromachi Period	(1392–1572), a time of constant civil wars
naginata	halberd; long pole ending in curved blade
naginata-jutsu	"way" of the naginata
Nambokucho Period	(1333-1391) a time when two emperors were vying for power
ninja	a group of specially trained men and women, usually from the lower classes, employed by the *daimyo* to assassinate enemies and infiltrate enemy strongholds
rensho	assistant to the regent
ronin	"wave people," a term applied during the Tokugawa Period to master-less *samurai*
seii tai shogun	military commanders
Sengoku jidai	the Warring States period
seppuku	ritual suicide by disembowelment
sessho	regent who was named to assist either a child emperor before his coming of age, or an empress
shikken	regent for the *shogun* in the Kamakura shogunate
shogun	"barbarian-subduing" general
shugo	military governor
sohei	warrior monks
su-yari	straight spear
tachi	generic name for a sword
tanko	one of the types of armor worn during the Kofun Period
tenno	emperor
yari	spear
yumi	bow
yumiya	bows and arrows
Zenkunen gassen	Former Nine Years War

The History of Japan

Generally, the history of Japan is regarded as falling into three main eras: legendary (from earliest times up to about 60AD), pre-history (from about 60AD to 500AD), and historic (from 500AD onwards). Within those eras, Japanese history is generally accepted as being divided into the following periods and sub-periods:

Dates	Major periods	Periods	Sub-periods
30,000–10,000BC	Paleolithic		
10,000–3000BC	Ancient	Joomon	
900BC–250AD		Yayoi	
250–538		Yamato	Kofun
538–710	Classical	Yamato	Asuka
710–794		Nara	
794–1185		Heian	
1185–1333	Feudal	Kamakura	
1333–1336		Kemmu restoration	
1336–1392		Muromachi	Narboku-cho
1392–1573			Sengoku
1573–1603		Azuchi-Momoyama	
1600–1867	Early Modern	Edo	
1868–1912	Modern	Meiji	
1912–1926		Taisho	Taisho Democracy
1926–1945		Showa	Expansionism
1945–1952			Occupied Japan
1952–1989			Post-occupation
1989–present		Heisei	

the north, during the Paleolithic period. These people lived for thousands of years as nomadic hunter-gatherers; later, as subsequent waves of immigrants brought over technologies from the continent, a pottery-making culture known as the *Jomon* developed from about 10,000BC. By 500BC this was being replaced by a unique rice-farming and metal-using culture, again developed with continental knowledge, called *Yayoi*.[4] Through farming, these people came to live in clan-like communities called *uji*, and sought to defend themselves and their lands from aggressors. It may be that certain among them were distinguished in some way because of their martial skills, and if that is true then these were the first Japanese warriors.

All of this knowledge comes to us from archaeology, and there is still much debate in academic circles about the nature of society in prehistoric Japan. The first real insight to Japan's history comes much later, from China, where a land across the sea is mentioned in a text[5] dating to about 57AD. The Chinese scribes called this land "Wa" and said that it was populated by a hundred or so tribal groups living independently of, and in sporadic conflict with, each other. This confirms that Japan had links with the mainland,[6] as ties between Korea and "Wa" people are also mentioned. As we shall see, both countries exerted considerable influence on the development of Japan's state institutions and, importantly, her military.

Above: Asakura Norikage left an invaluable written record about military matters, including the thought: "The warrior may be called a beast or a dog; the main thing is winning." *(British Museum/Jo St Mart)*

Left: An okodate or chivalrous commoner brandishes his *shakuhachi* (flute) at the beginning of a brawl. He wears one sword, as distinguished from a *samurai*'s two. Young men like this tried to protect commoners from the abuses of arrogant *samurai* and often became folk heroes. *(Asian Art & Archaeology, Inc./CORBIS)*

Above: Because of their close geographical proximity, both China and Korea had an influence in Japan's institutional development, including her military. Here, two great armies of cavalry face each other prior to the Battle of Kawanakajima in 1561. *(Library of Congress)*

NOTES

1 I use the term 'feudalism' with caution, as it is inappropriate to make too many comparisons between Japanese and Western political systems
2 An alternative thesis proposed by Wayne Farris William W. Farris, *Heavenly Warriors: The Evolution of Japan's Military 500-1300*, is that the *samurai* did not suddenly appear but evolved over 700 years.
3 Only much later, at around the turn of the 7th century, did the Japanese begin to chronicle their own history. The first accounts, the *Kojiki* (The Record of Ancient Matters) and *Nihonshi* (the Chronicles of Japan), were completed in the 8th Century, during the Nara Period. Although colourful and entertaining, these huge tomes reveal more about the authors than anything else. Although the genealogy of the kings to 400AD is generally accurate, much of what is contained therein is fabulous (the birth of Japan and her people is ascribed to a divine act) and therefore has been largely discounted by most historians.

However, in lieu of other sources the Kojiki was for many years invariably used alongside contemporary Chinese records.
4 For a more detailed look at Yayoi culture see Charles T. Keally's website http://www.t-net.ne.jp/~keally/yayoi.html
5 *The Shan Hai Jing or "Classic of the Mountains and Seas"*.
6 Cornelius J. Kiley *State and Dynasty in Archaic Yamato*: JAS 33:1 (Nov 1973) p.26

THE FIRST OF THE SAMURAI

From various sources it can be reasonably ascertained that, by the end of the Yayoi Period (300BC–250AD), Japan was populated by a host of widespread *uji*, ruled by a patriarch who was worshipped as a deity by the group's members and who in turn took responsibility in the devotional rites to the *ujigami* (clan deity). These men formed the basic ruling class of early Japan.[1] Progressively, the disparate, independent *uji* began to coalesce into larger groups or polities through religious, political, and military alliances.

Although Chinese accounts are vague in their descriptions of "Wa," the chronicle *Wei Chih* speaks of a 3rd century queen, Himiko,[2] who ruled over a confederation of tribes called Yamataikoku, and which evidence suggests was centered on a court that was in Kyushu. However, the first clearly defined polity emerged in the Yamato region (the modern day Kinki region near Osaka), which was initially settled by people who had traveled east through Japan, and had strong cultural and political ties with both China and Korea. According to the *Kojiki* the Emperor Jimmu led a group of migrants from Kyushu east onto Honshu in around 660BC, fighting with local clans along the way before settling at Kashiwabara, near present day Nara. Archaeologists put forward a much later time for this transition, suggesting the 3rd century AD as a more likely timeframe. During the movement there seem to have been efforts to colonize the area around Agi (Hiroshima) and then (Kibi) Okayama, before the Yamato region was settled.

We do not know much about those early Yamato settlers, or the court that governed them, or the limits of its authority. We can say with confidence that, by the later 4th century, a recognizable polity had been established at Yamato, in which we can see the germs of a more cohesive Japanese state, or "proto-government."[3] At the apex of this had emerged a dominant ruling line, the Yamato Sun Line. The supreme authority was a king (Yamato-okimi, or Great king of Yamato) who resided at the Yamato capital of Naniwa (modern-day Osaka). Three successive lines of Yamato kings (the current emperor traces his lineage to the third, or new, dynasty

which dates to about the year 500) took the regnal seat, control of which was fought over between the stronger clans in numerous bloody *coups d'etat*.

Note that authority was based not on any military superiority over other *uji*, or their subjugation, but the promulgation of Yamato rule by them. In practice, many local polities, particularly in places such as Kibi (current Okayama prefecture), Izumo (current Shimane prefecture), Koshi (current Fukui and Niigata prefecture), Kenu (northern Kanto), Chikushi (northern Kyushu), and Hi (central Kyushu) were largely independent, and could even rival the Yamato in terms of importance.[4]

Progressively, the Yamato court extended its control over most of southern Japan, by suppressing other clans and claiming agricultural lands. By the middle of the 7th century, its authority was such as to necessitate a new system of rule to administer the recently conquered and united lands and people under the emperor.[5] In 645, Prince Naka-no-oe (who later reigned as Emperor Tenj, 661–671) and Nakatomi-no Kamatari successfully carried off a palace coup,[6] which overthrew the domineering Soga[7] clan. The two then oversaw the drafting of a set of edicts called the Taika reforms, which called for the creation of a new centralized administration under a revitalized imperial court, and which drew heavily on the *Ritsuryo* political system that was then

Below: The two Soga brothers, from one of the most powerful clans in Yamato Japan, were orphaned when very young. While still teenagers, they succeeded in avenging their father by killing his murderer. At one point during their many adventures, Goro sensed that his brother needed him and galloped madly to his rescue. Members of the Soga clan were influential in the spread of Buddhism in Japan during the 6th century. *(Asian Art & Archaeology, Inc./Corbis)*

employed by the Tang Dynasty in China.[8] Central to the reforms was the institution of a court rank system to classify both the court and provincial nobility. Also proposed was a system of conscription, prompted by events on the continent that are described below.

Of fundamental importance was the implementation of new systems of land reform and taxation. Thus far, land had been under the ownership of the powerful *uji*. However, beginning in the 8th century, all land was claimed by the state, which then redistributed rights not of ownership of the land, but to work the land for profit, a proportion of which was returned as tax. Although, ostensibly, this was an effort to secure state revenues, it signals a clear attempt to subordinate local rulers to the central government, and to prevent rival centers of power from developing.

In practice, efforts to implement the reforms met with only partial success,[9] due in part to the fact that the government lacked the power to enforce them, and that they were "too elaborate and unwieldy for Japan."[10]

Above: "War is conducted at a run." One of a series of modern illustrations in the sequence "The Face of Battle" by R. Knutsen, this shows Muromachi or Sengoku *jidai* period *ashiguru* (foot soldiers), running into battle with *yari* (spears), urged on by cavalry, between 1336 and 1573. *(via Clive Sinclaire)*

Furthermore, although *uji* lands were nationalized, the government used grants of land as a reward for support, thus undercutting its own efforts to keep control over the land, and allowing some individuals to build up substantial estates (*shoen*).

Scholars attach great significance to these efforts. It has been argued that this laid the foundations for a "feudalist" system, by making provision for local *uji* to retain power and title over land that in theory belonged to the emperor. Ultimately, this economic and political power allowed them to maintain their independence of the central government, and in later years to challenge its power.

The other significant political development of concern to us came a half-century later in 701, under the Emperor Mommu. This was another attempt at administrative reorganization and again took as its model the governmental system of the Tang Dynasty. Under this Taiho Code two branches of state were created to deal with state and religious matters, and the country was divided into (initially) sixty-six provinces (excluding

Left: Buddhist monks clean the dust from the fifty-foot-high Great Buddha at the Todaiji Temple in Nara. The statue was completed in 752AD. It is believed that Buddhism was introduced to Japan around the 5th century. *(Koichi Kamoshida/Getty Images)*

Above: Tombs from the Silla Dynasty are excavated in Kyongju, South Korea. The Yamato court in Japan ordered the construction of coastal defenses to protect Japan from attack by the country's mainland enemies. *(Edward Kim/National Geographic/Getty Images)*

northern Japan, which had not been subjugated) administered by government-appointed *gunji* (governors). These provincial governors would later assume great significance.

The early Japanese warrior

Turning our focus on to the evolution of the Japanese warrior, until the Taika Reforms, Japan possessed no

semblance of a formal national army, and warriors were privately conscripted under the banners of individual clans that on occasion were commissioned to fight for the emperor.[11] These men fought on foot, with sword and shield, both owing much to Chinese models,[12] and therefore have little in common with the mounted *samurai*.

Sometime in the early 5th century, there was a development of great significance, and that was the

Right: An Ainu village chief (left) holding court. The Ainu are believed to be the indigenous people of Japan, living on the northern island of Hokkaido. *(Alfred Eisenstaedt/Time & Life Pictures/Getty Images)*

Above: The inhospitable Kyushu region in which coastal fortifications were built for the protection of Japan against mainland raiders. *(Steve West/Getty Images)*

importation from the continent of techniques for fighting on horseback. At this time the Yamato and the ancient Korean kingdom of Baekje (in southwestern Korea) enjoyed strong ties, and Yamato warriors frequently fought on behalf of the Baekje against the rival Silla and Koguryo kingdoms. In 366 a mission was sent from the Yamato court to Baekje and subsequently established a military outpost at Gaya[13] (Japanese Mimana) at the tip of the peninsula, which subsequently formed part of the Yamato court's domain. During these continental expeditions, Japanese armies encountered cavalry, and were quick to note how the speed and maneuverability of horse-mounted troops were devastatingly effective against regular infantry. As soon as horses were brought to the peninsula, and bred domestically, Japanese warriors began to refine their skills

as cavalrymen, and their new skills were employed to good effect in subsequent expeditions. Certain prominent historians in this field, notably William Farris,[14] have concluded that these men were the distant progenitors of the *samurai*.

During the first year of the reign of Emperor Tenji, architect of the Taika reforms, there was an incident of wider importance to the development of the Japanese military. This was the annexation of Baekje by the neighboring Silla Kingdom, an act that prompted the Yamato court to dispatch 37,000 men to the aid of its ally on the mainland. In August 663 a combined Yamato-Baekje army fought a disastrous engagement against the armies of Tang China and Silla at Baekgang (this is also known as the Battle of Hakusukinoe), in the lower reaches of the Geum River in Jeollabuk-do province. The Silla-Tang forces won a decisive victory, forcing the Japanese to withdraw completely from Korean affairs.

In the aftermath of this catastrophic reversal, Japan underwent widespread military reforms. Fearful of an invasion from the Tang or Silla (or both) the Yamato court ordered the construction of extensive coastal defenses, to be manned. In 664, *sakimori* (literally "defenders of the edge") frontier guards and beacons were established in Tsushima Island, Iki Island, and northern Kyushu.[15] Between 665 and 667, fortifications were built in Nagato province, two others in Kyushu, and yet more in the Yamato region, at Sanuki, and Tsushima Island. This program of construction continued over the next thirty years.

In 672, following the death of Tenji, a succession dispute erupted that culminated in a civil war,[16] in which Prince Ohama defeated his brother Prince Otomo for the throne. Ohama became Emperor Temmu, the first ruler of Japan to bear the title "Heavenly Warrior Emperor." Acutely aware of how his own ascent had been achieved through force, during his reign Temmu actively sought to bring the military under central control.

To this end, Temmu instituted various laws designed to prevent military power being concentrated in the hands of individual clan leaders. He also decreed that the *Ritsuryo* conscript army proposed in the Taika Reforms was to be properly formalized,[17] with ranks filled by members of the peasantry. All healthy males between the ages of twenty and fifty-nine were henceforth required to spend a total of thirty-five days per year in the military divisions (*gundan*) of their particular province, or else at the coastal defenses in Kyushu as *sakimori* or as *chinpei* (pacification soldiers) on the northern border. They were also expected to supply their own weapons and equipment, all of which must have been a major burden on a poor family.[18] In each province the supreme commander was the governor, and he personally selected the senior officers from among the provincial aristocracy. However, as William R. Wilson points out, "with the elevation of the Imperial House to a transcendent position, as in China, warriors were subordinated."[19]

Below: Eighth-century gold Buddhist scriptures were found in a Silla tomb. Kyongju, South Korea. In 663 Japan's Yamato lost an important battle on Korean soil, and for some time afterward feared an invasion by Korean and Chinese forces. *(H. Edward Kim/National Geographic/Getty Images)*

Above: The story of Yamato Takeru is one of the earliest legends of Japan. He is seen bearing the fabled sword Kusanagi no tsurugi during a battle with a teacherous lord who set fire to grassland to kill him. *(via Clive Sinclaire)*

Although, by the end of the 7th century, the need to guard against invasion from the continent appeared to have diminished, this *ritsuryo* conscript army found itself severely tested in fighting against Yamato enemies within Japan itself—the *emishi*. In these campaigns its many inherent shortcomings were revealed, and further impetus was provided for the emergence of a professional warrior class.

The place that fostered the martial skills of the Japanese mounted warrior is the Kanto plain, in central Honshu, where farming communities had for generations prospered on fertile land well suited to the cultivation of rice and the raising of horses. The Kanto plain, encompassing polities such as Kenmu and Musashi, lay distant from and beyond the direct authority of the Yamato court. Over time, however, the Kanto polities were drawn into alliances with the Yamato court, and engaged in government wars against the peoples of northeastern Japan (present-day Tohoku region) that they called the *emishi* or "northern barbarians."

Although some tribes of *emishi* (whose origins have yet to be fully determined) entered into alliances with the Japanese, between the 7th and 10th centuries, others fiercely resisted attempts to conquer their lands and subjugate them. The more aggressive launched cross-border raids, which became an increasing concern for the central government. Beginning in the late 8th century, the imperial army, and mounted warriors from the Kanto, were sent on major expeditions[22] against recalcitrant *emishi*[23] tribes.

In the engagements they fought on the northern borders the *emishi* tribes proved to be an elusive enemy. Fighting in small, mobile, mounted groups on ground they knew well, more often than not they defeated the slow-moving conscript armies sent against them.[24] Far more successful were the Kanto warriors, who quickly established a reputation as good fighting men. According to Martin Chollcutt, "through fighting in the northeast, *bushi*[25] tightened their feudal bonds of personal loyalty and honed a technology of fighting that emphasized the role of mounted warriors in man-to-man fighting."[26]

Nonetheless, the inconclusive campaigns in the north quickly became a major headache for the Yamato government. Along with the expense of procuring weapons, the available pool of conscripts was "diminished by famine and outbreaks of smallpox." Beginning in 770, conscription began to be slowly replaced by a system of regular soldiers trained in military matters.[27] Here too is a significant milestone in *samurai* history, for at this point we see the start of the division between the peasantry and the class of professional warriors, to whom the central government was happy to devolve responsibility for military matters. From this time onwards, for almost a thousand years, the Japanese military consisted of professional soldiers. Initially, they owed their loyalty to the emperor but by the middle of the Heian Period, they had gradually merged into the private armies of provincial lords.

Thus, "by the end of the eighth century, a new breed of Japanese soldier had clearly evolved, out of necessity, in response to the requirements of fighting in the north."[28] Armed with bow and arrow, he had adopted lighter, more flexible leather armor better suited to his needs, and also a new type sword with a curved blade, the *katana*,[29] which was much easier to draw and sheath. In many ways, he can be distinguished as the progenitor of the *samurai*.

NOTES

1 Cornelius J. Kiley *State and Dynasty in Archaic Yamato*: JAS 33:1 (Nov 1973) p.27.
2 Joseph Ryan *Methods of Early Japanese State Building and Tactics of Legitimation* p.4.
3 Anthony J. Bryant *Early Samurai* p.7.
4 Karl F. Friday *Hired Swords: The Rise of Private Warrior Power in Early Japan* p.10.
5 The word *tenno* or "emperor" was by this time being used for the monarch. See Cornelius Kiley *The Journal of Asian Studies* 33: 1; p.25-26.
6 Karl F. Friday *Hired Swords: The Rise of Private Warrior Power in Early Japan* p.10.
7 Cornelius J. Kiley *State and Dynasty in Archaic Yamato*: JAS 33:1 (Nov 1973) p.23.
8 Two scholars with positions high in the administration, Takamuko no Kuromaro and a priest Min, and who had spent more than a decade in Sui Dynasty China are likely to have had a hand in the drafting of the reforms.
9 Minoru Shinoda *The Founding of the Kamakura Shogunate* p.27.
10 Martin Chollcutt *Harvard Journal of Asiatic Studies* 56: 152.
11 Karl F. Friday *Hired Swords: The Rise of Private Warrior Power in Early Japan* p.11.
12 Here as with so many aspects of Yamato society and culture, the influence of the continent can be easily discerned in the early Japanese military. During this time there was a large influx of foreign immigrants brought to Yamato for their advanced knowledge and skills, among them artisans skilled in weapons making.
13 This is a contentious topic. Although Japanese history books are clear in their conviction that

Mimana existed, despite their research for the last five decades, both Korean and Japanese historians have failed to verify this theory. Whatever the truth about this presence, it is clear that from the earliest days of the Yamato there was a flow of culture and technology, including weaponry, from the continent. According to the Nihon Shoki : 247, the first diplomatic missions from Baekje reached Japan around 367. According to Japanese sources, the war on the Korean peninsula eventually led to the expulsion of the Yamato from Mimana in 562.
14 William W. Farris *Heavenly Warriors: The Evolution of Japan's Military 500-1300*.
15 Karl F. Friday *Hired Swords: The Rise of Private Warrior Power in Early Japan* p.21.
16 The *Nihongi* mentions the use of mounted archers during the battle of the succession, which some scholars suggest as a possible early model for the future *samurai*.
17 Karl F. Friday *Hired Swords: The Rise of Private Warrior Power in Early Japan* p.12-14.
18 Minoru Shinoda *The Founding of the Kamakura Shogunate* p.28.
19 William R Wilson *The Way of the Bow and Arrow. The Japanese Warrior in Konjaku Monogatari* Monumenta Nipponica 28: 2; p.186.
20 See Karl F. Friday *Samurai, Warfare & the State* for a more detailed analysis of the evolution of the bow in Japan. (p.68-74).
21 More detail on the history and construction of this armor can be found in Anthony J. Bryant *Early Samurai AD 200-1500* p.28-46.
22 See Karl F. Friday *Hired Swords: The Rise of Private Warrior Power in Early Japan* (p.26-28) for

more on this topic.
23 One of the commanders of these expeditions, Tajihi Agatamori, was assigned the temporary rank of *jeisetsu sei-I-shogun*, a title inspired by similar Chinese military ranks. This may have been the first conferment of the rank of "shogun" on an individual in Japanese history. The title of *sei-I-shogun* meant "barbarian-quelling general," while *sei-to-shogun* meant "general who quells the eastern barbarians." The actual extent of authority a *sei-I-shogun* carried is unclear, but he was clearly considered a commander-in-chief on his given assignment.
24 In 784, Otomo Yakamochi was given the title of *sei-I-shogun* and dispatched to quell rebellious *emishi* in Mutsu province. Despite the bestowment of this honor, it was an assignment that he proved unable to complete. Likewise, three years later Emperor Kammu made Ki no Kosami *shogun*, gave him an army and sent him to Mutsu. Once there, Ki was soundly defeated and his army recalled in shame.
25 The term *bushi* was used to describe warriors until late Heian. The term *samurai* was adopted much later.
26 Martin Chollcutt *Harvard Journal of Asiatic Studies* 56: 157.
27 For a description of the changes to the imperial military institutions during the 8th century see Karl F. Friday *Hired Swords: The Rise of Private Warrior Power in Early Japan* p.33.
28 David Lay *Origins of the Samurai* www.samurai-archives.com.
29 The design seems to have been inspired by the swords used by the *emishi*.

ASCENT TO POWER

In 794, the thirteenth year of Emperor Kammu's rule, the imperial court was re-established at Heian-kyo (Kyoto), between the Katsura and Kamo Rivers in the central Kansai region. The name chosen by Kammu means "city of peace" and, either by fate or by providence, the relocation of the seat of power ushered in a long and welcome period of peace and stability at court after the internecine strife of the Nara Period (710–794). In this atmosphere of comparative tranquility Japan blossomed culturally; her arts, which had long adhered to continental influences, began to develop a distinct character of their own. The driving force for this cultural, and spiritual, awakening was Buddhism, introduced from China over previous centuries, and modified by Japanese monks.

The four centuries of the Heian era bore witness to many important developments in Japanese politics and society. The most important of these centered on efforts to build on the framework laid out by the Taika and Taiho reforms. To this end, an extensive administration was built under the emperor, at the pinnacle of which was a Council of State on which sat the chief ministers of government. Below this council was a vast army of lesser civil servants, the great majority of whom served the imperial household.

Government continued to be concerned primarily with the matters of the court. Away from the capital, in sixty-six provinces, the government appeared satisfied to devolve responsibility to court-appointed governors, and allowed many of them to become almost self-governing. Initially,

Below: Minamoto Yoshitsune is a popular figure in Japanese myth and legend. Here he is seen fleeing from his enemies with his older brother, Yoritomo. *(via Clive Sinclaire)*

Provinces of Feudal Japan

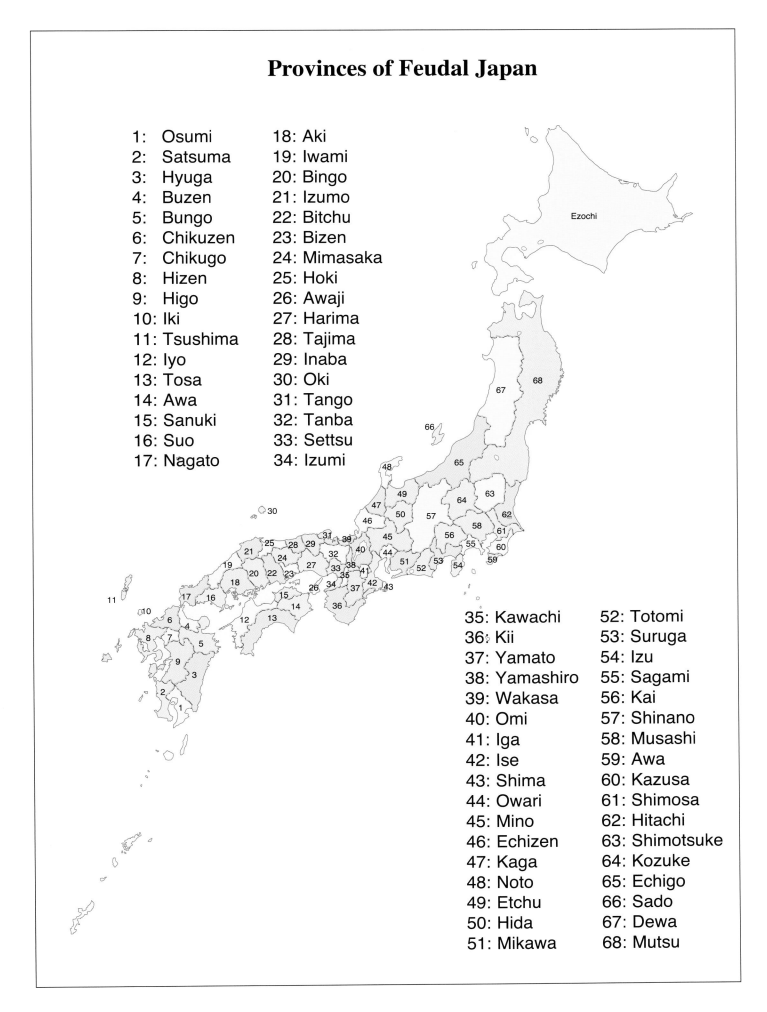

1:   Osumi
2:   Satsuma
3:   Hyuga
4:   Buzen
5:   Bungo
6:   Chikuzen
7:   Chikugo
8:   Hizen
9:   Higo
10: Iki
11: Tsushima
12: Iyo
13: Tosa
14: Awa
15: Sanuki
16: Suo
17: Nagato

18: Aki
19: Iwami
20: Bingo
21: Izumo
22: Bitchu
23: Bizen
24: Mimasaka
25: Hoki
26: Awaji
27: Harima
28: Tajima
29: Inaba
30: Oki
31: Tango
32: Tanba
33: Settsu
34: Izumi

35: Kawachi
36: Kii
37: Yamato
38: Yamashiro
39: Wakasa
40: Omi
41: Iga
42: Ise
43: Shima
44: Owari
45: Mino
46: Echizen
47: Kaga
48: Noto
49: Etchu
50: Hida
51: Mikawa

52: Totomi
53: Suruga
54: Izu
55: Sagami
56: Kai
57: Shinano
58: Musashi
59: Awa
60: Kazusa
61: Shimosa
62: Hitachi
63: Shimotsuke
64: Kozuke
65: Echigo
66: Sado
67: Dewa
68: Mutsu

this worked well, for there was remarkably little friction within the government or between government and the state-appointed officials. That is not to say, however, that there was none, for in the later Heian Period there were significant and major outbreaks of violence that were to have a significant impact on Japanese society.

There were two key areas of conflict. The first was at tertiary level, and centered on the struggle for power and influence at court. This manifested itself as maneuvering by aristocratic families for positions of influence on the Council of State, which exerted great influence over the ruler, and in other branches of the government hierarchy. In this struggle the Fujiwara *kuge* (court nobility family) emerged the clear winner, for by the mid-9th century it had gained almost total control over the emperor and the ruling power structure. For the best part of the Heian era, the Fujiwara and their scions dominated the government of Japan.[1]

The second was a breakdown in the government authority in the provinces; beginning in the early 10th century the inherent weakness of the central government, and its growing inability to control developments away from the capital, began to be exposed by warfare and rebellion.[2] Although the provincial governors were theoretically answerable to the state, in practice some of them were able to rule more or less autonomously, and in many cases corruptly, and attempted to assert their independence, bringing them into violent dispute with the central government.

The Taira Clan

During the Heian Period (794–1185) there were four important clans dominating Japanese politics—the Taira, Fujiwara, Minamoto, and Tachibana clans. Some emperors of the period (grandsons of the Emperor Kammu) were given the name Taira from about 825, while other descendants of emperors Nammyo, Monotku, and Koko also received the surname Taira. The most dominant line emerged as the Kammu Heishi line from 889, with Taira no Kiyomori forming the first *samurai*-dominated government in Japan's history, it is claimed.

One of Heishi Takemochi's descendants, Taira no Korihira, established an important *daimyo* dynasty in Ise Province, while another, Kiyomori, was honoured as great minister of state after his successes in the Hogen and Heiji Disturbances in 1156 and 1160, respectively.

However, when Kiyomori installed his infant grandson as Emperor Antoku in 1180 this led to the Genpei and Taira-Minamoto Wars in the 1180s. As described in the *Heike Monogatari*, During these wars, Kiyomori's sons lost out in the Battle of Dan-no-ura in 1185 against the mighty Minamoto no Yorimoto, which led to the destruction of the head family of the Kammu Heishi line.

Above: Taira Koremori (right) was a Taira clan commander during the Genpei War. However, he lost both the battle of Fujigawa (1180) and the battle of Kurikara (1184) before he fled the field at the battle of Yashima. *(via Clive Sinclaire)*

There were other significant developments. First, there was a noticeable rise in the power of certain provincial land-owning families, several of which grew rich and powerful from their lands. This in turn allowed them to build up private armies of professional soldiers, and to gain further stipends by employing them in the service of the Heian government.[3] The two greatest beneficiaries of this phenomenon were the Taira (or Heike) and the Minamoto (or Genji), about whom we will hear much in the subsequent chapter.

Militarily, the focus therefore gradually shifted from conflict *without* to conflict *within*. Although battles were still fought in the north-east portion of Honshu (the Tohoku region) against the *emishi*, "between 791 and 803 Sakanoue Tamuramaro succeeded in bringing the entire region under imperial control after a series of military victories."[4] Disputes between clans now became the key source of conflict.

And, as the sources of conflict altered, so did the fighting forces.

With the abdication of responsibility[5] for military matters to the powerful clans, the structure of the imperial army was altered drastically. After the final dismantling of the *ritsuryo* conscript system in 792, reliance on conscripts decreased[6] as the government instead came to rely on a military system based on local militias composed of mounted horsemen. While it is often stated that the later Heian Period witnessed the "emergence" of the true *samurai*, it could be argued that these men were, in essence, the first *samurai*. Karl Friday and others in fact argue that there was a process of continual evolution from the horse-riding warriors of the 8th century; Wayne Farris contends that they were an outgrowth of a seven-hundred-year-old military tradition. As William R. Wilson points out, this can be styled as the "ultimate success of tribalism" as "warriors never ceased to perform an essential function on the periphery of Imperial circles."

Revolt of Taira no Masakado

By fault or design, government authority gradually diminished outside the capital and, as it did, rebellions arose. One of the most prominent and well recorded of these insurrections occurred in the mid-10th century, in the Bando (Kanto) region. This was the revolt of one Taira no Masakado,[7] an event depicted in detail in a contemporary account called the *Shomonki*.

The rebel Taira no Masakado[8] had spent many years serving the powerful politician Fujiwara Tadahira. Apparently he was refused the office of Kebiishi (police chief) by the emperor, after the death of his father, *chinjufu-shogun* Taira no Yoshimochi, so he returned to the Bando region and rose to become one of the most powerful landowners. As Giuliana Stramigioli states, "It is not clear what kindled the spark" that set off the rebellion. It seems to have started in 931 as a dispute between Masakado and Taira no Yoshikane over a woman who may have been Masakado's wife.[9] Another catalyst may have been attempts by his uncle to gain control of his father's lands, and he may have been at least partly provoked by the attempts of government officialdom to raise taxes in his domain.[10] This was not unusual—there were frequent complaints from provincial families of exploitation by the *zuryo* (local governors).

The unrest broke out in 935, when Masakado was apparently attacked by members of the Minamoto family at Nomoto in Hitachi. In the event, Masakado turned the tables on his attackers, and many of his opponents were killed (including his uncle Taira no Kunika, although the circumstances are unclear). Later in the year Masakado's cousin Yoshimasa took up arms against him but was defeated at Kawawa no mura in Niihari. In the following year his uncle Yoshikane marched into Hitachi, where he joined up with Yoshimasa and Kunika's son Sadamori, and fought Masakado in an engagement at the Hitachi-Shimotsuke border. Together they commanded several thousand men, in contrast to Masakado's few hundred, but nonetheless the attackers were routed and forced to flee.[11]

In late 936 Masakado was called to Kyoto to explain his actions. After staying in the capital for several months he eventually received an amnesty and returned to his lands. Shortly thereafter he was attacked by Yoshikane's forces at the Kogai-kawa and retreated. Less than two weeks later he suffered another reversal at Shimo-okata.

With Masakado now firmly on the back foot, Yoshikane struck at him in Sashima, and succeeded in capturing Masakado's wife and children.

This act seems to have finally galvanized Masakado into action; in the fall of 937 he marched on Yoshikane's stronghold of Hatori in Hitachi, forcing him to escape to the nearby mountains. Yoshikane then rallied troops for one last attempt to defeat his nephew, leading a surprise attack on Masakado's stronghold at Ishii, but was soundly beaten and ceased thereafter to be a threat.

For much of 938 there was a hiatus in the fighting, as neither Sadamori nor Yoshimasa seemed willing to take up where Yoshikane had left off. Things took a dramatic turn in 939 when, in response to a government order to arrest an ally, Fujiwara no Haruaki,[12] Masakado led 1,000 men to attack the quarters of the central government in Hitachi Province. After a series of battles against numerically superior forces he occupied the buildings, capturing the zuryo (governor) Fujiwara no Korechika in the process.

The consequences of this were potentially grave. Whereas thus far the central government had taken a "conciliatory" approach with him, by this open act of rebellion he was directly challenging the authority of the state. Nonetheless, by this time Masakado had already won considerable support for his cause in the Bando region, a fact that may have persuaded him to occupy Shimotsuke and then Kozuke province.

At this point he decided to stage an investiture at Soma (Shimosa) and declared himself *shin no tenno* (new emperor)[13] over a new autonomous state, appointing new governors for the Kanto provinces. In the following months he moved to occupy the other Bando, whose governors willingly abandoned them to his army and fled to Kyoto, spreading panic in the capital with news of his conquests. Fearing that Masakado planned an attack on the capital itself,[14] the government ordered the revolt to be quashed.

In the first month of 940, Masakado led an army out of Shimosa into Hitachi, in an attempt to bring Sadamori to battle. Enlisting the help of Fujiwara no Hidesato,[15] whose province bordered Shimotsuke, Sadamori marched out to engage Masakado's army. Masakado was defeated at the Battle of Kojima by his cousin Sadamori and Fujiwara no Hidesato, dying in the midst of the plain.[16] His head was sent to Kyoto and displayed in the capital as a warning to any prospective rebels. There was apparently much rejoicing at his demise. Modern historians attach considerable significance to Taira no Masakado, despite this somewhat ignominious end. Many see his revolt as symbolic of the fall of Kyoto sovereignty and the rise of the provincial clan leaders, who were later called *daimyo*. In many respects Taira no Masakado could be seen as their archetype.

Fujiwara no Sumitomo

Another event often presented as an indication of the government's loss of control is the entirely coincidental uprising of Fujiwara no Sumitomo.[17] He was the son of Fujiwara Yoshinori, a member of the powerful Fujiwara clan that held much influence on the Council of State.[18] Yoshinori himself was an official in the government at Dazaifu[19] as well as a governor of Chikuzen Province (modern day Fukuoka). His son Sumitomo was also initially a courtier, and an official in Iyo Province (Shikoku), and in 936 he received an Imperial Decree to arrest Inland Sea pirates.[20] However, he decided to desert his court post to lead the pirates,[21] and at one point commanded as many as 1,500 ships, "killing men and despoiling the cargoes of ships plying between the provinces."[22]

With this powerful fleet, from 936 to 941 he effectively controlled the Inland Sea, and may have aided

Fujiwara Kiyohira (1056–1128)

Fujiwara Kiyohira was a late Heian Period *samurai*, and founder of the Fujiwara dynasty (*Hiraizumi*) that ruled Mutsu from about 1100 to 1226. Kiyohira was the son of Fujiwara no Tsunekiyo, a middle-ranking official at Taga Castle (in present-day Sendai, Miyagi Prefecture) who left his post to live with the unidentified *emishi* woman who was Kiyohira's mother. Thus, Kiyohira grew up in an *emishi* community which at that time was at war with the Kyoto government authorities.

During the Earlier Nine Years War he lost his father, his grandfather Abe no Yoritoki, and his uncle Sadato, and all of his mother's brothers were deported to Kyushu. His father was personally beheaded by Minamoto no Yoriyoshi with a blunt sword. Subsequently, the Kiyohara clan brought up Kiyohira, together with his elder brother-in-law Sanehira and younger half-brother Iehira, The complex fraternal relationship between these three instigated the Later Three Years War from which Kiyohira emerged as the victor in 1087.

Above: Following victory in the Later Three Years War Kiyohira returned home to Fort Toyoda. *(British Museum/Jo St Mart)*

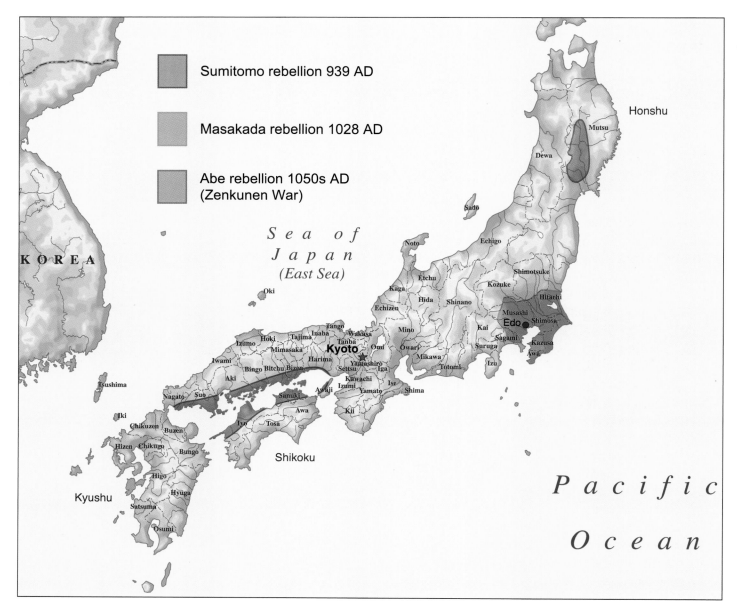

Sumitomo rebellion 939 AD

Masakada rebellion 1028 AD

Abe rebellion 1050s AD
(Zenkunen War)

the Taira clan in their series of revolts against the government. In 939 Sumitomo fomented a revolt in Iyo, and soon afterwards invaded the provinces of Harima and Bizen in western Honshu. However, when Sumitomo tried to invade the Kyushu capital Dazaifu from neighboring Hakata Bay, his band was scattered and a number of ships burnt by Ono Yoshifuru, who had been dispatched by the court to confront him. In May of that year he appeared at Dazaifu again, attacking, looting, and finally putting Government Office to the torch.

The court quickly dispatched another army (under Tachibana no Toyasu) to Hakata. Sumitomo temporarily withdrew to Ura-no-jo Castle in the eastern part of Dazaifu, from where he continued to resist the imperial army, but was eventually defeated and escaped to Iyo. He was later captured, and summarily executed. His head and that of his thirteen-year old son were taken to the capital, and presented to the government.[23]

Although the government had been successful in quashing these upstart provincial leaders, it is clear that Masakado and Sumimoto had presented it with very real challenges, and both had been defeated not through the strong hand of the government but due to the willingness of other clan leaders to respect the wishes of the government and offer battle on the emperor's behalf.

Whether this was a deliberate policy, or evidence that the government was losing control is still hotly debated. These rebellions were certainly another milestone on the path to warrior-led government. The escalation in the

Minamoto no Yoriyoshi (998–1082)

Minamoto no Yoriyoshi was leader of the Minamoto clan in mid-eleventh century, and hence leader of one of the four great families that dominated Japanese politics during the Heian Period. Yoriyoshi is notable among the many prominent Minamoto for commanding the imperial government forces against the Abe family of Mutsu in the *Zenkunen kassen* (or Former Nine Years) War. He also fought some years later in the *Gosannen kassen* (Later Three Years War).

The Minanoto clan had for many years provided support to the dominant Fujiwara clan, and enjoyed their patronage. Yoriyoshi often accompanied his father Yorinobu on military expeditions on behalf of the imperial court and in 1031 went with him on just such a mission to subdue a rebellion fomented by Taira Tadatsune. From these experiences he learnt much about the art of war.

In 1051, he was commissioned to lead an expedition against the upstart Abe clan in Dewa Province, and was bestowed, like his father and his grandfather before that, the title of *Chinjufu-shogun* (Commander-in-chief of the Defense of the North). The Zenkunen War would occupy him (with brief periods of peace) for the next twelve years. In 1057 Yoriyoshi was defeated at the Battle of Kawasaki by Abe Sadato, but saw the Minamoto emerge victorious five years later when his son Yoshiie beat Abe Sadato at Kuriyagawa. For his services against the Abe, Yoriyoshi was awarded the governorship of Iyo Province.

power of such provincial leaders continued until Minamoto no Yoritomo established the Kamakura Shogunate in 1192.

The Zenkunen Kassen (Early Nine Years War)

Although the defeat and capture of Fujiwara no Sumimoto earned the Minamoto great acclaim, this action was soon to be overshadowed by the endeavors of one of their most famous sons, Minamoto Yoshiie. More than a century after the defeat of Taira no Masakado and Sumitomo, the government faced a threat from the provinces, this time focused on another of the powerful provincial families—the Abe. For more than two centuries, the Abe had held sway in Mutsu province, in the far north of Honshu (comprising Fukushima, Miyagi, Iwate, and Aomori Prefectures), and profited

from the rich trade in gold and iron mined in the area. Furthermore, the powerful position of *chinjufu shogun* had long been held by a member of the Abe clan.[24]

Compounded by the remoteness of the region, and the fact that the court seemed satisfied to let the clan act as a local policing force, by the mid-11th century the Abe were living in Mutsu with a great deal of autonomy—often openly defying the state-appointed governor. There were many conflicts between the two over administrative control of the province, and these finally came to a head in 1050.

The spark was provided when the current incumbent, Abe no Yoritoki[25] began to levy taxes and confiscate property on his own, in open defiance of the government. Frustrated by these blatant acts of disobedience, the governor sent word to the capital in Kyoto asking for help. In 1053 the court responded by ordering an army to be raised. To lead it north they commissioned Minamoto no Yoriyoshi and gave him the position of *chinjufu shogun*.[26]

The fighting between Yoriyoshi and Yoritoki actually lasted for twelve years, including temporary periods of ceasefire and peace. However, although there was much ferocious skirmishing between the two sides, few major battles were fought until the battle of Kawasaki in 1057. The previous year Yoritoki's eldest son, Sadato,[27] engaged the Minamoto army in some small-scale actions, which within a year had flared into full-scale war. At a battle south of the Koromogawa River, Abe no Yoritoki was killed by an arrow. He was succeeded by Sadato as head of the clan and leader of the military effort against the Minamoto. At Kawasaki (in modern-day Miyagi Prefecture) Sadato's 4,000-strong entrenched force were attacked by the Minamoto army. Much of the battle took place during a snowstorm, but wave after wave of Minamoto assaults failed to break the defenders' lines, and the attack was broken off. Sadato now turned his troops onto the attack and pursued Minamoto through the blizzard for a short time. Other battles followed, during which Sadato's attacks further weakened the imperial army.

The reversals continued for some time, acerbated by the harsh northern terrain and freezing conditions.

Above: During a battle in the Later Three Years War, Minamoto Yoshiie determined the position of the enemy by watching the flight of wild geese. *(The Art Archive/Laurie Platt Winfrey)*

Above right: Minamoto no Yoshiie became famous for his *samurai* skill and bravery. This earned him the name Hachimantaro, meaning the son of Hachiman, the god of war. *(via Clive Sinclaire)*

Reprieve came in the form of fresh troops, including many offered by the governor of the neighboring Dewa Province, who was a leading member of the Kiyohara family. During 1062, Sadato attacked the now much-strengthened force, and eventually had to retreat into a fort near the Kuriya River.[28]

In the ensuing siege Yoriyoshi employed a tactic that we hear of time and again in Japanese military history. In simple terms, this entailed denying a castle its water supply, and thereby weakening the physical and mental resolve of the defenders. With this accomplished, Yoriyoshi and Yoshiie led a spirited assault on the fort, set it aflame, and put Sadato to flight. In the account given in the *Mutsu Waki*, during the chaotic retreat Yoshiie is supposed to have engaged Sadato in an impromptu *renga* (linked verse) session with his enemy from horseback, afterwards allowing him to escape. However colorful, like many such legends surrounding the *samurai*, this seems scarcely credible.

What is more certain is that Yoriyoshi and Yoshiie returned to Kyoto in early 1063 with the heads of Abe no Sadato and a number of others. Upon their triumphant return to the seat of power, Yoritoki was appointed governor of Dewa, and elevated in rank. Some time later the *Mutsu Waki* (The Story of Mutsu), an account of the war, was written. Yoshiie was bestowed with the name Hachimantaro, or child of Hachiman, the god of war, and went on to further glories. Subsequently, Yoshiie became something of a paragon of *samurai* skill and bravery, in many ways the archetype of the *samurai* martial tradition.[29]

NOTES

1 William R. Wilson *Hogen Monogatari: Essay on the Tale of the Disorder in Hogen* p.109.

2 Martin Chollcutt *Harvard Journal of Asiatic Studies* 56:152.

3 Martin Chollcutt *Harvard Journal of Asiatic Studies* 56:153.

4 Karl Friday *Teeth and Claws. Provincial Warriors and the Heian Court* Monumenta Nipponica 43:2 p.164

5 Karl Friday (*Hired Swords: The Rise of Private Warrior Power in Early Japan*) makes the assertion that the government *consciously sought* to increase its reliance on private armies.

6 Karl Friday *Hired Swords: The Rise of Private Warrior Power in Early Japan* p.69.

7 Masakado has received different treatments in different accounts. In the *Konjaku monogatari* and *Shomonki* he is portrayed as something of a villain (see Monumenta Nipponica, Vol. 28, No. 2, (Summer, 1973), pp. 177-233), whereas the *Masakadoki* is more sympathetic.

8 Paul Varley *Warriors of Japan as portrayed in the War Tales* p.10-11

9 Giuliana Stramigioli *Preliminary Notes on Masakadoki and the Taira no Masakado Story* Monumenta Nipponica 28: 3; 271.

10 Paul Varley *Warriors of Japan as potrayed in the War Tales* p. 11.

11 Giuliana Stramigioli *Preliminary Notes on Masakadoki and the Taira no Masakado Story*

Monumenta Nipponica 28: 3; 275.

12 The *Shomonki* is scathing in its description of this man, calling him a "hooligan," and a "blight on the people."

13 Wayne Farris *Heavenly Warriors: The Evolution of Japan's Military, 500-1330* Chapter 5.

14 *Hogen Monogatari* (William R. Wilson trans.) p.50.

15 See Karl Friday *Teeth and Claws. Provincial Warriors and the Heian Court* Monumenta Nipponica 43:2 p.168-170 for a discussion of the men who finally defeated Masakado.

16 William Ritchie Wilson *Konjaku Monogatari* xxv.II

15 William Ritchie Wilson *The Way of the Bow and Arrow. The Japanese Warrior in Konjaku Monogatari* Monumenta Nipponica, Vol. 28, No. 2 (Summer, 1973), pp. 177-233.

16 Matthew Lamberti *Harvard Journal of Asiatic Studies,* Vol. 32, (1972), p. 100.

17 From the Nara Period through the Heian Period and until the Kamakura Period, Dazaifu was one of the military and administrative centers of Japan.

18 Karl Friday Monumenta Nipponica 43:2 p.170.

19 Piracy was a problem for many centuries. The Heike Story mentions that Taira no Kiyomori had accompanied his father Tadamori on an expedition against Inland Sea pirates in 1135, and there were complaints from the Korean government about them prior to the Mongol invasions.

20 William Ritchie Wilson *Konjaku Monogatari*

xxv.III.

21 William Ritchie Wilson *Konjaku Monogatari* xxv.III.

22 Like Taira no Masakado, the Abe had been tasked with subduing these so-called *emishi*, who had been subjugated when the Japanese took over the area in the 9th century,

23 William Ritchie Wilson *The Way of the Bow and Arrow. The Japanese Warrior in Konjaku Monogatari XIII (How the Noble Minamoto no Yoriyoshi Chastised Abe no Sadato and His Followers)* Monumenta Nipponica XXVIII, 2 p.222.

24 Karl Friday *Hired Swords: The Rise of Private Warrior Power in Early Japan* p.26

25 *Hogen Monogatari* (William R. Wilson trans.) p.62.

26 William Ritchie Wilson *The Way of the Bow and Arrow. The Japanese Warrior in Konjaku Monogatari XIII (How the Noble Minamoto no Yoriyoshi Chastised Abe no Sadato and His Followers)* Monumenta Nipponica XXVIII, 2 p.229.

27 Karl F. Friday *Samurai, Warfare, and the State in Early Medieval Japan*, p.69.

28 William Ritchie Wilson *The Way of the Bow and Arrow. The Japanese Warrior in Konjaku Monogatari XIII (How the Noble Minamoto no Yoriyoshi Chastised Abe no Sadato and His Followers)* Monumenta Nipponica XXVIII, 2 p.229.

29 Karl F. Friday *Samurai, Warfare, and the State in Early Medieval Japan*, p.69.

SAMURAI & THE COURT (1086–1160)

In the years following the Zenkunen War, and throughout the 12th century, the amity that had prevailed in the early years of the Heian era was progressively and irrevocably eroded, and the outcome of this was fighting and bloodshed.

The three conflicts that we focus on were the product of power struggles between discordant factions within society. The first, the so-called Gosannen War (*gosannen kassen*), also known by the English translation Later Three Year War, was a local war fought between two of the increasingly powerful warrior clans, the Kiyohara and Minamoto.[1] Then, a long and relatively peaceful eighty years later, the *Hogen no Ran* or the Hogen Rebellion erupted between the Minamoto and Taira over matters of court influence and the imperial succession. Following shortly after, in 1159, Taira Kiyomori seized power during the Heiji Incident[2] and reigned supreme for a decade. Together the events described can be seen as the prolog to the Genpei War of 1180–1185, and the outcome of that was the formation of the first recognizable *samurai* government.

In a neat summary of the prevailing *zeitgeist* in Heian Japan, Hasegawa Tadashi[3] wrote that, "The culture of the Heian Period was the product of a small aristocracy which flourished in the metropolis of Heian or Kyoto, capital of a highly centralized political system. It bloomed in the soil of luxury consumption maintained by the produce of lands which the aristocracy held in every province of the country."

The most powerful element within that small clique was still the Fujiwara, who maintained their centuries-old domination of the high offices of government and used this position to further their own ends. The imperial court

Above: Minamoto Yoshiie, encamped near the battlefield, receives his aides. After being appointed governor of Mutsu in 1083 he put down the Kiyowara revolt in the northern provinces in the conflict known as the Later Three-Year War. *(The Art Archive)*

and its government, both of which the Fujiwara monopolized, had thus far tended to exclude the warrior clans, which had grown strong in the provinces. As the Heike points out, "the Fujiwara aristocrats regarded the warriors as no better than slaves. They were valued only for their ferocity."[4] Throughout the Heian Period they remained on the "periphery of political power." However, as politicians in the capital came to depend more and more on the powerful warrior families of Eastern Japan (the Minamoto and the Taira) to back up their claims (as few of them had a substantive source of military power of

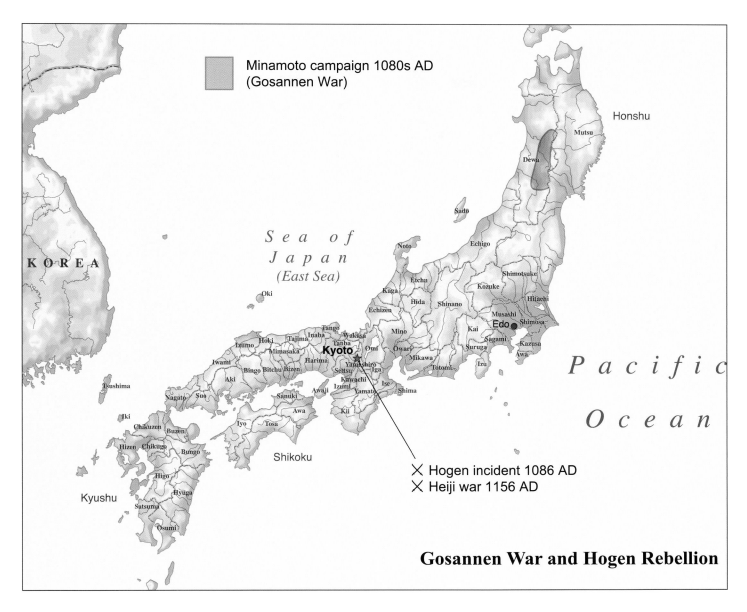

Minamoto campaign 1080s AD
(Gosannen War)

✕ Hogen incident 1086 AD
✕ Heiji war 1156 AD

Gosannen War and Hogen Rebellion

their own), the strength and influence of these families grew exponentially, as did their willingness to challenge the established order.[5] In these disputes, "the Fujiwara, despite its great display of wealth and power, was dependent to a large degree on upon the armed might of the Minamoto for the maintenance of its position and influence."[6] When factions centering on Emperors Go-Shirakawa and Go-Toba sought to wrest control of the court from the Fujiwara, they called on the Taira.

The Gosannen War

In 1086, the Gosannen War (*gosannen kassen*) broke out in the far north of Japan's main island of Honshu.[7] The Gosannen War bore certain similarities to the preceding Zenkunen War (see previous chapter), and the various conflicts that were to follow, in that it was a struggle for

power within the competing warrior clans of the time. The roots of the conflict are rather complex, best explained with reference to the Zenkunen War. During that conflict, Kiyohara had contributed warriors to the victorious Minamoto effort. In recognition of their support the Kiyohara clan were given the administration of Mutsu, along with Dewa, and the clan wielded significant power in the Tohoku region from around 1063 to 1089. However, during these two decades the Kiyohara quarreled among themselves and conflicts arose within the family over differing interests arising from intermarriage with different warrior families.

Three men were at the center of these familial disputes. First was Fujiwara no Kiyohira, the son of Fujiwara no Tsunekiyo and an unnamed daughter of Abe no Yoritoki, who had been one of the chief combatants

Above: Portion of a scroll showing the Emperor Go-Shirakawa being protected by *samurai* during the Heiji Rebellion, during which his Sanjo Palace was attacked. *(Burstein Collection/Corbis)*

in the Zenkunen War. His mother had become the second wife of the Taira clan chief, Takesada, who had a son and heir named Kiyohara no Sanehira by a previous marriage. To further these already complex fraternal ties, Kiyohira's mother gave birth to a son, Kiyohara no Iehira, by Takesada.

Sanehira took the mantle of leadership upon Takesada's death, but his relations with clan elder Kimiko Hidetake quickly soured and developed into a feud that rapidly turned violent. Hidetake sought aid from Kiyohira and Iehira, while Minamoto no Yoshiie, who had succeeded as governor of Mutsu in 1083 and had territorial ambitions of his own, acted without the approval of the court by allying himself with Sanehira. The conflict would likely have become protracted had it not been for the fact that Sanehira fell ill and died, bringing hostilities to an abrupt halt.

With Sanehira's death, Iehira saw a possible way to accelerate his own rise to power. A spat developed between him and Kiyohira, prompting Iehira to attack his brother's estate. In this assault, Kiyohira's family was slaughtered and he was moved to petition his former adversary, Yoshiie, for help. After much fighting, the two warriors crushed Iehira and three years of warfare came to an end. Both Iehira and his uncle Kiyohara no Takahira were killed, and the other Kiyowara leaders surrendered. Control of both Dewa and Mutsu then passed to Kiyohira, who eventually moved his base of operations to Hiraizumi.

During the Gosannen War, a poorly documented engagement[8] took place at Numa, one of Iehira's strongholds. Numa, like most early Japanese fortresses, was more a wooden palisade than a fortress, as it is sometimes described. What *is* known is that Yoshiie lost many men trying to invest the position, a large number due to cold and lack of supplies. In 1087 Yoshiie countered by establishing a camp around the stockade at Kanezawa, with the forces of Kiyohara no Takahira. After a period of inactivity and relative peace, Yoshiie and his

Above: Kiyohara no Iehira was a member of the Kiyohara clan, which wielded significant power in the Thoku region from around 1063 to 1089, during the Heian Period. He was also a key participant in the Gosannen War which grew out of conflicts within the clan. *(British Museum/Jo St Mart)*

Fujiwara Nobuyori (d. 1160)

Fujiwara no Nobuyori was a late Heian era courtier and one of the chief allies of Minamoto no Yoshitomo in the Heiji Rebellion of 1159. Nobuyori had ambitions for the position of regent, either for the *sessho* (infant) or *kampaku* (adult) emperor, but was overshadowed by Fujiwara no Michinori.

In the late 1150s a dispute arose between the followers of the reigning Emperor Nijo and those who favored the retired (cloistered) Emperor Go-Shirakawa. Michinori and the Taira clan supported Nijo, while Nobuyori and his Minamoto allies supported Go-Shirakawa's bid to retain some influence and power. Nobuyori saw this as an opportunity to advance his cause, and in early 1160, with a faction of supporters, including members of the Minamoto clan, attacked and burned the Sanj Palace, and abducted both Emperors Niji and Go-Shirakawa They then turned on Michinori, destroying his home and killing all those inside, with the exception of Michinori himself, who escaped only to be captured and beheaded soon afterwards.

Nobuyori then forced Niji to appoint him chancellor. His reign was all but brief, as Taira no Kiyomori, who had been absent, presently returned to the capital and quickly retook it. The emperors were both freed, the Minamoto were defeated, and Nobuyori was killed.

Above: Fujiwara no Nobuyori. *(British Museum/Jo St Mart)*

brother Minamoto no Yoshimitsu, who had arrived from Kyoto, began a siege of the stronghold.

The siege was drawn out for several months, but finally succeeded after an assault on the fortress with the aid of Fujiwara no Kiyohira.[9] [10] The stockade was set aflame, and Iehara was defeated. The Minamoto forces suffered great losses as well. It is said that during the fighting Yoshiie exhibited great leadership, maintaining morale and discipline among the warriors.[11]

The Hogen Rebellion

Ultimately, however, the Gosannen War was largely a provincial matter and its outcome was of little consequence to the Kyoto government. So too was another dispute that Yoshiie was drawn into in 1091, between Fujiwara Sanekiyo and Kiyowara Norikiyo. However, in 1156, the powerful Fujiwara clan once more became embroiled in a much more significant dispute

over imperial succession and control of the position of regent. This shortly led to the so-called *Hogen no ran* (Hogen Rebellion), which succeeded in establishing the dominance of the clans and eventually the first *samurai*-led government in the history of Japan.

After the death of the cloistered Emperor Toba,[12] Emperor Go-Shirakawa and the retired Emperor Sutoku,[13] both sons of Go-Toba, disputed over succession to the throne and continuation of the cloistered government. In this dispute, Fujiwara no Tadamichi, first son of regent Fujiwara no Tadazane, sided with Go-Shirakawa while his younger brother Fujiwara no Yorinaga declared for Sutoku. Each rival side in turn called on the Minamoto and Taira clans for military

Right: Fujiwara Yorinaga fought against the Go-Shirakawa party. He was one of the last major advocates in favor of restoring the once powerful Fujiwara Regency. *(British Museum/Jo St Mart)*

assistance.[14] Minamoto no Tameyoshi, head of the Minamoto, and Taira no Tadamasa took up with with Sutoku and Yorinaga,[15] while Minamoto no Yoshitomo and Taira no Kiyomori, head of the Taira clan, allied with Go-Shirakawa and Tadamichi.

Throughout late June and into the first days of July 1156, the antagonists assembled their forces in Kyoto, as people fled the capital[16] to escape the fighting. Then, on the night of July 11, Kiyomori and Yoshitomo led 600 cavalry in an attack on the Shirakawa Palace (at the time occupied by Yorinaga's troops). The fierce battle raged on into the night,[17] with Tametomo's archers holding off spirited assaults by Kiyomori and Yoshitomo on the West Gate. With the attack in danger of stalling, Yoshitomo was pressed to advise that they burn the enemy out. The palace was duly set aflame and Sutoku's *samurai* were forced to flee the conflagration.[18]

Go-Shirakawa's forces later defeated Sutoku, clearing the way for Emperor Nijo to be appointed to the throne, while Go-Shirakawa became the cloistered emperor in 1158. Of the others, Sutoku was banished to Sanuki Province on Shikoku, Fujiwara no Yorinaga was killed in

Above: Protecting a royal carriage, scroll painting details from "The Burning of the Sanjo Palace." *(Burstein Collection/Corbis)*

Top right: Detail of a *samurai* beheading an enemy, from a scroll painting of "The Burning of the Sanjo Palace." *(Burstein Collection/Corbis)*

Right: Detail of a mounted *samurai*, from a scroll painting of "The Burning of the Sanjo Palace." *(Burstein Collection/Corbis)*

battle, and Minamoto no Tameyoshi and Taira no Tadamasa were publicly executed on the banks of the Kamo River.[19] Tametomo survived the battlefield but was later captured and sent into exile on the Isle of Devils.[20]

The Taira and Minamoto were handsomely rewarded for their service, with gifts of land and positions in government. Yoshitomo assumed leadership of the Minamoto after the death of his father and, together with Taira no Kiyomori, succeeded in establishing the two clans as major new political powers in Kyoto. Soon these two would fight their own battles, during the Heiji Rebellion of 1159. This event has been described as "chronologically the first conflict in a historical process culminating in warrior domination of society in Japan."

The Heiji Rebellion

Prefacing the chapters describing the Heiji Rebellion the Heike Story says: "In the two years since the end of the Hogen War, many changes had taken place in Kyoto. The emperor's palace was rebuilt. New ministers headed the various departments of state, and new laws were enacted...a general air of peace prevailed, when without warning or apparent cause the Emperor Go-Shirakawa was dethroned and the Emperor Nijo ascended the throne."[21]

Thus, just three years after the Hogen Rebellion, war again broke out between rival subjects of the cloistered emperor, the "sly and wily" Go-Shirakawa.[22] This was known as the Heiji Rebellion or *Heiji no ran*, and has often been seen as a direct outcome of the preceding conflict.[23]

The rebellion unfolded in early January of 1160, when Taira no Kiyomori departed the capital with his family on a pilgrimage to Kumano.[24] Seizing upon his temporary absence Fujiwara no Nobuyori and Minamoto no Yoshitomo moved to wrest control of the capital. The Sanjo Palace,[25] residence of the Cloistered Emperor Go-Shirakawa, was attacked and the former emperor was taken as a hostage. Emperor Nijo, ally of their enemies, the Taira clan and Fujiwara no Michinori, was placed under house arrest. They next moved on Michinori, attacking and burning his mansion, and killing all inside except Michinori himself. He escaped, only to be captured later and executed. To legitimize the claim, Nobuyori then forced Emperor Nijo to recognize him as imperial chancellor.

By this time, however, Taira no Kiyomori had already received news of the coup and was rushing back, with his son Taira no Shigemori and a small force of troops. Once his troops had gained the capital, Kiyomori sought shrewdly to lull the usurpers into a false sense of security by offering them his surrender. Appearing to present no threat, he was thus allowed to return to the Taira mansion in the Rokuhara district, where he set about winning over allies for a planned counter coup.

Left: Dramatic print of Taira Shigemori and his magnificent horse. Shigemori took part in the Hogen and Heiji rebellions. *(British Museum/Jo St Mart)*

Right: Statue of So Yoshitomo. *(via Jo St Mart)*

At the end of January, the Taira smuggled the Emperor Nijo and his empress consort out of the Sanjo Palace and into the Rokuhara Palace, disguised as a lady in waiting. Go-Shirakawa, too, was helped to escape.

By the end of January, a Taira assault on the (occupied) Sanjo Palace appeared imminent; Kiyomori had already received an imperial grant from the emperor to attack Yoshitomo and Nobuyori, and Minamoto no Yoshitomo and his men were preparing to defend it. The first attacks were led by Taira no Shigemori[26] at the head of 3,000 cavalry on the morning of February 5. Nobuyori, it seems, ran away immediately, but Minamoto no Yoshihira (the eldest son of Yoshitomo) stood his ground. Initially at least, the defense held firm and the two armies were soon locked in a fierce exchange. Then, at a crucial moment, a portion of the Taira feigned a retreat, luring Minamoto warriors out of the palace, and giving the rest of their force the opportunity to rush the gates. Soon afterwards, the Minamoto were driven out. Yoshitomo's men then attempted to attack the Rokuhara Palace, but the assault failed and they fled Kyoto *en masse*, meeting resistance along the way from the warrior monks of Mount Hiei who they had attacked in decades past. Ultimately, Taira no Kiyomori defeated Yoshitomo, killed his two eldest sons and Nobuyori, and released Go-Shirakawa. Yoshitomo was eventually betrayed and killed by a retainer in Owari, while escaping from Kyoto. The whole sorry episode was, in the words of Karl Friday, a "poorly conceived and clumsily executed attempt by Yoshitomo to eliminate his rival."[27]

However, although it was comparatively brief and highly localized, the Heiji Rebellion and its aftermath deeply affected the course of Japanese history. Afterwards, Taira no Kiyomori banished Yoshitomo's sons (including Minamoto no Yoritomo, who was sent to Izu in eastern Japan[28]) and seized Minamoto's wealth and land, and subsequently went on to form a government led by the Taira.

Kiyomori himself dominated Kyoto politics for the next decade, but as we shall see in the following chapter, he overreached his political position by trying to have his infant grandson installed as emperor. When that happened many rallied to the banner of Kiyomori's old rival, the Minamoto, and the result was another war.

Right: The priest Mongaku goads Minamoto Yoritomo into rebelling by showing him the skull of his father. *(British Museum/Jo St Mart)*

Minamoto no Yoshiie (1039–1106)

Minamoto no Yoshiie was a noted military commander in the mid-Heian Period, and the man often described as the first progenitor of the *samurai*. Yoshiie was the son of Minamoto Yoriyoshi. He accompanied his father on his expedition to suppress the Abe clan in Mutsu (*Zenkunen kassen* or Former Nine-Years War), and soon proved his talent for fighting. Successes against the Abe (including Sadato in 1062) gained him governorship of Mutsu and the epithet *Hachimantaro* or Great Son of Hachiman (the God of War).

In 1083 Yoshiie became embroiled in a power struggle within the Kiyowara clan in the Tohoku region, sparking off the conflict known as the *Gosannen kassen* or Later Three-Year War. In the subsequent siege of Kanazawa, Yoshiie defeated the Kiyohara. Receiving no commission from the court, he recompensed his men from his own holdings, enhancing his already impressive reputation.

Right: Minamoto no Yoshiie. *(via Clive Sinclaire)*

NOTES

1 The first test of strength between these two clans had been in 1028, when the Minamoto were called to suppress Taira Tadatsune's attempts to expand into Awa Province. Ref: Minoru Shinoda *The Founding of the Kamakura Bakufu 1180–1185* Columbia (1960) p.39 and Karl F. Friday *Samurai, Warfare and State in Early Medieval* Japan p.116.

2 This event is the focus of the *Heike Monogatari* (The Heike Story), one of the classic works of early Japanese literature.

3 Hasegawa Tadashi *The Early Stages of the Heike Monogatari* Monumenta Nipponica 22: 1; p.65.

4 Eiji Yoshikawa *The Heike Story* (Fuki Wooyenaka Uramatsu trans) p.11.

5 There is some disagreement as to the exact date of the start of the war. Some scholars date the war to the period of 1086 to 1089, others place it a few years earlier, lasting from 1083 to 1087.

6 As Karl Friday points out, "'written sources from the tenth and twelfth centuries, other than literary texts, tend to be terse in their accounts of battles, making it difficult to assemble meaningful statistics on Heian strategy and tactics." *Valorous Butchers: The Art of War during the Golden Age of the Samurai* Japan Forum 5: 1 p.8.

7 Much of the war is depicted in an e-maki narrative handscroll, the Gosannen Kassen E-maki, owned today by the Watanabe Museum in Tottori city, Japan.

8 Fujiwara no Kiyohira's maternal grandfather was Abe no Yoritoki and his uncle was Abe no Sadato, both Minamoto enemies who perished during the Zenkunen War. All of his mother's brothers were deported to Kyushu, while his father, Fujiwara no Tsunekiyo, was personally beheaded by Minamoto no Yoriyoshi using a blunt sword. These experiences may well have persuaded Kiyohira to remain loyal to the Minamoto

9 During this siege the two Minamoto brothers apparently dissected bodies of fallen enemy soldiers in order to study their anatomical structures. This practice was said to have helped Yoshimitsu in perfecting unarmed fighting skills.

10 *Hogen monogatari* William R. Wilson trans. p.5-7,

11 He had come to the throne as an infant in 1141 *The Heike Story* (Fuki Wooyenaka Uramatsu trans.) p.116

12 Hogen monogatari William R. Wilson trans. p.11

13 According to the Heike (p.201, Fuki Wooyenaka Uramatsu trans) Tameyoshi was reluctant to do so.

14 Eiji Yoshikawa. *The Heike Story* (Fuki Wooyenaka Uramatsu trans) p.181

15 Most of the latter part of Chapter XV of the Heike Story is devoted to a description of this battle.

16 The episode is described in detail in Volume II

of the *Hogen monogatari* (p.35-51, William R. Wilson trans.)

17 Eiji Yoshikaw *The Heike Story* (Fuki Wooyenaka Uramatsu trans.) p.236

18 See P.100-107 *Hogen monogatari* (William R. Wilson trans.)

19 Eiji Yoshikawa *The Heike Story* (Fuki Wooyenaka Uramatsu trans.) p.273

20 As Jane Goodwin says, "Go-Shirakawa has not fared well in history, nor was he honored in his own time." *Go Shirakawa and Todai-ji Japanese Journal of Religious Studies* 17: 2; 3 p.223

21 Richard A. Gabriel and Donald W. Boose Jr *The Great Battles of Antiquity* Greenwood Press (1994) p.573

22 Eiji Yoshikawa *The Heike Story* (Fuki Wooyenaka Uramatsu trans.) p.279

23 Karl F. Friday *Samurai, Warfare and State in Early Medieval Japan* p.10

24 The eldest son of Kiyomori, who assumed the clan leadership and leadership of imperial forces in 1167.

25 Karl F. Friday *Samurai, Warfare and State in Early Medieval Japan* p.10

26 Eiji Yoshikawa *The Heike Story* (Fuki Wooyenaka Uramatsu trans.) p.388

27 Karl F Friday *Samurai, Warfare and Stae in Early Medieval Japan* p.10

28 Eiji Yoshikawa *The Heike Story* (Fuki Wooyenaka Uramatsu (trans)) p.388

THE GENJII & HEIKE (1180–1185)

The ultimate conflict of the Heian Period was the Genpei Wars *(Genpei gassen)*, fought between 1180 and 1185. During its five-year course some of the most celebrated battles in Japanese history took place. Most scholars attribute great significance to the outcome of the war as an influence on subsequent events, most notably the establishment of a form of military government controlled by the *samurai*—the Kamakura *shogunate*. This was the final act in the displacement of the court nobility *(kuge)* by the *samurai* class. From this point forward *shogunates* would dominate Japanese politics for nearly seven hundred years (1185–1868), undermining the power of the emperor and of the court.

Thus far, conflict within Japan had been largely localized and comparatively small in scale.[1] However, between 1180 and 1185 much of central and western Japan became a battleground for competing factions centered on one side on the Minamoto, and on the other the Taira. Although there has been a tendency to explain the war as a conflict between these two powerful warrior clans, this oversimplifies what in reality was far more complicated.[2] Complex alliances were formed that saw Minamoto pitted against Minamoto and likewise with the Taira. More accurately, the conflict was borne out of "intra-familial and inter-class frustration with the structure of land-holding and administrative rights in the provinces, and was fought between those on the one side who were sufficiently dissatisfied with their lot under the status quo…and those who were content with their current situation."[3]

One of the major problems with assessing the Genpei Wars has always been the lack of reliable historical information on the conflict. Given the relative paucity of information available, the most commonly used sources of information on this pivotal period in Japanese history have traditionally been the *Heike Monogatari*, and the *Azuma kagami*. However, there are many frustrating omissions and inconsistencies in both accounts. The characters of Minamoto no Yoshitsune and Minamoto no Noriyori, who both played a major role in the prosecution of the war, are conspicuously absent for a large part of the account. It is also widely acknowledged that figures given for the troop strengths are commonly exaggerated,[4] often grossly so, and the validity of certain other information is also highly questionable.

Background

In 1165, the Emperor Nijo died, and was succeeded by Rokujo as the Titular emperor. However, as before, the cloistered emperor, Go-Shirakawa, and the Fujiwara family wielded the real power. In the year following Rokujo's assumption Fujiwara noble Motofusa became regent, a title he would hold until 1179.

However, within three years of his accession to the Chrysanthemum throne, Rokujo was forced to abdicate by Go-Shirakawa in favor of his seven-year-old son Taira no Takakura.

Much of this had been at the prompting of Taira no Kiyomori, whose wife was older sister to the boy's mother, Taira no Shigeko. Kiyomori was by this time the most powerful noble in Japan. The story of this critical period in Japanese history, and that of Minamoto no Yoritomo, is inextricably linked with his name.

It will be remembered that after the death of his father, Taira no Tadamori, in 1153, Kiyomori had assumed control of the Taira clan and entered the

The Genpei Wars

political realm, in which he had previously held only a minor post. In 1156, he and Minamoto no Yoshitomo, head of the Minamoto clan, suppressed the Hogen Rebellion. This established the Taira and Minamoto *samurai* clans as the leading warrior clans in Kyoto. However, their new strength in effect caused the allies to become bitter rivals, which culminated three years later during the Heiji Rebellion in 1159. Kiyomori, emerged victorious from that conflict and the Taira became the single most powerful warrior family/clan in Kyoto.

Due to his status as the head of the sole remaining courtier/warrior clan, Kiyomori was in a unique position to manipulate the court rivalry between the retired sovereign Go-Shirakawa and his son, Nijo tenno (*tenno* – sovereign). Via this manipulation, Kiyomori was able to climb the ranks of government, though the majority of his promotions as well as the success of his family in gaining ranks and titles at court were due to the patronage of the retired sovereign Go-Shirakawa, who

continued to exercise power as a cloistered emperor until his death in 1192.

In 1167, Kiyomori became the first courtier of a warrior family to be appointed *Daijo Daijin*, chief minister of the government, and *Naidaijin* or Home Minister. The holding of these titles was a first for a member of a military clan. As was the norm, he soon relinquished the position and leadership of the Taira clan. Both ambitious and astute, Kiyomori also garnered a reputation as something of a degenerate, "seeking the social and political prestige of the highest office in the land without the burden of the attendant duties."

In early 1172 Kiyomori's daughter, Tokuko, became Emperor Takakura's consort, further consolidating his position at court. Increasingly, these and other of Kiyomori's actions were judged with resentment by Go-Shirakawa and the Fujiwara family. For them it seemed apparent that the power of the Taira should be limited in some way. Thus, Go-Shirakawa and the Fujiwara became

Above: Minamoto Yoshitsune is a popular figure in Japanese myth and legend. Here he is seen fleeing from his enemies with his older brother, Yoritomo. *(via Clive Sinclair)*

Right: Minamoto Yoritomo was the founder and first *shogun* of the Kamakura *Shogunate*. He had Imperial blood from his father and Fujiwara noble blood from his mother. *(The Art Archive)*

embroiled in a plot against Kiyomori, one that opened an irreparable breach between the Heike, and the Retired Emperor and the Genji.

The affair became known as the Shishigatani Incident (*Shishigatani jiken*) or the Shishigatani Conspiracy or Plot, and is the most famous of a number of conspiracies and uprisings against Kiyomori.[5] The plot, which was hatched with the full knowledge of Go-Shirawaka, centered on group of several nobles that included Fujiwara no Narichika, his son Naritsune, Fujiwara no Saiko, Taira no Yasuyori, and Tada Yukitsuna. Unbeknown to them, Kiyomori had recruited the latter as a spy, and was thus fully appraised of their plot. In June 1177 the conspirators were arrested and either executed or exiled. In the aftermath of the incident, Kiyomori castigated Go-Shirakawa for his passive role in the plot, while the Fujiwara had certain properties seized. Kiyomori then purged the government of suspected enemies, including the regent Fujiwara no Motofusa, and replaced them with trusted members of his own family.

Resentments seethed, storm clouds continued to gather, and the threat of war loomed ever larger. When in 1179 the head of the Taira, Shigemori (Kiyomori's eldest son) died and was replaced by his brother (Munemori) Go-Shirakawa interpreted this as a chance to regain lost advantage, and began to dismiss Taira from their positions within the court officialdom.

In reaction to this affront, in December 1179 Kiyomori marched into the capital with several thousand troops, ostensibly in retaliation for Go-Shirakawa's having confiscated some Taira property earlier in the year. The emperor of the time, Takakura, was forced to abdicate, and Kiyomori's two-year-old grandson Antoku was elevated in his place. Go-Shirakawa was placed under house arrest and Kiyomori's rivals were removed from all government posts and subsequently banished. Kiyomori then filled the vacant positions with his allies and relatives.[6]

The other noble families were outraged by this. Takakura immediately sent emissaries to the Minamoto for support, and on May 5, 1180, Prince Mochihito (who had been bypassed for the throne in favor of

Antoku) issued a general call to arms against the Taira.[7] This act marks the beginning of what has come to be called the Genpei War,[8] a five-year struggle that would cast a long shadow over Japan and change its political landscape forever.

The Battle of the Uji Bridge

The first battle of the Genpei War was fought at the 1,400-year-old Uji Bridge, located near the historic Byodo-in temple complex in the picturesque Uji River valley near Kyoto. It is said to have first been erected in 646 by Doto, a priest of the Gango Temple in Nara, and with the Seta Bridge upriver was one of the two key eastern entry points to Kyoto. Stretching along the Uji River are various places noted in connection with the last ten chapters (*Uji-jujo*),

of the *Tale of Genji*, a masterpiece of Japanese literature written by the Lady Murasaki Shikibu.

On a hot June day in 1180, this tranquil valley rang with the sounds of battle, which continued to echo across Japan for half a decade. In the days beforehand Prince Mochihito had been pursued by Taira forces to the Mii-dera, a temple just outside Kyoto.[9] But, due to the interference of a Mii-dera monk with Taira sympathies, the Minamoto army arrived too late to help defend the temple. With the Taira pressing close at his heels, Minamoto no Yorimasa[10] led Prince Mochihito, along with the Minamoto army and a number of warrior monks (*sohei*), from Mii-dera, south towards Nara. They crossed the Uji River over the Uji Bridge—and as they crossed, the planks of the bridge behind them were torn up to halt the progress of the pursuing Taira.

Warrior monks (*sohei*) first appeared in a significant way in Japan in the middle of the 10th century, when bitter political feuds began between different temples following different sub-sects of Buddhism, over imperial appointments to the top temple positions (i.e. abbot, or *zasu*). Much of the fighting over the next four centuries was over these sorts of political feuds, and centered around the temples of Kyoto and Nara, namely the Todai-ji, Kofuku-ji, Enryaku-ji, and Mii-dera, the four largest temples in the country. In 970, following a dispute between Enryaku-ji and the Gion Shrine of Kyoto, the former established the first standing army of warrior monks. Disputes continued through the 11th and into the 12th centuries. The armies became larger, and the violence increased, until in 1121 and 1141 Mii-dera was burned to the ground by monks from Enryakuji. Other temples became embroiled in the conflicts as well, and Enryaku-ji and Mii-dera united against Kofuku-ji, and, at another time, against Kiyomizu-dera.

At the Uji bridge, the monks[11] fought bravely, repulsing the Taira warriors with their traditional *naginata* polearms, bows and arrows, swords, and daggers. But their ruse to sabotage the bridge failed, since the river was fordable and Taira forces were able to cross. Soon they overtook the fleeing Minamoto band and ultimately defeated them. Yorimasa made valiant efforts to ensure that the prince did

Above: Minamoto no Yoritomo enjoying his first battle, despite the snow. *(via Clive Sinclaire)*

Right: Portrait of Minamoto no Yoritomo. *(British Museum/Jo St Mart)*

not fall into enemy hands, but in so doing was felled by Taira bowmen. Rather than surrender, the wounded Yorimasa chose to take his own life by *seppuku* at the the Byodo-in, setting a precedent for subsequent generations of *samurai*.[12] His sacrifice, however, proved to be tragically futile, since the prince was captured and killed by the Taira warriors shortly afterwards.

In the aftermath of the defeat at Uji Bridge, Kiyomori[13] exacted bloody revenge on the monks who had opposed him. Mii-dera was burned to the ground once again, and Kiyomori next moved on Nara.[14] Taira no Shigehira and Tomomori, both sons of Kiyomori, led the attack.

They were opposed again by *sohei* from nearly every major monastery and temple in Nara. The monks dug ditches in the roads, and built many forms of improvised defenses. However, whereas the Taira were mounted, the *sohei* fought on foot, putting them at an acute disadvantage. Despite the monks' superior numbers, and their strategic defenses, their enemy succeeded in destroying nearly every temple in the city, including the Kofuku-ji and Todai-ji. At Todiji the destruction was catastrophic. The huge copper and gold Daibutsu, a statue of Vairocana Buddha, was "melted into a shapeless mass."[15] In all, an estimated 3,500 people died in the burning of Nara. Only the Enryaku-ji managed to repel the attackers and survive.

Minamoto Yoritomo

In mid-August, the exiled Minamoto warrior Yoritomo finally moved to take up Mochihito's call to arms and declared war on the Taira. It will be remembered that after his defeat in the Heiji Rebellion, Yoritomo had been exiled to Hirugashima, a Hojo-controlled island in Izu province. During his twenty-year incarceration, Yoritomo had succeeded in winning over his court-appointed guard, Hojo Tokimasa, to his side, and in 1179 he also made a marriage of convenience with Tokimasa's daughter, Masako.

At the death of Minamoto no Yorimasa and Prince Mochihito himself at the Battle of Uji, Yoritomo declared

himself the rightful heir to leadership of the Minamoto clan. During the Genpei War, Yoritomo proved himself a wily and resourceful man and, although his power in the Genpei War was primarily through his role as a statesman, not a soldier, less than a decade later he became *shogun*. His rise is all the more remarkable when one considers that "Yoritomo held no government posts or titles on private estates, led no warband of his own, and controlled no lands," and that "His one and only asset was in fact his tenuous claim to a rightful pre-eminence among his surviving kinsmen."[16]

But this position was not won easily, since Yoritomo's early efforts to attract followers to the cause were frustrated by complex inter-family politics, alliances, and fear of reprisal.[17] Having issued his declaration of war, Yoritomo found himself facing an awkward dilemma. He could not afford to hesitate long, for fear that he would be surprised by an attack by local Taira lords. However,

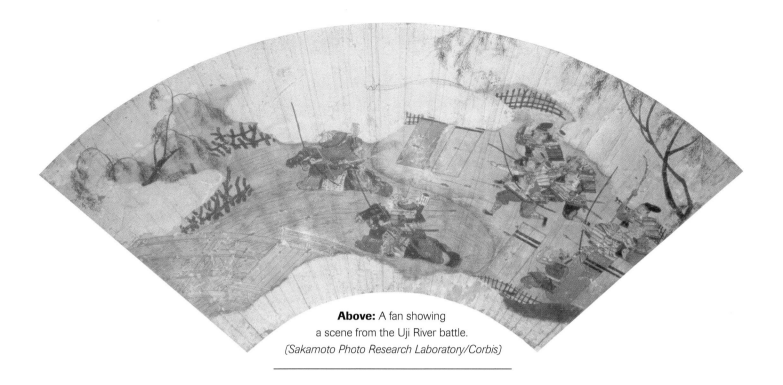

Above: A fan showing
a scene from the Uji River battle.
(Sakamoto Photo Research Laboratory/Corbis)

he lacked the strength in numbers for any major action; with reinforcement from the Miura and Chiba he could count on only a small force of three hundred. Thus, only by the slenderest of margins was Yoritomo able to drum up sufficient support for his first action of the war, a cautious attack on August 17 on the Yamagi headquarters of Deputy Yamamoto Kanetaka, who was in due course executed. After that Yoritomo tried again to rally others

Below: Gochin no Tajima—also known as Tajima the arrow-cutter—was a warrior monk who fought alongside the Minamoto clan forces at the Battle of Uji in 1180. *(via Clive Sinclaire)*

to his flag, moving around the Kanto in an attempt to gather followers. He sent out messages to the now widely dispersed Minamoto elders, but many of those in the vicinity of Izu still rejected his pleas, and some in fact sided with the Taira.

Above: Minamoto Yorimasa was a Buddhist monk and court poet, and during his long career served eight different emperors. He also fought many battles, in particular leading the Minamoto armies and the warrior monks from Mii-dera into battle at the beginning of the Genpei War. His ritual suicide following defeat at the Battle of Uji (1180) is the first recorded *seppuku* by a defeated *samurai*. (British Museum/Jo St Mart)

Battle of Ishibashiyama

In September 1180, as Yoritomo sallied his tiny army eastward out of Izu into Sagami, he was in a precarious position. His army was outnumbered ten-fold and his hold on Izu tentative at best. Nevertheless, Yoritomo marched on towards the pass in the Hakone mountains, through which he planned to advance.

Already appraised of the movement, Kiyomori had appointed Oba Kagechika to halt the advance. Like many of this age, the battle began with a surprise attack at night. On September 14, at Ishibashiyama, in the Hakone Mountains, near Mount Fuji, the forces of Ito

Sugechika attacked Yoritomo's men from the rear. After much bloody fighting Yoritomo was forced to concede defeat and flee.[18]

In the aftermath of the battle, Yoritomo and his men scattered and found a few days' sanctuary in the Hakone mountains. On August 29 Yoritomo escaped to the relative security of Awa province at the tip of the peninsula across the bay from Sagami. He had been lucky to escape. The defeat at Ishibashiyama had been an inauspicious beginning for Yoritomo as commander of the Minamoto forces. To compound his problems, the Minamoto cause had been dealt a body blow at Kingusa,

Samurai Armor

The Heian Period was marked by progressive development in the weapons and armor of the Japanese soldier. The two distinct types of armor that had been developed in the Yamato and Nara Periods—the *tanko* and *keiko* (scale armor)—began to be superseded by the familiar *o-yoroi* or great armor. This is the armor that most people associate with the *samurai*, and has the appearance of a heavy, square, boxy suit.

The remnants of the oldest surviving *o-yoroi* (on display at Oyamazumi Jinja) show that the earliest designs were just leather boards made of *kozane* (scales) laced together and then lacquered to form a solid, overlapping plate. (This is in contrast to earlier *keiko*, on which the scales hung loose.) The advantage of the new design was that it offered increased protection; conversely, it also placed more restriction on the wearer's movements. *O-yoroi* was very ornate, with six different colors of lacing.

A significant feature of the *o-yoroi* is that it was completely open on the right side. Three large, heavy

Above: A *do*, known as *haramaki*, in *murasa-ki-ito odoshi*, or deep purple lacing, with *sode*, from the 16th century. *(via Clive Sinclaire)*

Above: White-laced *domaru* with sixty-two-plate *suji-bachi*, believed to date from the 18th century. *(via Clive Sinclaire)*

sets of skirt plates of *kozane* boards hung from it—one in front, one at the back, and one on the left. A solid metal plate called a *waidate*, from which hung the fourth set of skirt plates, protected the right side. Two large square or rectangular shoulder protectors called *o-sode* were attached at the shoulder straps.

Small rounded flanges stuck up from the shoulder straps to give added protection to the side of the neck. Hanging in the front of the armor to protect the armpits were two plates called the *sendan-no-ita* and *kyub-no-ita*.

The entire front of the torso was covered with a printed or patterned

---

where a force under Miura Yoshiaki had met with defeat as it advanced to meet him.

But now, it seemed, the tide began to turn in his favor. A steady stream of followers began to join the revolt, and some (such as the Kai Minamoto) even began to launch attacks. On September 17 a newly confident Yoritomo left Awa and journeyed to the fishing village of Kamakura in Sagami,[19] a traditional Minamoto stronghold, which he reached on October 10. Here, with financial help from the Hojo, he set up his capital, settled his army, and prepared to meet the expected Taira counterattack. The journey itself was "one of the more remarkable events of the war and constituted a turning point in the young

conflict."[20] Remarkable indeed, as he was able to increase his following from barely three hundred to an estimated 27,000, many of whom had only recently engaged Yoritomo at Ishibashiyama.

There were several motives for the *volte face* of many former Taira supporters. Minoru Shinoda succinctly puts it thus: "Yoritomo's successes in rallying local lords to his standard after the Battle of Ishibashi Mountain can be attributed in a large measure to his willingness—in fact his eagerness—to embrace his former enemies."[21]

Battle of Fujigawa

As the cooler weather began to settle over the landscape,

Above: Kuroda-family-style brown-laced *domaru* with gold-lacquered horns (18th century). *(via Clive Sinclaire)*

leather apron called *tsurubashiri* ("bowstring-running"). The purpose of this covering was to keep the bowstring from catching on the scales as the warrior fired his bow. Mounted

warriors in Japan often shot arrows with their hand along the breast rather than by their ear (the large helmets typically prevented usual firing methods). This same leather pattern was used all over the armor.

Early warriors only wore one armored sleeve (*kote*) on the left arm; this was tied across the body with long leather straps. The sleeve's primary purpose was to keep the bulky armor-robe sleeves out of the way of the bow. Around camp, warriors typically wore the *waidate*, *kote*, a throat guard (*nodowa*), and their leg armor (*suneate*) as a sort of "half-dress" armor. These items together are referred to as *kogusoku* (small armor).

The *o-yoroi*, as well as being bulky and heavy, was also expensive. A full suit could take as long as six months to make. For subordinates, the *do-maru* and *haramaki* armors were developed. These had more skirt plates and fitted closer to the body, obviating the need for a *waidate* (part of the *cuirass* providing separate defense of the right side). The *do-maru* opened under the right arm; the *haramaki* opened at the back

Above: Sendai-style white-laced, five-plate armor for samurai boy's coming of age ceremony (18th century). *(via Clive Sinclaire)*

Yoritomo assembled his forces at Kamakura and plotted his next move. Already, on September 29, a large force under Taira Koremori had departed from Kyoto and by October 13 was in Suruga. On the 16th, a much larger army set out under Yoritomo to confront them. There are many estimates of its strength; the *Jisho* records that more than 200,000 marched west over the Ashigara Pass, but the figure is likely less than half that.[22]

As he moved through the region below Mount Fuji and into Suruga Province, Yoritomo rendezvoused with the Takeda clan and other families of the provinces of Kai and Kozuke to the north. On the 20th a vastly more formidable Minamoto army drew up on the east bank of

the Fujigawa River.[23] Facing them on the opposite bank lay the army of the Taira. It was the first time since the outbreak of the war that the two had met.

What happened next was therefore something of an anticlimax. To describe it as a battle is somewhat misleading, for actual instances of combat there were none. According to the most accounts, late on the night of October 20, a Minamoto scout put to flight a vast flock of nesting waterfowl as he tried to reconnoiter the Taira rear. The great noise made by the birds as they rose into the air snapped something within the Taira soldiers, already made nervous by the presence of thousands of camp fires on the opposite bank.[24] Their commanders, fearing a Minamoto

Above: Triptych showing the "Ghosts of the Slain Taira Clan above the Ship of Yoshitsune" by Kuniyoshi, 1794. *(Christie's Images/Corbis)*

surprise attack, fled back in the direction of Kyoto whence they had come, without any actual fighting taking place. Twelve days later they were back in the capital, "never again to challenge Yoritomo on his own ground."[25]

This scenario, if it is true, says much about the apprehension with which the Taira now viewed any battle with Yoritomo's army. Indeed, battle reports by their commanders, as documented in the *Jisho*, indicate that many were gripped with fear at the prospect. However, as Gabriel and Boose point out, "some historians believe the story of the wild geese and the frantic retreat has been exaggerated…[as] a Taira strategic withdrawal from Fujigawa would have been a sound course of action in view of the strength of the Minamoto forces and the recent defections of war bands from the Taira army."[26]

Fortunately for them, Yoritomo, who wanted to pursue the Taira army to Kyoto, was persuaded to err on the side of caution by his commanders. Instead he turned back to Sagami, choosing to postpone military operations against the Taira in the interest of unifying the east, where internal discord between the various Minamoto factions threatened his leadership.

The inconclusive Fujigawa battle marked the end of several highly eventful months of campaigning, and by comparison the winter of 1180–81 proved relatively quiet. However, there were several incidents of significance worth detailing. The first was the

capitulation of the Oba clan, and its leader Oba Kagechika, to Yoritomo on November 23. Kagechika, who only two months previously had defeated Yoritomo at Ishibashiyama, was decapitated. The second was Yoritomo's defeat in December of the powerful Satake clan in Hitachi, who had been unwilling to give their loyalty to his cause and threatened to occupy the Minamoto territories in the east. This victory, together with Yoritomo's now conspicuous military strength, had the effect of drawing others to his flag.

One exception to these helpful events concerned Yoritomo's uncle, Shida Yoshihiro, who despite initial pronouncements of loyalty turned on Yoritomo once he quit Hitachi and sent a 30,000 strong force to attack Kamakura.[27] It was defeated, and thereafter few of the Minamoto would try to oppose him. Nonetheless, perhaps conscious of his shortcomings as a military leader, henceforth he trusted more capable generals with the conduct of the war. Safe in his well-protected base at Kamakura, Yoritomo had little to fear from Taira attacks, as he now took no active part in the fighting.

One such general, who was to prove invaluable to Yoritomo, was his brother, Yoshitsune. Like his sibling, Yoshitsune had spent the two decades since the Heiji Rebellion in exile, but entirely isolated from Yoritomo in Oshu in northern Japan. From his place of incarceration Yoshitsune traveled south to be reunited with his brother,[20] escorted by guards somewhat surprisingly provided by his custodians. From this time his star was firmly in ascendance, as he rose to become one of the most celebrated of the samurai commanders.[29]

By spring of the following year, Yoritomo had drawn most of the Kanto families into his camp. But before any effort could be made to move into the Taira heartland the strategically important Chubu region had to be fully subjugated. Instead of risking weakening his position by moving the armies west, Yoritomo, typically, erred on the side of caution. Rather than take on the Taira in large scale actions, he sought to strengthen his grip on those territories he already held; instead, small bands of his supporters took up the fight,[30] engaging the enemy in small harassing actions around the Kyoto stronghold and in the western provinces of Kyushu and Shikoku.

Battle of Sunomata

As the war entered its second year, the Yoritomo camp had begun to adopt a new policy of containment and consolidation.[31] In the Taira camp too, there was a noticeable downscaling of military operations. Early in the year, old Taira no Kiyomori fell gravely ill, and then died; with his death began "a long decline in Taira fortunes."[32] As his eldest son Shigemori was already dead, Kiyomori declared from his deathbed his wish that all control of the Taira clan should pass to Taira no Munemori. Although—unlike his cautious father—Munemori was eager for a more aggressive policy against the Minamoto, Taira campaigning in the east was curtailed, never again to be resumed. Instead, the armies were employed in local actions in the vicinity of Kyoto against rebellious monasteries.

During this two year hiatus in the Genpei War there were but two large scale clashes: one was at the Sunomata River, one of the three major rivers of the Nobi Plain that covers southwest Gifu and northwest Aichi.[33] Here, as the weather became favorable for campaigning again, Yoritomo's brother Yukiie, in his first action as commander,[34] attempted to carry off a surprise attack on Taira no Tomomori's army. On the night of April 25, finding Taira's army camped directly opposite from his, Yukiie ordered his men to ford the river and slay their

Above: *Samurai* warriors Ichijo Jiro Tadanori and Notonokami Noritsune locked in combat. The latter was known for a famous battle with Yoshitsune. *(Library of Congress Prints and Photographs Division LC-DIG-jpd-00292)*

unsuspecting foes. Their ambush failed, apparently because the Taira could easily distinguish friend from enemy by their sopping wet clothes—even in the pitch dark of night. Consequently, Yukiie and the other surviving Minamoto were forced back across the river. He fled, and tried to take a stand by tearing up the bridge over the Yahagi-gawa and forming a shield wall.

There followed another battle in which Yukiie was again routed, having lost nearly 700 men.[35] Fortune now played a hand, for when their leader Tomomori suddenly fell ill, the Taira halted their pursuit, and withdrew.

In the fall, with the two sides locked in stalemate, a dark new cloud came over the land. The harvest failed,

and famine set in. This, coupled with the factors already discussed, forced a hiatus in the fighting that was to endure for nearly two years. Also in the fall, away from the battlefield, there was a surprising new development when Yoritomo sent emissaries to the Taira with the offer of a peaceful resolution to the conflict. His entreaty called for the partition of the country between the two families, with Yoritomo taking the eastern half of the country. Given the strength of his position at the time, it is curious that Yoritomo should feel so moved. Regardless, despite an apparent willingness at court to at least consider favorable reactions,[36] the peaceful overtures were ultimately rejected.

Minamoto no Yoshinaka

Yoritomo's motives for extending the hand of friendship have never been made fully clear, although some suggest that he was prompted by concerns over the growing power of his cousin, Minamoto Yoshinaka. The latter hailed from Musashi province, where his father Minamoto no Yoshikata once held a large domain. While Yoshinaka was still an infant these lands were seized, and his father was killed by Minamoto no Yoshihira. Thereafter he was raised by the Nakahara clan in Shinano Province (present-day Nagano Prefecture).

Yoshinaka used the lull in the fighting in the Genpei War to build up his powerbase in the rich provinces of Japan's mountainous north east coast, on the Sea of Japan.[37] He had a strong contingent of warriors from Shinano province and although nominally allied to Yoritomo, he was soon to prove an immediate threat both to the Taira, and to Yoritomo's claims of Minamoto leadership.

His motivations require some elaboration. In 1180 Yoshinaka had received Prince Mochihito's rallying call to the members of the Minamoto clan to rise against the Taira. He raised an army in Shinano and quickly conquered the province. In October he raised suspicions as to his loyalty when he moved east from Shinano into Kozuke, instead of westward toward Taira-held territory. Then in 1181, he began attempts to regain his father's domain in Musashi.

Before matters could come to a head, the two cousins were reconciled and resolved not to fight one another. Nonetheless, Yoritomo demanded that he be accepted by Yoshinaka as the leader of the Minamoto clan, that Yoshinaka give up his aspirations for his father's domain, and that he would send his son Yoshitaka to Kamakura as a hostage. The humiliation rankled, and Yoshinaka determined to take Kyoto, defeat the Taira, and take control of the Minamoto for himself.[38]

Yoshinaka's rise to a position of dominance in North Central Japan was viewed with growing alarm in both Kamakura and Kyoto.[39] But as Yoshinaka was a

Below: Minamoto Yoshitsune joined Yoritomo in the Genpei War of 1180. *(British Museum/Jo St Mart)*

Minamoto, the Taira had greater cause for concern; fearing further Minamoto territorial gains, Taira Munemori began planning a campaign to defeat Yoshinaka, who presented a more serious threat even than Yoritomo. Furthermore, Yoshinaka had on a number of occasions raided Taira lands, and the clan was eager for retribution. An attempt was made against him in mid-1181, but met with failure.

By spring of 1183, the worst effects of the famine mentioned above had passed, and conditions were conducive for the launch of a major new offensive—the first in two years—at Yoshinaka's Shinano base. In March 1183 an army of 100,000 men marched out of Kyoto, led by the Taira generals Koremori, Michimori, Yukimori, Tsunemasa, Kiyofusa, and Tomomori.

Koremori was entrusted with overall command of the campaign. Over the course of three years of war, his forces had been severely reduced by battle and famine, and they had to replenish these losses with warriors recruited from lands surrounding Kyoto. The recruitment was clearly a success, for when the host departed from Kyoto, it numbered some 100,000 men.[40] Opposing this formidable army, Yoshinaka could count on the forces of his uncle Minamoto no Yukiie, and the so-called *shitenno,* Imai Kanehira, Higuchi Kanemitsu, Tate Chikatada, and Nenoi Yukichika.

On gaining Kaga Province, Koremori divided the Taira army into two, trying to outflank his enemy. Tomomori was ordered to lead a contingent north and then into Noto Province. The other, led by Koremori, headed east into Echizen Province, which is today the northern part of Fukui Prefecture.

Siege of Hiuchiyama

On his line of march to Echizen Koremori met with sporadic resistance from small bands of Minamoto, but these were easily brushed aside. In the account given in the *Heike,*[41] Yoshinaka's forces had built fortifications at Hiuchiyama, and upon crossing into Echizen, this was where Koremori's force drew up. During April and May Koremori laid siege to the Minamoto who had taken refuge inside. The fortress, long since destroyed, was built on rocky crags, and was well defended; there was also a moat to repel attackers. For two months the defenses held firm, and Koremori could make no progress; however, it seems that at some point a weak area within the fortress defenses was exposed, possibly by someone within the castle, allowing Koremori to breach the dam holding back the waters of the moat, and drain the water. Without this vital barrier the fortress lay exposed. Koremori was able to storm the castle, only to find that it had already been abandoned.

Above: After winning the battle of Kurikara Pass, Yoshinaka and his army marched to Kyoto where his troops looted and burnt the city. He captured Emperor Go-Shirakawa and forced him to make him *shogun*, but Yoshinaka was soon driven out of Kyoto and then killed by his cousins at the battle of Awazu, in Omi Province. *(British Museum/Jo St Mart)*

Battle of Kurikara

Despite the loss of the fortress at Hiuchiyama, Yoshinaka now rallied his troops for a counter-attack, leading a seven-pronged advance at Koremori's army as it pushed further northeast up the coast into Etchu. By June 2, 1183, the Taira had advanced to the Kurikara Pass, a breach in the mountain range up to Tonamiyama that divided western Honshu from the east and Yoshinaka's Shinano stronghold.

During the approach, Koremori had again divided his forces, one part moving up the pass, and the other entering Etchu through Noto Province to the north to threaten from the rear. Acknowledging that he was at a disadvantage in numbers, Yoshinaka decided to employ a clever sham[42] to deceive the enemy. As the Taira forces approached the pass, Yoshinaka had a great host of white war banners (white being the Minamoto clan color) planted on a hill a few miles distant, giving the impression that he commanded a far larger force. The ruse worked. Seeing the banners, the Taira commanders halted, and Yoshinaka was afforded a few precious hours before nightfall, when he planned to use the cover of darkness to pull off his masterstroke.

He separated his own forces into three groups, sending one to attack the Taira from the rear, a second beneath the Pass, as an ambush party, and the third he accompanied and held centrally. To distract the enemy as the troops moved into their respective positions, Yoshinaka made as if he intended to fight according to established conventions. As was customary before battle he ordered his archers to begin firing special arrows fitted with whistling-bulbs, before rival *samurai* challenged each other to single combat.

But Yoshinaka had no intention of "fighting by numbers," as it were, and as the dusk settled his armies moved undetected into position. When the Taira commanders finally realized that the demonstration in front of them had in reality been a grand bluff, it was already too late, for behind them was a Minamoto detachment, again displaying a great profusion of flags to give the illusion of strength beyond their true numbers.

In the center, Yoshinaka's signalers began to blow their conch shells and beat drums, announcing the imminence of the attack. But it was not men who came charging down to meet the Taira warriors, but cows, five hundred of them with torches fastened to their horns in a bellowing, surging stampede. For the men in their path, already exhausted by the long march from Kyoto, the sight must have been truly terrifying. Some brave souls charged headlong into the herd; others were trampled underfoot or swept off the pass and down the steep mountainside onto the rocks below.

The *Heike* here talks of *gansen no chi* (or "streams of blood") which "flowed from rocks." Those still alive simply fled in disarray, but became lost in the warren of paths leading off the pass and were slain by Minamoto forces that lay waiting in the rear. The surviving Taira, confused, demoralized, and having suffered heavy losses, retreated to Jigoku valley.[43]

Now the Taira became the quarry, as Yoshinaka took up the chase. From Etchu the Taira were pursued south west into neighboring Kaga (now part of southern Ishikawa prefecture), and were finally caught at Shinohara. The ensuing battle was largely a formal affair. An archery duel by champions on both sides preceded general fighting, which included several celebrated instances of single combat.

One warrior in particular, Saito Betto Sanemori, has achieved fame, not least because he was reputedly seventy years of age when he fell at Shinohara. As by tradition his armor was presented to Tada *jinja* (shrine) by his vanquisher, Kiso Yoshinaka. In 1689, the famous haiku poet (and spy) Matsuo Basho passed by during his epic tour of Japan and was inspired to write about Sanemori: "*piteous creature, under the pitiless helm, grasshopper lies still.*"

But no degree of heroics could turn the tide of battle; victory went to the Minamoto[44] and Yoshinaka now began a relentless drive all the way to the capital.

The advance on Kyoto

Now, what had begun as a defensive war for Yoshinaka war turned into an offensive war on Kyoto itself, for by the middle of the seventh month he had penetrated Omi Province, directly adjacent to the capital."[45]

In August, with a major battle for control of the capital seemingly imminent, Go-Shirakawa escaped

Kyoto (where he was still under the house arrest ordered by Kiyomori in late 1179) and sought refuge to Mt. Hiei, while the emperor and his consorts hid at a monastery in the suburbs. The flight of both emperors actually seemed to lend weight to the claim that the Minamoto were the legitimate power as they closed in on the capital.

But there was to be no battle for Kyoto. With his warriors demoralized and in disarray, on August 25 a shaken Munemori ordered an evacuation in the face of Yoshinaka's advance. Taking the child-emperor Antoku, the emperor's mother, a few retainers and the imperial regalia, Munemori departed for Dazaifu in the west. Three days later, on August 28, 1183, Yoshinaka and Yukiie entered the capital, bringing with them the retired Emperor Go-Shirakawa from Mt. Hiei.

Yoshinaka's capture of the capital dramatically changed the complexion of the war. Whereas previously Yoritomo had always been the focus for the Minamoto opposition, it was now Yoshinaka and Yukiie who

Above: Minamoto Yukiie (on horseback) was defeated by Taira no Tomomori at the Battle of Sunomatagawa, 1181. He escaped but was eventually betrayed and subsequently beheaded in 1186 on charges of high treason. *(British Museum/Jo St Mart)*

received the mandate from Go-Shirakawa to take the battle to the Taira. It is interesting to note that almost overnight the Taira had become the rebels and the Minamoto the defenders of the imperial court. Furthermore, Yoshinaka was given several offices of high rank and bestowed with gifts of land confiscated from Taira lords, while Yukiie was made governor of Bizen. Such are the fortunes of war.

Within a short time of Yoshinaka's assumption of the role of protector of Kyoto, his relationship with Go-Shirakawa began to deteriorate. Welcomed at first as a liberator, his rough country manners, arrogance, and the indiscretions of his warriors bred discontent and resentment among Kyoto's genteel courtiers.[46]

But the real source of tension was Yoshinaka's procrastination over the conduct of the war; despite receiving an immediate mandate from the emperor to pursue the Taira, Yoshinaka lingered in the capital for a full month, seemingly disinclined to carry on the pursuit. It seems probable that his attention was now focused on the growing prospect of conflict with his brother Yoritomo, whom he had so clearly usurped in taking the capital. Whatever his thoughts, communications between Yoshinaka and Go-Shirakawa indicate the emperor's growing frustration that the Taira were able to retreat more or less intact to Dazai-fu in Kyushu and rally their forces.

Battle of Mizushima

In September a second mandate was issued and Yoshinaka was finally persuaded to leave the city, moving west toward Bitchu. Ultimately, this expedition was to prove his undoing. Already, at the end of August, the Taira had left Dazai-fu and moved to Yashima Island,[47] a small island off the coast of Shikoku, and a point closer to Kyoto. Yashima was one of the most important Taira bases, and they were well placed to hold it; nevertheless, on November 17, Yoshinaka sent an amphibious force under Yata Yoshikiyo across the Inland Sea to attack.

En route to Yashima, Yoshikiyo's force encamped on the island of Mizushima, off Bitchu, where they were attacked by a Taira fleet. The battle has many interesting features, one of which is the lengths to which the Taira commanders went to enable them to fight, using tactics unusual in a naval battle and highly reminiscent of the battles fought on land. Horses were taken onto the ships that were then grouped together, to form a concentrated fighting platform. This gave archers a base from which to launch a fusillade of arrows upon the Minamoto boats. After the initial exchanges of fire, the boats approached and the opposing warriors engaged in hand-to-hand combat. Taira warriors then swam their horses from ship to the shore, and defeated the remaining Minamoto warriors.

From here the Taira were able once more to gain a foothold on the mainland, and set out to advance on the capital. Yoshinaka, the tide of battle now against him, began planning for a counter attack, but these plans were frustrated by unconfirmed reports of an attempt by Go-Shirakawa to undermine his authority in the capital. It transpired that the manipulative emperor had been engaged in surreptitious dialog with Yoritomo regarding Yoshinaka's growing power. The latter returned in great haste to investigate, and began to pressurize Go-Shirakawa to suspend the mandate against the Taira and issue another authorizing him to defend Kyoto from Yoritomo. When Go-Shirakawa refused, Yoshinaka's fears of a plot were heightened, while his relationship with Yoritomo plunged to fresh depths.

In the meantime, the Taira army had advanced as far as Harima. But in Kyoto, the in-fighting continued. Go-Shirakawa continued to refuse to bow to Yoshinaka on the issue of the mandate against Yoritomo, instead delivering up a further demand that he move against the Taira. Frustrated by this test of his already limited patience, in December Yoshinaka conspired with the Taira and Fujiwara leaders to take over the capital, seize Go-Shirakawa, and set up a new government in the Northern provinces.

Battle of Muroyama

Meanwhile Yukiie, eager to make amends for the loss at Mizushima, decided to move against the Taira independently. Just prior to his departure he disclosed to Go-Shirakawa information regarding Yoshinaka's plan to take him hostage and move him north, should Kyoto come under attack. The day after the issue of the new mandate, having advanced to Harima, Yukiie's troops engaged the Taira at Muroyama. After fierce fighting, the surviving Minamoto were surrounded and massacred. Yukiie himself made a fortuitous escape out of the cordon with a few other survivors.

In Kyoto, once appraised of Yoshinaka's connivance, Go-Shirakawa had sent word to Yoritomo, calling him to Kyoto to deal with his troublesome cousin. Initially, Yoritomo ignored the request, thinking it more important to solidify his position in the eastern provinces. However, after repeated requests Yoritomo called on his brothers, Yoshitsune and Noriyori, to advance on the capital.

Without wishing to speculate, it seems that Yoshinaka now became gripped with paranoia, or delusions of grandeur, or perhaps both. Early in 1184, soon after Yukiie had departed the capital, Yoshinaka torched the Hoju-ji temple, where he suspected a gathering of troops and officials were plotting against him. His troops then sacked Kyoto and kidnapped Emperor Go-Shirakawa, while Yoshinaka had himself named *shogun*. At the Hoju-ji he was opposed by a number of court nobles and warrior monks from Mount Hiei and Miidera. In the aftermath, over a hundred of them were decapitated, and their heads were placed on display in public to warn against any further attempt at insurrection. Yoshinaka demanded the removal of fifty high-ranking officials from their posts.

The death of Yoshinaka

With the Minamoto armies under Yoshitsune and Noriyori now surrounding the capital, the stage was now set for a climactic encounter between the rival Minamoto factions. The opportunity was not long in coming. On February 19, Yoshinaka tried to flee Kyoto across the Bridge of Uji, scene of one of the earliest encounters in the Genpei War. Even though Yoshinaka tried to prevent him from crossing, using much the same tactic as in the first battle, only four years earlier, Yoshitsune led his horsemen across the river, quickly defeated Yoshinaka's troops, and pursued him away from the capital.

Two days later, northeast of Kyoto at Awazu in Omi Province (modern-day Shiga Prefecture), Yoshinaka made his final stand at Awazu. During the retreat he had met up with his companion Imai Kanehira at Seta. Their armies fought valiantly, holding off thousands of Noriyori's men for a time, but were eventually overwhelmed; Yoshinaka was struck dead by an arrow when his horse became mired in a paddy field. The final moments of the courageous mountain warrior are described thus in the *Heike*:

"At his side he wore a magnificent oversized sword; high on his back, there rode a quiver containing the few arrows left from his earlier encounters, all fledged

with eagle tail feathers. He grasped a rattan-wrapped bow and sat in a gold-edged saddle astride his famous horse Oniashige (Roan Demon), a very stout and browny animal. Standing in his stirrups, he announced his name in a mighty voice: "You must have heard of Kiso no Kanja in the past; now you see him!.. He galloped forward shouting." [48]

According to legend, his companion Imai died an equally heroic death, committing suicide by leaping off his horse with the tip of his sword clenched in his mouth. Before leaping, Kanehira apparently proclaimed: "See how the bravest man in Japan chooses to die." Their heads were carried back to Kamakura, "for the edification of Yoritomo"[49] and placed on public display.

Battle of Ichinotani

In early 1184, at his stronghold at Yashima on the north coast of Shikoku, the Taira commander Munemori had begun to lay plans to exploit the infighting in the Minamoto clan and retake the offensive. On March 14, a large Taira force embarked for the Honshu coast, bringing with them the young emperor and the symbolically important royal regalia.[50]

The Taira fleet anchored off Fukugawa (modern-day Kobe) in Settsu (which today comprises the eastern part of Hyogo Prefecture and the northern part of Osaka Prefecture). While the emperor remained onboard ship with guards near Wada Misaka (Cape Wada), troops were landed at various points between Fukugawa and Ichinotani. At the valley of Ichinotani they fortified the stockade, and commenced building defensive positions in the mountainous country to the north of Fukugawa, using boulders and felled trees to block the narrow eastern and western approaches.[51] However, before these defensive positions could be completed they were suddenly confronted with the white war banners of Yoshitsune's and Noriyori's armies.

On March 17, informed about the landings at Fukugawa, the Minamoto commanders had led their troops out of the capital, moving west along the south coast of Honshu, with the support of a flotilla of ships offshore.

Above: After winning the battle of Kurikara Pass, Yoshinaka and his army marched to Kyoto where his troops looted and burnt the city. He captured Emperor Go-Shirakawa and forced him to make him *shogun*, but Yoshinaka was soon driven out of Kyoto and then killed by his cousins at the battle of Awazu, in Omi Province. (*via Clive Sinclaire*)

On gaining Mukomachi, southwest of the capital, on the 18th they held a council of war at which a battle plan was formulated. This was to be a classic pincer envelopment of the Taira position, with Noriyori's main force of 15,000 moving to Ikuta no mori to assault the front lines from the east, and Yoshitsune's 2,000 mounted troops positioned at Mikusayama in the north for a simultaneous strike.[52] Before moving off on separate routes of march, they agreed on dawn two days hence as the time of the attack.

On the eve of the battle, Noriyori's troops were camped on the east bank of the Ikuta River, and were ready to move on to their start lines. Yoshitsune, however, now twelve miles to the north of Ichinotani at the village of Miki, could at last fully comprehend the strength of the Taira positions at Ichinotani. He saw that the valley was well defended with cliffs to the north, a harbor to the south where the Heike fleet was anchored, and narrow entrances to the east and west, which were heavily guarded by Heike soldiers.

Instead of a costly frontal assault, Yoshitsune made the inspired (and courageous) decision to lead a small party of troops down a narrow and dangerous path called the Hiyodorigoe Track, and attempt a surprise flanking attack. As the main body, under his deputy commander Toi no Jiro Sanehira, moved off to position itself on the west flank, Yoshitsune led seventy of his best horsemen south into the snow-covered mountains, and by narrow tracks to the heights above the Taira position on the valley floor. Meanwhile, Sanehira marched his men to Shiyoya, west of Ichinotani, and awaited the dawn.[53]

As the time for the attack drew near, several impatient *samurai*, eager for glory, broke rank and charged at the Taira lines. At first they were ignored, but soon their shouted boasts were answered as twenty Taira *samurai* appeared from behind the barricades to confront them. At this, Sanehira ordered his men to attack, followed in short order by the movement of Noriyori's forces across the Ikuta River and into the Taira defenses.

Troops on the flank were brought in to bolster the frontal positions, and Yoshitsune seized his chance. Taking his troops down a precipitous path leading from the Ichinotani heights, he rushed headlong into the Taira camp, quickly putting the enemy soldiers to flight. Hundreds of men tried desperately to flee by ships, but many vessels quickly became overloaded and sank, taking men to the bottom. In the aftermath of the battle, the bodies of many other poor souls littered the shoreline.

Above: The final battle of Taira no Masakado. He had rebelled against the government, which made him a hero to local peoples, but after a price was put on his head he was killed by his cousin Sadamori and Fujiwara no Hidesato at the battle of Kojima. *(via Clive Sinclaire)*

The cost to the Taira forces had been considerable. Many of their leaders were killed or captured, and only a few thousand men were able to retreat by ship to Yashima. However, the emperor and the imperial regalia were spirited away, and the Minamoto troops, lacking any seaborne transport, were unable to continue the pursuit, thus missing an opportunity to finally quash their rivals.

Yoshitsune returned in triumph to Kyoto with the heads of nine of the defeated Taira commanders[54] (including Taira Atsumori, Taira Michimori, Taira Narimori, and Taira Tomoakira), to receive the plaudits of Go-Shirakawa. This was to be the first of a trio of famous victories he would win for the Minamoto.

After Ichi-no-Tani, the Genpei War entered a six-month lull. Problems had now begun to manifest themselves that were to vex Yoritomo mightily, causing

"the Minamoto offensive in Western Japan which had begun so auspiciously at Ichinotani…to come to a virtual standstill." [55] The problems were twofold. First was the fact that from here on the Minamoto would be operating far from their eastern powerbase, in hostile territory peopled predominantly by Taira sympathizers. Conscious of this fact, Yoritomo, exercising typical caution, sent out ambassadors to the west to try and win over as many of the Taira as possible before resuming military action.

The other major obstacle was a lack of available boats with which to carry the fight further into western Japan, compounded by a dearth of experience in naval matters among the Minamoto troops. It was clear that operations in the west would depend heavily on movements on the Inland Sea, and rectifying deficiencies in equipment and skills essential to continued prosecution of the war.

Yoritomo was quick to try to address these problems, sending a trusted lieutenant to Kyoto in the spring of 1184 to look into the matter of provisioning boats. But little progress was made, and the problem continued to trouble Yoritomo throughout the year.

Finally, on October 8, Noriyori's army set out from Kyoto to attack the Taira. At Kojima, on the coast of the Inland Sea, he defeated a Taira army at the Battle at Kojima. The attack was led by Sasaki Moritsuna, who, lacking a vessel, swam his horse across a narrow strait between Kojima and the mainland of Honshu. But such heroics aside, when Noriyori's army finally reached the western tip of Honshu in the fall, two months after setting out from Kamakura with instructions to operate in Kyushu; "there it languished for the next three months because of Noriyori's inability to muster boats to take his army across the narrow channel to Kyushu."[56]

In the interim he had been plagued by desertions and logistical difficulties, deficiencies that were compounded by the blight of famine, which had struck again in 1184 and further weakened the resolve of the troops. In light of these problems, early in 1185 Yoritomo was forced to send thirty-two boatloads of supplies to Noriyori. The drain of provisioning an army with men and materiel for a protracted campaign posed him a serious dilemma, as any weakening of the Minamoto position in the east, where uprisings in Kai and Shinano in the spring of the previous year had already tested the fragile unity, was in every way undesirable. This necessitated that he remain in Kamakura to make strategic decisions and deal with the diplomatic problems of relations with and between the various factions of the *Genji*.

Yoritomo grew increasingly frustrated with Noriyori's prosecution of the campaign.[57] His choice of Noriyori for the expedition could be questioned, as Yoshitsune was clearly the better leader. However, it seems clear that Yoritomo had become suspicious of Yoshitsune's motives and prestige in the capital and wished to avoid providing him further opportunities to add to his growing status and influence.

Nevertheless, in March 1185, after a lull of several months in the fighting, it was Yoshitsune who sailed across the Inland Sea to carry the battle to the Taira. At his base in Kyoto, sufficient boats had been mustered at Watanabe (Settsu Province) to carry a small force across to Shikoku. During the preparations he argued with Kajiwara Kagetoki, one of his elder brothers and closest retainers, about strategy. Then, in the days before departing, many of his ships were destroyed or lost in a storm, and even though he made good some of the losses, a difficult passage was promised. On the night of March 22 Yoshitsune decided he could delay no longer, and ordered his men to board ship for the thirty-mile journey across the strait. But the weather was still so bad that many sailors refused to attempt the crossing. Typically, Yoshitsune abruptly issued a threat to kill any man who disobeyed his orders, but nevertheless during the passage a number of ships either became lost or slipped away from the fleet.

Landing at dawn with no more than about 150 men,[58] Yoshitsune struck out to attack the Taira fortress at Yashima (Sanuki), to where the clan had retreated after the defeat at Ichinotani. There Emperor Antoku was installed, together with the imperial regalia, in an improvised palace. From a local warrior he received welcome intelligence; despite the importance of the fort, the garrison at Yashima was presently much reduced owing to an expedition into Iyo.

The Taira camp at Yashima[59] was on a beach facing the mainland across a narrow stretch of water. Expecting the attack to come from the sea, not overland, the Taira had focused attention on their seaward defenses. As he approached with his tiny band of men, Yoshitsune once again showed the flair for opportunism so characteristic of his leadership in battle. Acknowledging that he stood little chance of success in a frontal assault, Yoshitsune ordered his men to raise large fires in the enemy rear to fool the Taira that a huge force was approaching on land.

The ruse worked. The Taira abandoned the fortress/palace and took to their ships, moored in the shallows directly in front, and taking with them Emperor Antoku and the imperial regalia. Yoshitsune's horsemen charged into the channel and a fight ensued around the ships, while another party torched the fort. By the time Munemori realized how few men Yoshitsune had, the fort was in flames. The fighting continued in the shallows until the dusk, at which point the Taira moved out beyond the reach of the Minamoto arrows[60] and withdrew.

The Taira had once again narrowly slipped through a Minamoto cordon. Within a month, however, as the net

was drawn inexorably tighter, they would clash in a final climactic encounter to decide the outcome of the five-year war.

On the morning following the loss of Yashima, the Taira set sail for nearby Shido harbor, while Yoshitsune pursued on shore. Grossly overestimating the number of troops the Minamoto had on Shikoku, they fled the island completely. The Taira army then regrouped at their main naval base of Hikoshima in Nagato while Yoshitsune, after viewing the heads of those taken, crossed over to Suo province and prepared for the final battle of the war.

During the following month, Noriyori maneuvered in Honshu and northern Kyushu to isolate Taira forces. Meanwhile Yoshitsune used the temporary lull to build up his force, incorporating new allies who, inspired by Minamoto victories, now flocked to the Minamoto cause. But more importantly, new ships and crews also became

Above: Taira Munemori, although the leader of the clan, was one of the very few Taira not to commit *seppuku* after their humiliating defeat at the battle of Dan-no-ura in 1185. He was later captured and executed in Kyoto as a completely shamed man. *(British Museum/Jo St Mart)*

available.[61] Thus far the Taira had enjoyed a superiority gained through experience in naval warfare, but this was now counterbalanced through the secondment of local shipping and seasoned sailors to Yoshitsune.

Battle of Dan no Ura[62]

On April 24, 1185, Yoshitsune's much-strengthened fleet was finally ready to sail. Moving east through the Moji Strait, the Minamoto advanced to Okutsu Island (Manshujima) while simultaneously the Taira fleet under Taira Tomomori, which had left Hikoshima two days previously, moved to Ta-no-ura, near the modern city of Moji. At dawn the next day the two fleets approached at a place called Dan no ura, in Akamagaseki (near Shimonoseki).

As Marder points out, both fleets were primarily comprised of "small, clumsy, oar-propelled junks. They are referred to as war vessels but they do not seem to have differed particularly in construction from ordinary ships and were probably mainly fishing or ferry boats commandeered for this purpose." [63]

Although Yoshitsune outnumbered his adversary in ships by almost two to one (850:500), the Taira planned on using the east-flowing morning tides to their advantage and encircle the Minamoto fleet. By 8.00AM battle had been joined, and initially at least, the tides and the experience of the Taira sailors in the tricky currents that flow in the Strait worked in their favor.

Taira Tomomori had divided his forces into three groups, and at the forefront placed his best archers under Yamaga Hideto. These bowmen fired devastating fusillades of arrows at a range of some 350 yards into the ranks of Minamoto warriors crammed in their boats. At around 8AM the opposing flotillas finally came into contact, and the sword and spear took the place of bow and arrow. For a time neither side was able to gain significant advantage and the outcome hung in the balance.

But by a cruel twist of fate, the tables were turned on the Taira. In mid-morning the tide began to recede and the flow of the current reversed. The Minamoto fleet, which thus far had been held, now began to make headway. The final blow was struck when, just as Tomomori had feared, his former ally Taguchi Shigeyoshi[64] suddenly broke rank and joined the enemy. Shigeyoshi made his way to Yoshitsune's boat and betrayed the identity of the ship sheltering the infant Emperor Antoku and his retainers. Yoshitsune pounced on his chance, exploiting the favorable shift in current to bear down on the Taira flagships, while his archers set about picking off the defenseless sailors.[65]

Faced with the imminent capture of their ship, the emperor's grandmother, Nii-no-ama (sometimes also called Lady Azechi), chose instead to throw herself into the sea bearing the infant and drown them both. Some

芳年武者兀類

畠山庄司重忠

Above: Hatakeyama Shigetada, riddled with arrows, rides from the battlefield after being attacked by the mutinous troops of his Lord Tokimasa. From the series Yoshitoshi mushaburui (Yoshitoshi's Finest Warriors). *(Asian Art & Archaeology, Inc./Corbis)*

accounts say that before stepping into the waves she comforted the unfortunate child with assurances that a better place lay beneath the waves.

Tomomori followed them into the water, along with hundreds of other Taira warriors who, weighed down by the great weight of their armor, quickly drowned. Only the unfortunate Munemori, who had been forced to jump by a Minamoto warrior contemptuous at his hesitation to die, was pulled from the ocean—only to be later executed.

By early afternoon the rout of the Taira fleet was complete. Messengers were immediately sent out to relay the news to Yoritomo in Kamakura that the Taira had been decisively defeated, and the Genpei War ended. For Yoritomo, it seems victory came at an unexpected juncture. Progress in the campaign in Kyushu had been slow—only recently he had been forced to send fresh supplies and edicts eliciting the support of the local lords.

But with the Taira clan all but eradicated as a threat to Minamoto power, nothing now stood in the path of Yoritomo's rise, culminating in 1192 with the grant of the the the title of *shogun*.

However, it should not be assumed that victory in the Genpei War made Yorimoto the absolute ruler of all Japan. As Minoru Shinoda points out,[66] Yoritomo did indeed rule the eastern and central provinces, but that represented only a third of the total. Kyushu and the north remained independent of his control. Nor did he win any significant lands from the defeated Taira.

NOTES

1 Karl F. Friday *Samurai, Warfare and State in Early Medieval Japan* p.166

2 See also Minoru Shinoda *The Founding of the Kamakura Bakufu 1180-1185* Columbia (1960) p.50

3 Karl F. Friday *Samurai, Warfare and State in Early Medieval Japan* p.12

4 Karl F. Friday *Samurai, Warfare and State in Early Medieval Japan* p.129-130 and Richard A. Gabriel and Donald W. Boose Jr *The Great Battles of Antiquity* Greenwood Press (1994) p.588

5 Jane Goodwin *Go Shirakawa and Todai-ji* Japanese Journal of Religious Studies 17: 2; 3 p.223

6 His nepotism was extensive– no fewer than sixty members of his family held major governmental offices.

7 Minoru Shinoda *The Founding of the Kamakura Bakufu 1180-1185* Columbia (1960) p.48

8 The name was a compound of Gen (from "*Genji*" or Minamoto), and Hei (from "*Heike*" or Taira)

9 Minoru Shinoda *The Founding of the Kamakura Bakufu 1180-1185* Columbia (1960) p.49

10 Minamoto no Yorimasa held high posts in the government, and opposed the Minamoto in the Heiji Rebellion of 1160. Although he was a one-time ally of Kiyomori, he sided with Go-Shirakawa at the outbreak of the Gempei War.

11 Three warrior monks in particular are named in the *Heike Monogatari*: Gochin no Tajima, Tsutsui Jomyo Meishu, and Ichirai Hoshi. Tajima achieved quasi-legendary status for resisting the *samurai* archers with his naginata, apparently chopping away incoming arrows. For this he earned the nickname of "arrow-cutter" and the lasting admiration of his enemies.

12 Yorimasa's death at the battle of Uji is in fact the first historical incidence where seppuku was chosen as a preferable alternative to capture. See Richard A. Gabriel and Donald W. Boose Jr *The Great Battles of Antiquity* Greenwood Press (1994) p.577.

13 During this time Kiyomori had forced the emperors (both titular and cloistered) to move residence to Fukuwara, (to the west of Kyoto), his residence outside of Kyoto on the Inland Sea. It was planned to move certain government functions there at a later date. His motivations for this upheaval are unclear, but the move was not a success and the entire court returned to the capital six months later.

14 Richard A. Gabriel and Donald W. Boose Jr *The Great Battles of Antiquity* Greenwood Press (1994) p.577.

15 *Heike*

16 Karl F. Friday *Samurai, Warfare and State in Early Medieval Japan* p.44.

17 Minoru Shinoda *The Founding of the Kamakura Bakufu 1180-1185* Columbia (1960) p.50.

18 Minoru Shinoda *The Founding of the Kamakura Bakufu 1180-1185* Columbia (1960) p.54.

19 Richard A. Gabriel and Donald W. Boose Jr *The Great Battles of Antiquity* Greenwood Press (1994) p.577.

20 Minoru Shinoda *The Founding of the Kamakura Bakufu 1180-1185* Columbia (1960) p.60.

21 Minoru Shinoda *The Founding of the Kamakura Bakufu 1180-1185* Columbia (1960) p.60. One example of this phenomenon is Kajiwara Kagetoki, who had fought against Yoritomo at Ishibashiyama and then joined his camp.

22 In the classic *Tale of Genji* 5- [11] the Taira forces hear that Yoritomo's forces are vast in number, that the warriors recruited in that area are especially fierce, and that Yoritomo might attack from behind as well as make a frontal assault. For a further discussion see Richard A. Gabriel and Donald W. Boose Jr *The Great Battles of Antiquity* Greenwood Press (1994) p.577.

23 Richard A. Gabriel and Donald W. Boose Jr *The Great Battles of Antiquity* Greenwood Press (1994) p.577.

24 They were actually the fires of peasants who had fled on the eve of the battle.

25 Richard A. Gabriel and Donald W. Boose Jr *The Great Battles of Antiquity* Greenwood Press (1994) p.578.

26 Richard A. Gabriel and Donald W. Boose Jr *The Great Battles of Antiquity* Greenwood Press (1994) p.578.

27 Minoru Shinoda *The Founding of the Kamakura Bakufu 1180-1185* Columbia (1960) p.56.

28 Minoru Shinoda *The Founding of the Kamakura Bakufu 1180-1185* Columbia (1960) p.67.

29 It is not until the final years of the war that Yoshitsune resurfaces in the *Heike Monogatari*. See above note.

30 Minoru Shinoda *The Founding of the Kamakura Bakufu 1180-1185* Columbia (1960) p.68.

31 During the lull, an important development took place at Kamakura, namely the establishment of the *Samurai-dokoro* (Board of Retainers), an office which regulated the affairs of the military—its privileges, obligations, property, ranks, and treatment in general—thus laying the foundation for the future military government, the Kamakura bakufu regime (although the term bakufu was used only later in retrospect).

32 Gabriel R.A and Boose D.W, p.578.

33 This was later renamed Nagara.

34 He later deserted to Minamoto no Yoshinaka.

35 Minoru Shinoda *The Founding of the Kamakura Bakufu 1180-1185* Columbia (1960) p.70.

36 The cloistered emperor was prepared to accept the peace offer, but his views were ignored by Munemori.

37 Richard A. Gabriel and Donald W. Boose Jr *The Great Battles of Antiquity* Greenwood Press (1994) p.578.

38 Also of interest is Yoshinaka's marriage to Tomoe Gozen, a woman who gained renown as a warrior and fought with her husband as an equal.

39 Minoru Shinoda *The Founding of the Kamakura Bakufu 1180-1185* Columbia (1960) p.81.

40 Minoru Shinoda *The Founding of the Kamakura Bakufu 1180-1185* Columbia (1960) p.81.

41 *Heike no Monogatari*, 7-[4]

42 Many authors make reference to the use of deception and trickery by Japanese field commanders. For a full discussion of this see Karl F. Friday *Samurai, Warfare and State in Early Medieval Japan* p.140 – 144.

43 A rare folding screen painting depicting "The Battles of Kiso Yoshinaka" is held by the National Museum of Japanese History, and can also be viewed online.

44 The site of the battlefield is now home to a visitor's center.

45 Shinoda, p81..

46 Richard A. Gabriel and Donald W. Boose Jr *The Great Battles of Antiquity* Greenwood Press (1994) p.579.

47 Yashima, a headland sticking out into the sea in the northeast of Takamatsu, used to be an island before the Edo Period. It was an important maritime base on the strait between Honshu and Shikoku.

48 *Heike Monogatari*, Chapter 9 (4).

49 Richard A. Gabriel and Donald W. Boose Jr *The Great Battles of Antiquity* Greenwood Press (1994) p.579.

50 Richard A. Gabriel and Donald W. Boose Jr *The Great Battles of Antiquity* Greenwood Press (1994) p.579.

51 Karl F. Friday *Samurai, Warfare and State in Early Medieval Japan* p.121.

52 Karl F. Friday *Samurai, Warfare and State in Early Medieval Japan* p.50.

53 The precise delegation of responsibilities in this battle is unclear. Some scholars think it likely that Sanehira led the daring assault from the Ichinotani heights, and it was later credited to Yoshitsune.

54 Taira Koremori committed suicide on April 15.

55 Shinoda, p.86.

56 Shinoda, p.89.

57 Richard A. Gabriel and Donald W. Boose Jr *The Great Battles of Antiquity* Greenwood Press (1994) p.594

58 Shinoda, p.98.

59 See above note.

60 Part of the legend surrounding this battle tells us that once safely beyond the range of the Minamoto bowmen, the Taira defiantly placed a fan atop the mast of one of their ships, and dared the Minamoto to try and knock it off. One Nasu no Yoichi rode out into the sea on horseback, and did just that, earning the plaudits of both friend and foe. This feat has since been widely celebrated in stories of the battle.

61 Shinoda, p.98.

62 An excellent account of this battle can be found in Arthur J. Marder's article *From Jimmu Tenno to Perry: Sea power in early Japanese history* The American Historical Review 51: 1; p.9-12.

63 Arthur J. Marder *From Jimmu Tenno to Perry: Sea power in early Japanese history* The American Historical Review 51: 1; p.9-10.

64 Arthur J. Marder *From Jimmu Tenno to Perry: Sea power in early Japanese history* The American Historical Review 51: 1; p.11.

65 It was traditionally considered a contravention of the unwritten rules of engagement to target enemy sailors.

66 Shinoda p.114.

THE GOLDEN AGE (1221–1281)

The Genpei War, and the profound changes to government and society that came out of it, became the prelude to a new age in which the *samurai* held sway over almost every aspect of Japanese society. The most important of the changes was the transition of power to the Kamakura *bakufu* established by Minamoto Yoritomo between 1180 and 1185, the first in a succession of military governments that would rule Japan for seven centuries. The 150-year period (1192 to 1333) of governance under the Kamakura *bakufu*, has been described by some as "the golden age of the *samurai*." Since we are concerned primarily with their military actions, the focus here is on the successful repulse of the Mongol invasions, first in 1274 and then again in 1281. These events were certainly the crowning achievement of "the golden age" *samurai*, and for many the most glorious of all their exploits are rightly attributed monumental importance in Japanese history; for many they were the most glorious of all their exploits.

However, as almost a century passed between the end of the Genpei War and the invasions, we need first to

Below: Hojo Tokimasa seated (top left), resting with his *samurai* during the Genpei War—the late Heian period (1180–1185) conflicts between the Taira and Minamoto clans. The former were defeated, to be replaced by the Kamakura *shogunate* under Minamoto Yoritomo in 1192. *(British Museum/Jo St Mart)*

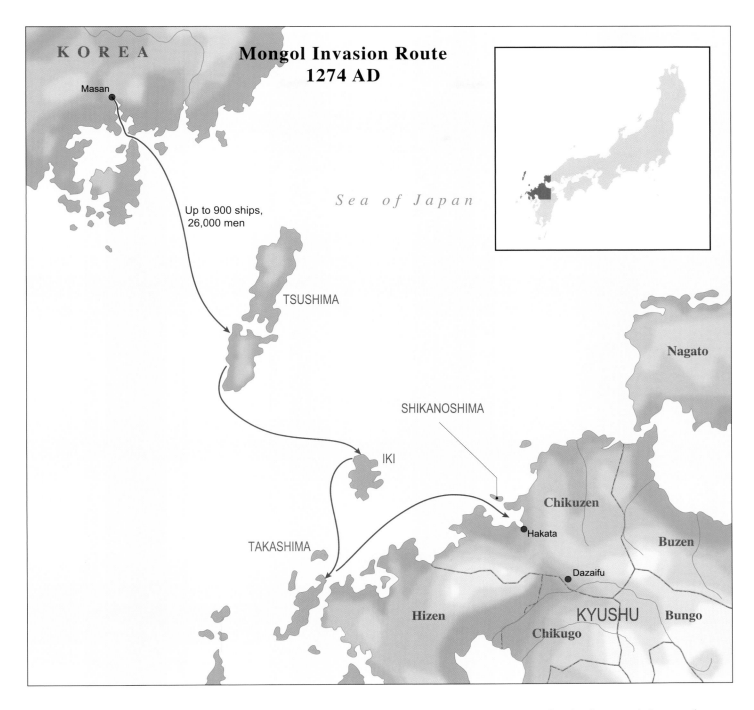

Mongol Invasion Route
1274 AD

KOREA

Masan

Sea of Japan

Up to 900 ships,
26,000 men

TSUSHIMA

SHIKANOSHIMA

Nagato

IKI

Chikuzen

Hakata

Buzen

TAKASHIMA

Dazaifu

Hizen

KYUSHU

Bungo

Chikugo

look at events during the intervening years. Briefly, in the years following his final triumph over the Taira, Yoritomo oversaw the transfer of many of the powers of the central government and the court aristocracy to the Kamakura *bakufu*. Under this system of government, the *samurai* took over many of the powers of government, while the emperor continued as the titular ruler in Kyoto.

Yoritomo swiftly sought to eliminate the last vestiges of opposition to his rule. The foremost of these threats he perceived to be his brother Yoshitsune. Perhaps motivated by jealousy over Yoshitsune's successes against the Taira,[1] and subsequent doubts as to his loyalty, the rift between

Yoritomo and Yoshitsune that had opened during the war widened to a gulf. Yoshitomo was eventually moved to openly declare Yoshitsune an enemy, forcing Yoshitsune to flee north in 1187 and find sanctuary with Fujiwara Hidehira."[2] Hidehira died that same year, to be succeeded by his son Yasuhira. Not wishing to incur the wrath of Yoritomo, he turned on Yoshitsune and by the early summer of 1189 had him surrounded at the fortress at Koromogawa no Tate in Mutsu. He died on June 13[3][4] by his own hand. Four years later, in 1193, the sole remaining threat, Minamoto Noriyori, was assassinated at the Shuzenji in Izu, on Yoritomo's orders.

Left: Hojo Yoshitoki was the second *shikken* (regent) of the Kamakura *Shogunate. (British Museum/Jo St Mart)*

In April 1192, the retired Emperor Go-Shirakawa died. Soon afterward, Yoritomo had conferred on himself the name *Seiitaishogun*, meaning "great barbarian-subduing general." The political system he had developed at Kamakura has become known as *shogunate*, headed by a succession of *shogun*. The adoption of the title *shogun*, a throwback to the honorary appointment of old,[5] reflected the transition of rule from the imperial court, and initiated nearly seven hundred years of warrior rule over Japan.

The reformation of the political apparatus under Yoritomo is a complex issue, and detailing it here is precluded by the limitations of space. However, one of Yoritomo's reforms is of particular relevance to us, and that was his forced reform of the *shiki* system of land control. This "can be regarded as the beginning of the feudalization of Japanese society."[6] The *shiki* system had been the basis of court power for centuries, and Yoritomo sought to bring it under his influence by appointing his own vassals to positions within the *shiki* hierarchy. Within this, each of the provinces had an assigned *shugo* or "constable," and each *shoen* agricultural estate a *jito* or "steward." The appointees were selected from among the warrior families that had demonstrated their support for the Minamoto in the Genpei War.

In their official capacity these officials were expected to regulate regional and local government, respectively, acting somewhat like military governors. Officially, they were also responsible for collecting taxes for military purposes, including from private estates. Privately, this was used an opportunity to extract great personal wealth from the lands they oversaw.

For the *shogunate*, increasing the power and wealth of the *samurai* held two benefits. First, it gave a guarantee of security in the provinces, and second, he could retain their loyalty through appointment to and dismissal from desirable posts.

In this and other ways the power and influence of the *samurai* grew under the successive *shogunates* of medieval Japan, until they became an intrinsic part of life; "their culture, their ethos, and their internecine struggles came to replace courtier traditions at the core of Japanese culture."[7] Furthermore, under the *bakufu*, a "*bushi*-class consciousness—a sense of warriors as a separate estate"[8] began to emerge, and "by the end of the [13th] century, the *shogunate* had assumed control of most of the state's judicial, military and foreign affairs."[9]

The rise of the Hojo clan

In 1194 Yoritomo took retirement, assuming a position that still commanded great influence over the government in the twilight years of his life. On February 13, 1199, the great Minamoto leader met his end in a riding accident, and so ended the life of one of the most remarkable of all the *samurai* leaders, and the dominance of the clan he had taken from virtual oblivion to the supreme seat of power.

Yoritomo's successor was Yoriie, another of the Minamoto line, but by the time of his appointment as *Seiitaishogun* in 1202, the real power in Kamakura was consolidating in the hands of his grandfather, Hojo Tokimasa, his daughter Masako (Yoritomo's widow), and his brother-in-law Yoshitoki. Thus, as the power of the Minamoto clan began to dwindle, that of another, the Hojo, rose to prominence.

This was ironic, perhaps, given that the Hojo were linear descendants of the Taira of Kammu, originating in Izu Province, and that most of them had been killed at Dan no Ura. However, despite his connection to the Taira, and the fact that he was a distant relation to the imperial family, Hojo Tokimasa had shrewdly chosen to distance himself from the interclan and succession disputes that engulfed western Japan in the mid- to late 12th century.

It will be remembered from the previous chapter that Minamoto Yoritomo served his exile in Izu, in the safekeeping of the Hojo clan, and that during his incarceration he won over Hojo Tokimasa and took one of the Hojo daughters as his wife. By 1180, Tokimasa had become his advisor on various affairs (and hence took a hand in the defeat of the Taira). Following the death of Yoritomo, Tokimasa became regent to the child *shogun*, and by this act effectively transferred control of the *shogunate* to his clan. The Minamoto and even the imperial princes now became puppets and hostages of the Hojo.

During the course of the next half century the Hojo, through guile and suppression, came to dominate the Kamakura *shogunate* and the imperial court. Although none of them ever became *shogun*, as regents they occupied a position akin to that of the Fujiwara family in relation to the retired emperor.

Beginning in 1203 the Hojo sought to eliminate opposition to their growing power. In October Hojo Tokimasa ordered the murder of Hiki Yoshikazu, and later most of the Hiki clan, after being informed that they plotted to revolt against him and against the Hojo family. Then, after killing his son Ichiman, the Hojo forced the *shogun*, Yoriie, into retirement and replaced him with Minamoto Sanetomo.

In 1204 Yoriie was assassinated at the Shuzenji, as were eventually most of the other sons and heirs of Yoritomo, including Sanetomo (in 1219). By 1221, regents from the Hojo clan exercised the real authority in Kamakura, and the *shogun* had effectively become a hereditary figurehead, selected for the most part from the Kujo family or clan.[10]

The imperial court began to voice increasing concerns over the growing power of the *shogunate* since, as John Brownlee points out, "its legal status and political significance remained obscure."[11] Soon these reached a critical point. In 1219, after the assassination of Sanetomo, the wily and resourceful retired Emperor Go-Toba took the opportunity to rein in the "eastern barbarians" in Kamakura. On June 6, 1221 Go-Toba issued a decree calling for the Hojo regent Yoshitoki to be reprimanded, signaling the start of the brief Jokyu War.[12] Only one major battle was fought, and again the locale of the Uji River was the battleground.

At Kamakura, Yoshitoki reacted quickly, assembling a large army under his eldest son, Yasutoki, to move on Kyoto. According to the *Heike*, "It was decided that the Kamakura forces should be divided into three armies, one to advance along the Tokaido Road, one along the Tosendo Road, and one along the Hokurikudo Road."[13]

Within two weeks they had gained the Tenryu River, near to Iwata-shi. Informed of the movements, the court ordered the emperor's forces out of the capital to mount a defense, but they were progressively pushed back onto a defensive line on the Uji River, which hinged on the vital Uji Bridge.

On July 5, the *bakufu* forces under Hojo Yasutoki attacked the entire line from Uji to Seta, crossing the river at Fushimi Ford south of Kyoto. The battle is described in some detail in the *Azuma Kagami*, which details how Yasutoki himself crossed on a raft made "by tearing down some commoners' houses."[14] The *Azuma Kagami* also reports that, whereas most of the imperial forces fled, others stood firm for many hours before they were eventually overwhelmed, killed or scattered. The way into the city now lay wide open, and victory for the *bakufu* forces was assured.

In the immediate aftermath of the brief uprising, Go-Toba, his third son Juntoku (the titular emperor), and first son Tsuchimikado (the former emperor) were all exiled.[15] The imperial court was brought under the direct control of the Kamakura *bakufu*, and henceforth the court was obliged to seek Kamakura's approval for all of its actions.[16] Furthermore, "after Yasutoki had

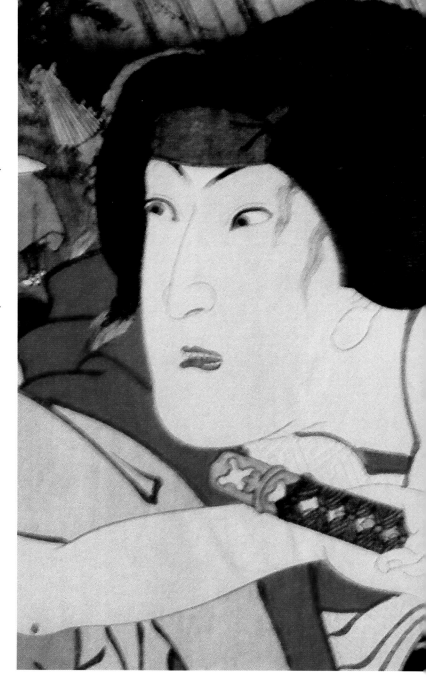

inventoried the more than three thousand pieces of land that had belonged to the rebellios court nobles and warriors, Masako redistributed them to Kanto retainers, giving each man what his bravery and service merited.[17]

In the aftermath of the Jokyu War, the Kamakura *bakufu* was controlled by a succession of Hojo regents in an atmosphere of comparative peace. The final incident of note was the brief Hoji War in 1247, a brief and unsuccessful challenge to the authority of the Hojo during Tokiyori's reign as regent. The uprising was quickly crushed, the Muira family was eliminated, and the Hojo tightened their hold on Kamakura politics yet further.

With regard to the political system, certain key legislation was enacted, formalizing *bakufu* rule, with "policies that would safeguard the position of the

Above: Hojo Yasutoki was the third *shikken* of the *Kamakura Shogunate*. (British Museum/Jo St Mart)

military."[18] The first was the establishment of the *hyojoshu*, a board of councilors which assumed the most important duties in the Kamakura government.[19] At the same time, Hojo Yasutoki issued the *Joei Shikimoku* (Joei Code), which served as the basis for principles guiding *samurai* law. The code established precedent and principle (*dori*) as the basis of law, and specific provisions were made for the respect for shrines and temples, specific duties of the *shugo* and *jito* provincial "constables," and the rights of women to inheritance and property.

Also interesting to note, in regard to the late Kamakura period, are Helen McCullough's observations in her translation of the *Taiheikei*. She describes the way that, in the post-Yoritomo Kamakura period, within the Hojo clan the spartan, martial atmosphere gave way to one of "snobbish officials, intricate ceremonies, luxurious habits, elegant diversions…." and that "Warfare became a novelty, rather than a way of life."[20] With soldiers concerned more with appearance than skill at arms. stagnation set in.

It is appropriate, at this juncture, to turn to developments abroad, which by now had become important: the story of the invasions, first by the Mongols, and then by the Japanese.

In 1263, after pirates (*wako*) from Tsushima[21] raided Ungjin, the king of Korea (then known as Koryo) sent a diplomatic mission to Japan protesting their depredations on the Korean coast. For centuries Japanese pirates had preyed on the rich shipping trade and coastal areas of Korea bordering the Sea of Japan, this created no undue concern.[22] Japanese negotiators simply reconfirmed the policies of limiting trade and prohibiting piracy. But it was the prelude to events far more perturbing, the unwelcome arrival from over the seas of emissaries from Kublai, the Mongol Khan.

The Mongol Empire

Some years earlier, in 1227, the great Mongol leader Genghis Khan had died. At his death the Mongol Empire covered nearly ten-and-a-half million square miles of Asia, about four times the size of the Roman Empire at its height. And although none of his successors achieved the greatness of the Great Khan, the Mongol Empire continued to swell and prosper in the years after his death. Under his successor, Ögedei Khan,[23] the speed of expansion reached its peak, with successful campaigns into Persia, against the Xia and the Khwarezmids. During the 1250s, Genghis Khan's grandson, Hulegu, operating from the Mongol base in Persia, destroyed the Abbasid Caliphate in Baghdad and moved into Palestine towards Egypt.

Then, during the reign of Kublai, the last of the Great Khans, the tight bonds that united the vast empire began to loosen, and it gradually unraveled into a number of smaller "khanates."

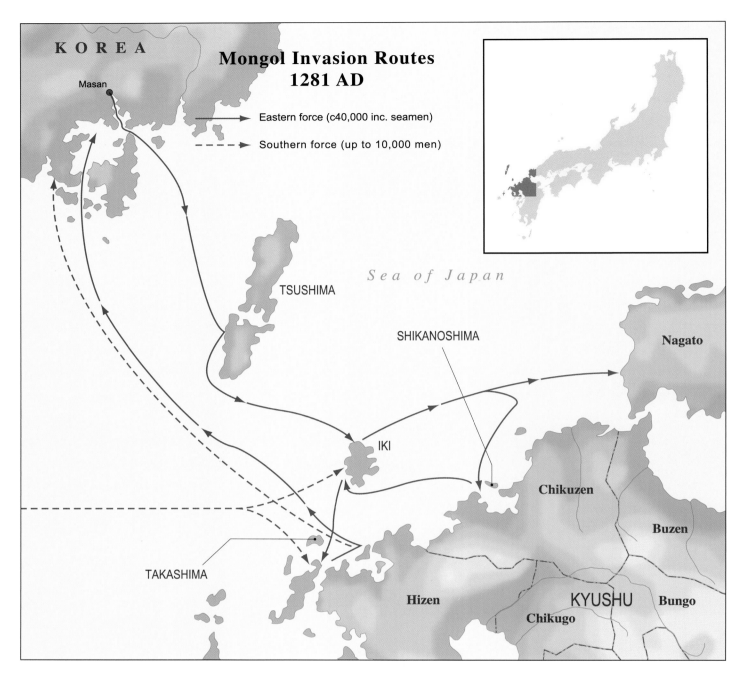

While Kublai concentrated on the war with the Song Dynasty in China, having himself assumed the mantle of ruler of that country, the more western "khanates" gradually drifted away. Inter-family rivalry and frequent succession crises further hastened the disintegration of the empire.

Already, in 1231, the Mongols had begun a series of campaigns on the Korean peninsula. After three tremendously costly decades of war, Korea signed a treaty in favor of the Yuan Dynasty and became a Mongolian dependency under Kublai.[24]

Kublai Khan's interest in Japan was aroused in 1265 when a courtesan of the Koryo royal house informed him that he believed Japan could be subdued easily. In the following year, Khan, whose empire now also included China, attempted to dispatch envoys across the Sea of Japan from Korea to demand tribute. Theories abound as to why Kublai did this; some suggest that his motives were entirely peaceful and that he merely wished to bring Japan into his sphere of influence. Others say that his ultimate strategic objective "was clearly the subjugation of Japan." It may also be that he was motivated by the belief that he would find gold there.[25] Whatever the reason, that first diplomatic mission was frustrated by bad weather.

Two years later emissaries He De and Yin Hong were successfully conveyed to Dazaifu, the ancient administrative capital of Kyushu. Khan's envoys met with the Chinzei Bugyo, or Defense Commissioner for the West (a post created in 1186 to oversee the defense of Kyushu), and they were given the customary Mongol ultimatum—submit to Mongol rule, or face invasion. The message was passed on to the *shogun* in Kamakura, and the emperor in Kyoto, and flatly rejected.

A number of messages were sent after that, some through Korean emissaries, and some by Mongol ambassadors, but all conveyed to Khan's court the same stubborn refusal to capitulate.[26]

The *bakufu* used this time to bolster the defenses in northern Kyushu, the closest point to the Korean peninsula from whence the invasion force was sure to come. Thousands of men from the Kanto region came to await the Mongol attack.

Khan had considered an invasion as early as 1268, but at that time the Mongol Empire had insufficient resources to provide him with an army or navy for such an undertaking. In 1273, after the rejection of his envoys, Kublai Khan sent a force to Korea to act as the advance guard while an invasion force was prepared. Kublai had asked Koryo to provide ships, sailors, soldiers, and provisions. Koryo mobilized some 30,000 carpenters and

built about 300 large ships. But in Korea, recovering from years of guerrilla war with the Mongols, there were barely sufficient means to support the local population, less still an invasion force, and they were forced to send to China for supplies. These logistical problems, and the difficulty in constructing a fleet to transport the troops, delayed the invasion for a year.

In October 1274, a Mongol army of 20,000 commanded by Hol Don arrived in Koryo. The Mongol army was joined by a Koryo army of 5,000, commanded by Kim Bang-gyong. Finally, on November 3, 1274, the Mongol fleet set out from Masan with roughly 20,000 Mongol and Chinese soldiers and 8,000 Korean warriors,[27] in 300 large vessels and 400–500 smaller craft manned by 6,700 Koryo sailors.[28] As Marder notes, "The Japanese fleet was so much weaker than the vast Mongol fleet that it made no attempt to intercept the expeditionary force at sea."[29]

Two days later, the Koryo army had overrun Tsushima and the Mongols had taken Iki Island. On November 14,

Below: The Mongol war: *samurai* boats fight the Mongols at sea. *(via Clive Sinclaire)*

they occupied Hirado and on the 19th landed at Hakata Bay, a short distance from Dazaifu. Despite superior weapons and tactics, which played a decisive role in the Mongol conquests, the force landing at Hakata Bay was grossly outnumbered;[30] estimates of Hojo Tokimune's command vary widely, some putting it as high as 102,000, but a more modest figure of 4,000 is more likely.

However, Japanese commanders had little experience in managing large bodies of troops; it had been a good half century since any fighting of significance had taken place in Japan, and there was a conspicuous lack of experience at command level. In addition, the fighting style of the *samurai* still involved single horse archery duels, even on large battlefields, and this was no match for the organization and close combat skills of the invaders. Against them, the Mongols fielded phalanxes of closely controlled infantry armed with shields and spears, concentrating at one point.[31] It is also important to remember that in certain military technologies the Mongols enjoyed superiority, particularly in long-range offensive armaments such rockets and a form of catapult.

Since the losses at Tsushima and Iki, the Japanese had been preparing, mobilizing warriors and reinforcing defenses at Hakata Bay for the Mongol onslaught.[32] For a few precious hours, the *samurai* held the Mongols in check in desperate fighting in the Hakata, Hakozaki, and Akasaka areas, enabling them to fall back onto prepared positions a few miles inland near Dazaifu under cover of darkness, from where to await the arrival of reinforcements for a counterattack. But as the Japanese pulled back, a severe storm began to blow up, causing the Korean ship captains much concern. They advised that the land force re-board the sailing vessels in order to avoid the risk of being cut off from their sea line of communication. With the threat of a night attack pressing on them, their unfamiliarity with the terrain, and the heavy losses already suffered, the Mongol generals withdrew to their ships.[33]

As dawn broke, only a few ships had not put to sea. As the force sailed out in the Sea of Japan, a typhoon[34] swept over the ships, sinking as many as 200 of them and causing the loss of 13,000 men.

Above: Hojo Tokimune was officially the eighth *shikken* (regent) of the Kamakura *shogunate*, but was in fact the *de facto* ruler at a time when Japan was threatened by the invading Mongols. He became known for extending *Bushido* (the Way of the Warrior) among the *samurai* and for helping the spread of Zen Buddhism across Japan.
(British Museum/Jo St Mart)

Some have questioned why, despite every indication that they were gaining the upper hand, and with the situation rapidly deteriorating for the defenders, the Mongols did not pursue the *samurai* further inland to the defenses at Dazaifu. Some analysts theorize that, given the relatively small size of the force, in fact this was never intended as an invasion, but merely a

The Second Invasion

But in Japan, Kublai Khan's decision to put off a second invasion was unknown and, with further attack seemingly imminent, very soon an atmosphere of crisis pervaded throughout Japan. This was heightened in May 1275 when the Korean emissary Suh Chan and colleagues, acting for Kublai Khan, arrived in Japan with a message calling for tribute and acceptance of Kublai as suzerain.[37] Hojo Tokimune responded by executing Suh and the other envoys and sending back their severed heads.[38]

Kamakura policy making was rapidly subsumed by issues of defense, and much government business was put off while the threat of invasion loomed.

In the aftermath of the failed landings, the *bakufu* ordered the construction of extensive defenses, including forts and other defensive structures, at the site of the most likely landing points, which included Hakata Bay in Kyushu. The dominant feature was a great stone wall at Hakata Bay, between six and ten feet high, that swept for twenty-five miles around the coastline from Shigashima to Imazu. The wall had a wedged profile, the sheer side facing seaward and the lee side sloped to allow *samurai* to ride to the crest and fire upon the attackers. Recognizing the dangers of placing too much emphasis on this one location, additional walls were constructed to the east and west at potential landing sites.

To man the defenses, the Dazaifu created a rotating pool of warriors. In addition, forces already in Kyushu were moved west and a reserve force was created to act as a sort of rapid reaction force should the enemy break through. All those who held fiefs in Kyushu were ordered to return to their lands. At sea, the defensive plans called for the use of small, maneuverable and fleet ships crewed by *wako* to harry the Mongol fleet as it disembarked its cavalry and foot soldiers. Construction of these began immediately.

One rather curious recourse, and of questionable military value, was to prayer. Much money was spent on organizing great prayer services at which the gods were called on for salvation,[39] and a new nationalistic sect of Buddhism even sprang up, named after its leader Nichiren. With its emphasis on duty to country,

reconnaissance. Alternatively, it may have been due to the stubbornness of the defenders, and the invaders' fears of a night attack that brought the attack to an end, as Arthur Marder suggests, or simply that they were running out of arrows.[35] We may never be sure of the reason the attack was brought to a halt, or Khan's precise motive for launching the invasion to begin with. But there is no doubt the venture was a calamitous failure and a mighty blow to his plans of conquest in Japan. Six years would pass before he was ready to try again. In the meantime, he concluded the subjugation of the Song Dynasty in southern China,[36] before once again turning his attentions to Japan.

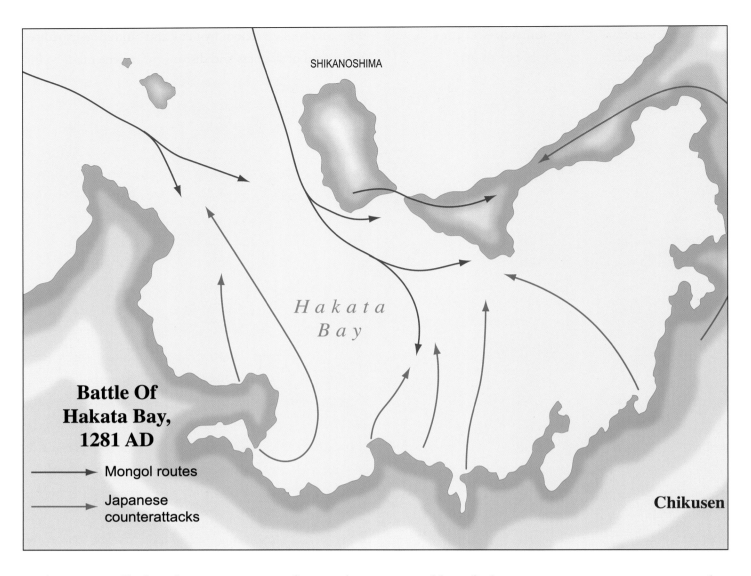

Battle Of Hakata Bay, 1281 AD

→ Mongol routes

→ Japanese counterattacks

SHIKANOSHIMA

Hakata Bay

Chikusen

Nichiren naturally found many supporters from within the *samurai* class.

In 1279, after a hiatus of four years, Kublai ordered preparations to begin for a second attack on Japan. Responsibility for this was delegated to an office within his government, created exclusively for the purpose. A fortress was built near Masan and a large garrison army was stationed there. Cheju-do was turned into a vast pasture for Mongol army horses. Korean shipwrights were set to work on building an invasion fleet, while their neighbors in southern China, also under Mongol rule, were directed to prepare an army to carry off the amphibious landings.

The force assembling at Aiura in Korea was to form one arm known as the Eastern Route Army, while the other, in what is now Kiangsu Province in China, would be called the Southern Route Army.[40] Again, reliable information on the size of these forces is almost

impossible to find—contemporary accounts suggest that together they may have numbered as many as 160,000, to be transported in 4,400 Korean and Chinese ships (900 and 3,500 ships respectively[41]), but these figures are impossible to verify. Given the propensity for exaggeration in medieval Japanese chronicles, it is probably safe to say that the stated ship totals are a gross over-estimation, and we shall just have to settle on "formidable." To lead the eastern force Kublai Khan appointed Hong Da-gu, a Mongol general, seconded by the Koryo General Kim Bang-gyong at the head of the Koryo army. The Southern Route Army, composed mostly of former Sung Chinese soldiers pressed into Kublai's service, was to be led by the Chinese General Bom Mun-ho.

Just after New Year in 1281, orders came down from Kublai that the attack was to proceed, as soon as was opportune. But as spring arrived, the Southern Route Army assembling just south of the Yangtze River in

China was still experiencing difficulties in provisioning and manning such a large number of ships.

The Korean fleet departed from Masan as scheduled on May 3, the plan being to rendezvous with the Southern Route Army off the island of Iki, before landing on Kyushu. En route, Tsushima was taken (June 9), and neighboring islands were occupied in quick succession. Iki itself fell on June 14.

But with the Chinese fleet still bottled up in port, the planned rendezvous off Iki could not take place as planned, and the commander of the Eastern Route Army decided to sail on alone. On June 6 he arrived off Nagato, where over the next two days several attempts were made to land, none of which succeeded in breaching the sea wall. The Mongol fleet withdrew and two days later tried again at Hakata Bay. The assault was presaged by a bombardment using crude bombs developed by Chinese engineers, rocks, flaming materials that may have been something like Greek fire[42] and iron balls. The Japanese, with no heavy projectile weapons of their own, responded with volleys of arrows.

As the Mongol assault boats drew up in the surf they were met by ranks of *samurai* rushing down from their positions behind the defenses. Again the Mongols were stymied; after much bloodshed, they withdrew to their ships to attempt a flanking maneuver via the narrow spit of land east of Shigashima (called the Umi no Nakamichi). The Japanese commanders were quick to act, sending their mobile reserve to head off this threat and denying them the beachhead.

The Mongols anchored offshore, and over the coming weeks made probing attacks along different parts of the shore, trying unsuccessfully to find a weak spot in the defenses. At night, under the cloak of darkness, small bands of *samurai* would venture into the bay in small boats, infiltrating among the Mongol fleet to sneak aboard the ships and kill the men, and then escape back to land before dawn.[43] In this way the Mongols lost an estimated 2,000 men. In an effort to prevent these raids the Mongols grouped their ships together in tight packs, but this served only to exacerbate another problem that began to manifest itself. On board the hot, humid, cramped ships, a lack of hygiene and sanitation expedited the spread of sickness and disease among the men.[44] This, coupled with the continual harassment by the raiders, prompted the Mongols to retreat to Takashima at the end of June, to await the arrival of the Southern Route Army from China.

In early August the much delayed Southern Route Army of General Bom finally arrived. Bom sent the main part of the fleet to Hirado, west of Hakata, and with an advance squadron rendezvoused with the Eastern fleet off Iki. This considerably strengthened combined force sailed for Takeshima, also to the west of Hakata Bay, where Bom planned to assault the flank of the Japanese defenses.

As the Mongol fleets positioned for a climactic encounter, they where harried by increasingly desperate Japanese naval attacks.

By August 12, the massed fleets were poised offshore, packed to the gunnels with tens of thousands of men ready to storm the beaches.

But now nature intervened again. On the eve of the attack[45] a powerful typhoon swept across the Tsushima Straits, wreaking havoc on the Mongol fleet for two full days. When the storm clouds finally cleared, most of the ships that had survived were forced to return to Masan, leaving behind a token army of about 20,000 soldiers. The Japanese descended on the outnumbered invaders and killed all but about 10,000 Chinese soldiers. Of the 9,960-strong Koryo army and 15,029 sailors, 19,397 made it back home.

The Mongol generals and army, fearing severe punishment by Kublai, went into hiding in Koryo. The Chinese captives became slaves in Japan and few of them made it back to China. Apparently undaunted by this second defeat, Kublai Khan in fact began to gather forces to prepare for a third invasion attempt in 1284. He ordered Korea to build more ships and stock up army provisions—this despite the horrendous cost to the economy and to his and Mongol prestige, and also the unanimous agreement of his advisors against such an attempt. Ultimately, he was distracted by a rebellion in Southeast Asia, and no third attempt was ever made. When he died in 1294, the plans died with him.

And so the second invasion and the threat from the Mongols passed, without a major battle between the two armies. There has been considerable speculation among historians about what the outcome would have been if the Mongols had landed successfully. Some historians point to the enormous numerical superiority, and the superior tactics and weaponry favoring the invaders. On the other hand, there is the fact that the Japanese had successfully defended for nearly two months, and were able to draw on considerable reserves.

While we may hypothesize over the outcome, much has come to light regarding the failure of the second expedition. It is sometimes believed that Japanese historians still persist in popularizing the *kamikaze* (sacred wind)[46] as the sole cause of the Mongol defeat.[47] However, scholarly research in Korea, China, *and* Japan has thrown up not one but a whole series of factors, some but not all of which were exposed by that terrible storm. Well established among these factors are the logistical problems that hampered the expedition throughout its course. This led to fatal delays and poor coordination between the Eastern and Southern Route armies,[48] and a weakening of the overall strategy.

Another factor, and one that is also subject to some controversy, concerns the type and quality of shipping the Mongols had at their disposal. Kublai gave his Korean shipwrights less than a year to rebuild the whole Mongol fleet, when it should have taken up to five. In order to achieve readiness, the Chinese had to supplement the shortfall with any available ships, including flat-bottomed riverboats. Such vessels (unlike ocean-going ships, which have a curved keel to prevent capsizing) would be highly unstable in typhoon swells.

Interesting investigative work has been undertaken by marine archaeologist Dr. Kenzo Hayashida, who headed an investigation that discovered the wreckage of the second invasion fleet off the western coast of Takeshima. After careful examination, Hayashida has concluded that the destruction of the Mongol fleet was greatly facilitated by another factor, in addition the use of hastily acquired, flat-bottomed Chinese riverboats. The archaeological evidence recovered from the site includes the remains of poorly constructed timber joints held together by weak nails. These ships, supposedly capable of blue-water operations, had been constructed by Korean forced-laborers, and the implication is that they might have introduced fatal flaws into many of the ships, either because of the pressures of time, or by deliberate sabotage. Had Kublai used a fleet entirely composed of standard, well-constructed, ocean-going ships, might then his navy have survived the journey to and from Japan and conquered it as intended?

Whatever, despite their ultimate failure, the invasion attempts are of a significant importance. These events marked the limit of Mongol expansion, and "shattered the myth of Mongol invincibility throughout Asia."[49] For the unity of the empire itself, the losses had far-reaching and damaging reverberations, as explained by the author John Pearson: "The cost of these defeats led the Khan to devalue the central currency, further exacerbating growing inflation. He also increased tax assessments. These economic problems led to growing resentment of the Mongols, who paid no taxes, among the Chinese populace."[50]

In Japan the events of 1274 and 1281 have an almost mythic significance, comparable to that which the defeat of the Spanish Armada has in English history.

However, for the Kamakura *bakufu*, victory was achieved at a high cost, for thereafter it entered a long decline that ended, in 1333, with collapse. In no small part this was due to the considerable strain imposed by the wars, which weakened the regime considerably.

"The gigantic defense effort of the Japanese lasted for some fifty or sixty years, utterly exhausting the resources of the *shogunate* and the Hojo family. Quite aside from military expenditures, huge outlays were made to temples and shrines…Moreover it was impossible to reward all of the warriors who had submitted claims, since there were no confiscated lands to distribute."[51]

As we shall see in the following chapter, this inability of the *shogunate* to satisfy demands for land made by powerful families "became critical as a result of the Mongol invasions of 1274 and 1281" and acted as a catalyst for the collapse of the Kamakura *bakufu*.

NOTES

1 Richard A. Gabriel and Donald W. Boose Jr *The Great Battles of Antiquity* Greenwood Press (1994) p.579.

2 Karl F. Friday *Samurai, Warfare and the State in Early Medieval Japan* Routledge (2003) p.47.

3 One of the great stories to emerge from this confrontation is that of the legendary warrior monk Benkei, who supposedly fought valiantly to his death on the bridge in front of the main gate, to protect Yoshitsune while he retired to the inner temple of the castle to commit seppuku. .

4 For a more detailed discussion of this see Shinoda p.122-130.

5 See Chapter 1.

6 McCullough p.xxxiii.

7 Source unknown.

8 Karl F. Friday *Samurai, Warfare and State in Early Medieval Japan* p.116.

9 Karl F. Friday *Samurai, Warfare and State in Early Medieval Japan* p.13.

10 In 1219, Masako invited Kujo Yoritsune from Kyoto to succeed to the 4th *shogun*. As she claimed herself as Kujo's guardian and handled the government business, she was called the Nun Shogun.

11 John S. Brownlee *Crisis as Reinforcement of the Imperial Institution: The Case of the Jokyu Incident, 1221* Monumenta Nipponica 30: 2; p.195.

12 John S. Brownlee *The Shokyu War and the Political Rise of the Warriors* Monumenta Nipponica, Vol. 24, No. 1/2 (1969), pp. 59-77.

13 The three old roads leading to the capital (William McCullough *The Azuma Kagami Account of the Shokyu War* Monumenta Nipponica 23: 1/2; p.113).

14 William McCullough *The Azuma Kagami Account of the Shokyu War* Monumenta Nipponica 23: 1/2; p.128.

15 William McCullough *The Azuma Kagami Account of the Shokyu War* Monumenta Nipponica 23: 1/2; p.153 and note p.154.

16 In reference to these events John Brownlee notes that "the survival of the Japanese imperial institution is one of the more unlikely phenomena of history….historical example suggests it should have disappeared." *Crisis as Reinforcement of the Imperial Institution: The Case of the Jokyu Incident, 1221* Monumenta Nipponica 30: 2; p.193.

17 William McCullough *The Azuma Kagami Account of the Shokyu War* Monumenta Nipponica 23: 1/2; p.147.

18 William McCullough *The Azuma Kagami Account of the Shokyu War* Monumenta Nipponica 23: 1/2; p.132.

19 Shigaku zasshi, Vol.92, No.9 *The Process of Founding the Hyojo System in Kamakura Shogunate.*

20 McCullough, xxxii.

21 Charlotte von Verschuer notes that the "Japanese called them Matsura-to, the Matsura band, indicating that they were based in Matsura, the coastal region of present-day Nagasaki prefecture in northwest Kyushu. *Japan's Foreign Relations 1200 to 1392 A.D: A translation from "Zenrin Kokuhoki"* Monumenta Nipponica 57: 4; 417.

2 Zuikei Shuho and Charlotte von Verschuer *Japan's Foreign Relations 1200 to 1392 A.D: A translation from "Zenrin Kokuhoki"* Monumenta Nipponica 57: 4; 417 – 418.

2 Zuikei Shuho and Charlotte von Verschuer *Japan's Foreign Relations 1200 to 1392 A.D: A translation from "Zenrin Kokuhoki"* Monumenta Nipponica 57: 4; 414.

2 Richard A. Gabriel and Donald W. Boose Jr *The Great Battles of Antiquity* Greenwood Press (1994) p.599.

25 Thomas Conlan *In little need for divine intervention - Rationales for the Mongol Invasion* Cornell University Press (2001) p.255.

26 Zuikei Shuho and Charlotte von Verschuer *Japan's Foreign Relations 1200 to 1392 A.D: A translation from "Zenrin Kokuhoki"* Monumenta Nipponica 57: 4; 414 – 415.

27 Richard A. Gabriel and Donald W. Boose Jr *The Great Battles of Antiquity* Greenwood Press (1994) p.599.

28 Arthur Marder suggests a figure of 900 ships. 300 large 100-ton warships, 300 landing craft and 300 water supply boats *From Jimmu Tenno to Perry: Sea Power in Early Japanese History* The American Historical Review 51: 1; p.13.

29 Arthur Marder *From Jimmu Tenno to Perry: Sea Power in Early Japanese History* The American Historical Review 51: 1; p.13.

30 Thomas Conlan *In little need for divine intervention - Rationales for the Mongol Invasion* Cornell University Press (2001) p.263.

31 Richard A. Gabriel and Donald W. Boose Jr *The Great Battles of Antiquity* Greenwood Press (1994) p.604. Also Thomas Conlan *In little need for divine intervention - Rationales for the Mongol Invasion* Cornell University Press (2001) p.256.

32 Karl F. Friday *Samurai, Warfare and State in Early Medieval Japan* p.52.

33 Richard A. Gabriel and Donald W. Boose Jr *The Great Battles of Antiquity* Greenwood Press (1994) p.599.

34 Thomas Conlan notes that contemporary Japanese accounts talk merely of a "reverse wind" whereas continental accounts make much more of the strength of the storm (p.266).

35 Arthur Marder *From Jimmu Tenno to Perry: Sea Power in Early Japanese History* The American Historical Review 51: 1; p.14.

36 Richard A. Gabriel and Donald W. Boose Jr *The Great Battles of Antiquity* Greenwood Press (1994) p.600.

37 Zuikei Shuho and Charlotte von Verschuer *Japan's Foreign Relations 1200 to 1392 A.D: A translation from "Zenrin Kokuhoki"* Monumenta Nipponica 57: 4; 416.

38 Zuikei Shuho and Charlotte von Verschuer *Japan's Foreign Relations 1200 to 1392 A.D: A translation from "Zenrin Kokuhoki"* Monumenta Nipponica 57: 4; 415

39 After the invasions gods were credited with intervening for the defenders.

4 Gabriel, R.A and Boose D.W, p.601.

41 Arthur Marder *From Jimmu Tenno to Perry: Sea Power in Early Japanese History* The American Historical Review 51: 1; p.14.

42 Greek fire was a burning-liquid weapon used by the Byzantine Greeks, Arabs, Chinese, and Mongols. The chemical composition is something of a mystery, but it was projected bomb-like from catapults and through some sort of siphon (like an early flamethrower). The Mongols had it from the Chinese, who had used it since at least the 10th Century.

43 The most celebrated instance was carried out in broad daylight by one Kusano Jiro, who led a small group of men under fire to an enemy ship, boarded it, set it aflame and returned with 21 enemy heads despite the loss of an arm! Arthur Marder *From Jimmu Tenno to Perry: Sea Power in Early Japanese History* The American Historical Review 51: 1; p.15.

44 Arthur Marder *From Jimmu Tenno to Perry: Sea Power in Early Japanese History* The American Historical Review 51: 1; p.15.

45 In fact, in Japan typhoons are not at all unusual in August, and Kyushu is particularly susceptible to them.

46 In Japanese history it is called the *Ise no Kami-kaze* or "Divine Wind of Ise."

47 Arthur Marder *From Jimmu Tenno to Perry: Sea Power in Early Japanese History* The American Historical Review 51: 1; p.17.

48 Richard A. Gabriel and Donald W. Boose Jr *The Great Battles of Antiquity* Greenwood Press (1994) p.608.

49 David Nicole *"The Mongol Conquerors."*

50 John Pearson, *Kublai Khan* (2005).

51 McCullough, p.xxxiii.

JAPAN DIVIDED (1331–1467)

In the years after the Mongols had been so adventitiously rebuffed from Japanese shores, the country entered a protracted period of upheaval, in which a dynasty rose and fell, and the *shogunate* asserted its preeminence amid a series of bitter disputes with the court.

This chapter examines events over a period of more than two hundred years, from the end of the 13th century to the start of the "Warring States" period (Sengoku jidai), and encompassing three major outbreaks of violence. The first was the brief Kemmu Restoration, in which the emperor was temporarily restored to a position of authority. The outcome of that was *Namboku-cho jidai* (Northern and Southern Courts Period), in which for the better part of half a century two separate and competing courts existed in Japan. Then, after a long and comparatively peaceful hiatus, the capital itself became a casualty of the decade-long Onin War, an ill-omened preface to the protracted period of civil war known as the Sengoku jidai.

During these turbulent times the functions and form of the military in Japan continued to evolve. Elaborating on this, Karl Friday says, "The Mongol invasions, and the long cold war of continued vigilance that followed, further expanded Kamakura's role in state military and police affairs. In assuming complete responsibility for national defense during the crisis, the *shogunate* significantly enlarged the formal limits of its authority— and thereby the weight of its countrywide presence."[1]

The nature of warfare also underwent a transformation. At a strategic level, the construction of the sea defenses at Hakata had taught Japanese commanders about the effectiveness of strong defensive walls, leading to experiments with positional castle

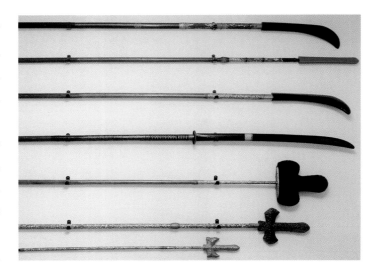

Above: A collection of polearms that would have been carried by *samurai* and *ashigaru* (foot soldiers), ranging from the small *makura* (pillow) *yari* that would likely have been kept by the bed for protection at night, to a *naginata* (top). *(via Clive Sinclaire)*

warfare. And in terms of the composition of forces, whereas previously there had been considerable reliance within Japanese formations on mounted warriors, this began to give way to a different model in which foot soldiers played a more prominent role. The small bands of armed and well-armored mounted *samurai* that were a dominant feature of the battlefield in the Genpei War were rapidly being replaced.

In the same way that they had adopted the horse from the continent, the Japanese military, taking as their model the Mongol forces, introduced infantry called *ashigaru* (literally meaning light foot) armed with the long iron-tipped pikes or glaives, which they called respectively *nagayari*, or *naginata*. As experience during the recent invasions had shown, such troops could be devastatingly effective, even against well-armed cavalry, provided they were used in large, disciplined groups. A battalion of pikemen standing behind solid, free-standing shields of

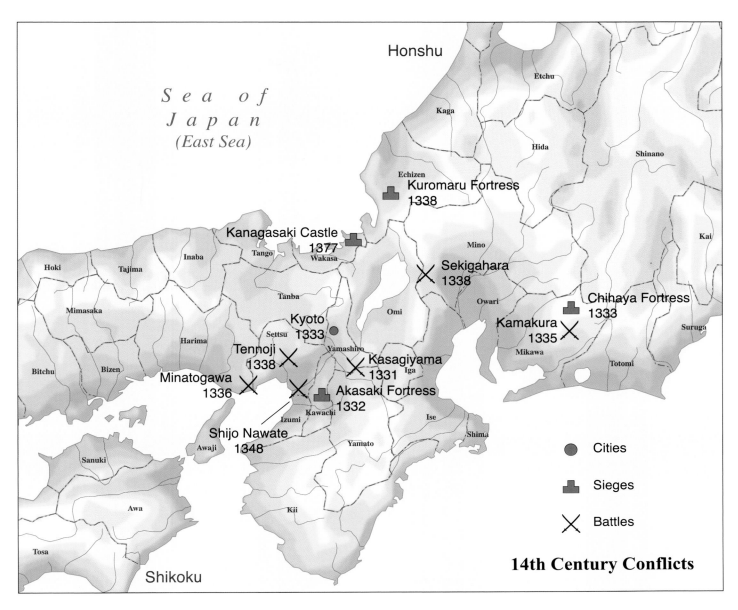

14th Century Conflicts

wood or bundled bamboo,[2] backed by ranks of archers, could withstand the fiercest cavalry attack. Not only that, they were cheaper to arm and easier to train, an important factor when considering that these new military technologies involved the use of much larger formations of men, thousands strong.

That is not to say, however, that the horseman simply disappeared from the battlefield. In the 14th century battles at Minatogawa and Shijonawate, cavalry was still a decisive element. Rather, "the way of the horse and bow" was gradually forsaken, with "warriors riding into battle with multiple striking weapons instead."[3] And whereas it might have been expected that, as warfare changed, there would be a corresponding loss of the chivalrous, heroic nature of combat as depicted in the old war tales, "It is now clear that there was no mysterious degeneration of warrior values and

standards of behavior between the late twelfth and early fourteenth centuries; *bushi* approached their craft with substantially the same attitudes in both areas. Military technology evolved, of course, and with it evolved tactics and methods of fighting. Heian *samurai* liked to fight on horseback, with bow and arrow; their medieval descendants preferred spears and short swords, wielded on foot."[4]

Of course the need for larger armies[5] changed the nature of political and administrative control as well. As tacticians experimented with complex strategies, the need arose for extensive training and drilling of troops to produce a disciplined and well-articulated corps. Furthermore, the need to coordinate the movements of large armies, and increase the degree of cooperation between cavalry and infantry, required better communications on the battlefield. A myriad of

battlefield communications and identification devices were employed for this purpose, including the *noroshi-dai* (signal beacon), *taiko* (drums), *horogai*[6] (conch-shell trumpet), *nagarehata* (battle flag), and gongs.

But of course all of these methods required a well-trained and disciplined military. Whereas, before, the *samurai*-farmer had been co-opted in times of war, left his fields and returned home after the fight, in due course the *samurai* left the rice fields, and the peasants left the battlefields. Henceforth, the *shugo* kept their *samurai* and *ashigaru* nearby and their farmers on the land producing food for the military.

Although often presented as a straightforward power struggle between the court and the *bakufu*, the path to the *Namboku-cho jidai* was convoluted, leading back beyond the Kemmu Restoration to the establishment of the Kamakura *bakufu* in 1185. This in effect had given rise to two different and in many ways competing political systems, one in Kamakura and the other in Kyoto. The product of the rivalry between the court and *bakufu* was a serious clash of arms in the brief Jokyu War in 1221, which ended with the total defeat of the court and resulted in it being quickly subsumed by the *bakufu*.

As part of this process the *bakufu* created an agency in Kyoto—the *Rokahara Tandai*[7]—to supervise the court and to control the legal and administrative business of the western provinces. It also appropriated the right to choose who sat on the imperial throne. This in effect represented the transition of political power away from Kyoto[8] and the effects of that were important, as Helen McCullough summarises: "In the opening decades of the fourteenth century, the atmosphere in Kyoto was gloomy and pessimistic. Profoundly dissatisfied with the present, the courtiers looked back nostalgically to the days before the *shogunate*, when decisions of state were made in the capital…."[9]

Beyond the imperial court, the *bakufu* was not without troubles of its own. As the Hojo clan turned increasingly inward and autocratic, other vassal houses were alienated. There were other strains on the relationship too. As touched on in the previous chapter, the defense of the realm against the Mongols had been "a hugely costly endeavor, crippling the Hojo-dominated *bakufu* both financially and politically," the latter so because the *shogun* had no confiscated lands with which to reward the so-called *gokenin*[10] who had borne the burden of the expense of military service.[11] Consequently many of them became mired in debt, amplifying feelings of discontent. Furthermore, certain structural changes within warrior families led to a weakening of the bonds between the Kamakura regime and its provincial vassals. Without them, the power base of Hojo and the *bakufu* diminished.

By the beginning of the 14th century, dark and troubled clouds were again threatening to blacken the land. It is at this point that the Kamakura period epic *Taiheiki* picks up the story, describing how in 1316 Hojo Takatoki became regent.[12] His tenure, as characterized by the author from the very outset, was an injurious blend of mismanagement, corruption and avarice. However, although Takatoki is the target of much criticism, he was first and foremost a self-indulgent pleasure-seeker, and had little involvement in the everyday administration. In fact, it was the corruption and unjustness of the men who manipulated him that were the real cause of malaise. Under Takatoki's vague stewardship, the Kamakura *bakufu* fell into disarray and terminal decline.

In Kyoto, the accumulating weaknesses of the *bakufu* prompted a movement among the nobility to regain political power from the military, and presented opportunities for advancement of the interests of the imperial court.[13]

At the end of the 13th century two separate imperial families had developed, and from the senior family, the Go-Fukakusa and the junior line, the Kameyama, the emperor was alternately selected. Initially, this arrangement worked well enough, as the emperor was invariably an infant and his position was manipulated by those behind the throne. But when the assertive and ambitious Go-Daigo came to the throne in 1318 (at the

Left: Part of a visual narrative depicting a *samurai* raid on the community during the power struggle between the court and the *bakufu*. *(Library of Congress)*

age of 29, somewhat unusual given that most of his predecessors had been mere infants), the happy concord was broken. Seeking to rule with genuine authority, and to realize his ambition of restoring the power and status of the imperial court,[14] he abolished the *insei* system (in 1321) and resolved to overthrow the *bakufu*.

In 1324, the intrigues of the ambitious emperor and his chief co-conspirators Hino Suketomo (the superintendent of police) and Hino Toshimoto (the chamberlain) were exposed in what is referred to as the Shochu Incident.[15] The Kamakura regime dispatched an expedition to the capital to arrest them. Although he was censured, the *bakufu* elected not to bring charges against Go-Daigo. The other members of the cabal were less fortunate; at least ten of them were executed. Suketomo was killed by the *Rokahara Tandai,* and Toshimoto was banished. Unabashed, Go-Daigo began afresh to scheme against the *shogunate*, and again, in 1331, his plans were discovered, this time through the betrayal of his close associate, Yoshida Sadafusa.

What became known as the Genko Incident quickly developed into open war. On September 27, taking the imperial regalia[16] with him, Go-Daigo fled to a fortified temple complex at Kasagiyama on the border between Yamato and Yamashiro (the modern town of Kasagi in Kyoto Prefecture). There he established a court and began raising an army.[17]

The force of men from Omi and Tamba under Sasaki Tokinobu was turned back and, in response, on October 5, the *bakufu* dispatched a 75,000-strong army south under Suyama Yoshitaka and Komiyama Jiro,[18] which laid siege to the garrison of 500 *sohei* warrior-monks. For three weeks the monks held out until, as graphically described in the *Taiheiki*, the temple was assaulted at daybreak by warriors who first scaled the seemingly impassable cliffs surrounding the fortress before setting it aflame.

Although the emperor got away under cover of darkness, he was soon caught at Rokuhara and in April 1332 exiled to Oki Province[19] (the Oki Islands in modern-day Shimane Prefecture). This marked a low point in his fortunes, for already in November, the key loyalist fortress at Akasaka[20] (on Mount Kongo, in Kwatchi) had fallen.

For three weeks, in the early fall, Akasaka had been

Above: The escape of Emperor Go-Daigo (the 96th emperor of Japan) from the Oki Islands in 1333, during the event known as the Genko Incident. *(via Clive Sinclaire)*

staunchly defended by troops under Kusunoki Masashige and Prince Morinaga, who had fled there from the Enryakuji Temple. In that time Masashige and his 500-odd men had fought valiantly against a numerically much stronger force, imposing a great many casualties on their enemy.[21] But the *bakufu* forces employed the familiar siege tactic of severing the castle water supply, which in this case was an aqueduct;[22] without this, the small garrison was doomed.

As he prepared for the inevitable loss of the fortress, Masashige had a great funeral pyre set within the compound. With the *bakufu* troops threatening on all sides, the castle was set ablaze. But when it was dark Masashige slipped out though the cordon. When the attackers finally broke in and saw the smoldering ashes of the pyre, all assumed that Masashige had met his end. Masashige, however, was not so easily beaten, and having made good his escape he set up base in the Yamato region, from where he took up the fight against the *bakufu* forces in the Kinai region.

Meanwhile, from where he was temporarily installed at Yoshino, Go-Daigo's son, Prince Morinaga, had busied himself issuing entreaties to others to rally against the Kamakura *bakufu*. Early in the following year, three large armies of *bakufu* troops were sent against him, and against Kusunoki Masahige at the Chihaya fort on Mount Kongo and Akasaka. Although the *bakufu* succeeded on March 1 in taking Yoshino,[23] and also Akasaka, once again Prince Morinaga evaded his would-be captors, this time escaping to Mount Koya. The *bakufu* troops now converged on Chihaya for a titanic and defining encounter that ultimately would decide the outcome of the campaign.

Meanwhile, on Oki Island, Go-Daigo's period of banishment was about to come to a premature end. He

Above: Ashikaga Takauji closing with the enemy on the field of battle. (via Clive Sinclaire)

had attracted considerable empathy among the nobility for his opposition to the *shogunate*, and it was one such family, led by Nawa Nagatoshi,[24] that assisted him in his escape. With Nawa's connivance, he got away from Oki in April and began to draw together loyalist troops at Funagami Mountain in Hoki Province (the modern town of Kotoura in Tohaku District, Tottori Prefecture), where he had several powerful allies.[25]

Throughout the early summer Masashige heroically defended Chihaya[26] castle (Kwatchi) against a *bakufu* army. This time, to preclude use of the siege tactics employed against him at Akasaka, Kusunoki ensured that Chihaya was provisioned to withstand repeated attacks. He also enjoyed some advantages. Principally, the position of the fortress atop a mountain clearly favored the defender.[27] And although he again had a numerically weaker force, he cunningly sited life-like mannequins in the defenses to give the impression of greater strength. Furthermore, Kusunoki and his warriors had intimate knowledge of the surrounding terrain and were thus able to use its ridges and ravines to launch surprise raids. Although the *bakufu* attackers employed a great range of

techniques and weapons, for more than 100 days they were unable to dislodge the well-provisioned defenders. As Helen McCullough points out "…it is difficult to exaggerate the importance of Kusunoki's contribution to the eventual success of the imperial arms. By containing the entire strength of the Hojo, he not only encouraged other rebels to rise, but also prepared the way for the loyalist capture of the virtually undefended capital."[28]

In Kyoto, the month of May had witnessed the departure of Ashikaga Takauji and Nagaoshi Takaie from Kamakura at the head of an army[29] they had been ordered to lead south on an expedition to find and destroy loyalist forces. However, when Takaie was killed *en route*, Takauji suddenly found himself sole commander of a massive host. Perhaps emboldened by his new strength, Takauji seems to have had a sudden change of heart, as he suddenly and quite unexpectedly switched allegiance to the emperor. His army, together with those of Go-Daigo and Masashige, seized Kyoto, while soon after forces led by another recent convert to the cause, Nitta Yoshisada, marched on Kamakura with 20,000 troops. After fighting in and around the town, the *bakufu* seat fell on July 5. *Shikken* Hojo Takatoki and many of the other prominent members of the *bakufu* committed suicide, while two days later, Hojo Hidetoki, the military governor of Kyushu, was overthrown by rebellious local families. In these actions, most of the Hojo leaders perished. Thus, after 140 years' rule, the Kamakura *bakufu* government was brought to an end, and with this the power and influence of the Hojo *Shikken*.

The Kemmu Restoration

Go-Daigo subsequently returned to Kyoto to be restored on the throne, marking the beginning of a three year period known as the *kemu no shinsei* or Kemmu

---

Below: *Samurai* warrior Ashikaga Takauji became *shogun* and opened his *bakufu* at Muromachi, Kyoto. Under his rule the economy prospered as did the merchants and peasants. *(British Museum/Jo St Mart)*

Restoration. One of his first acts was to officially announce his reformist intentions. Go-Daigo, it seems, was persuaded that under his sovereignty the power of the *shogunate* and other usurpers would be diminished, and that the emperor would once again take on the mantle of supreme authority. To this end he reformed certain branches of the civil administration and established a *mandokoro* to keep order among the warriors in Kyoto. Prince Morinaga was placed in charge of his military forces and members of the imperial family set up provincial governors in the northern and eastern provinces.

His attempts at reform proved to be naïvely formulated and ineffective. The *samurai* clans soon became disillusioned with a reestablished imperial court

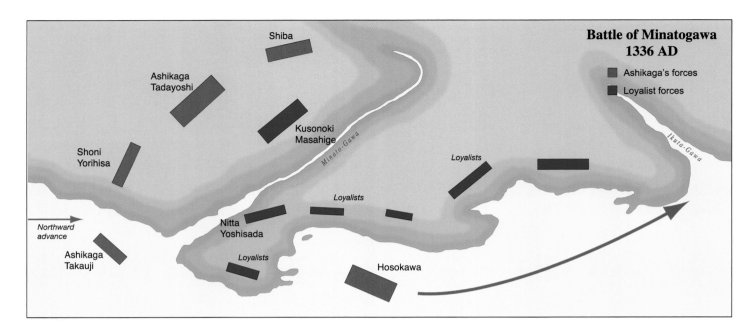

that apparently sought a return to the social and political systems of the Heian period. Furthermore, the administration that he established had neither administrative experience nor the influence in the provinces to survive in a society dominated by warriors. Sensing the discontentment, Takauji pleaded with the emperor to counter the mounting threat of rebellion, but his warnings were ignored. And in fact very soon he fell out of favor with Takauji too, for refusing to appoint a member of the Ashikaga family *shogun*.

In August 1335, Hojo Tokiyuki, son of former regent Hojo Takatoki, implemented the *Nakasendai no Ran* (Nakasendai rebellion) in an attempt reestablish the *shogunate* at Kamakura. Takauji swiftly put down the rebellion, took Kamakura on September 8 and seized this opportune moment to install himself instead. Taking up the cause of his fellow *samurai*, he claimed the title of *seii taishogun*. Then in mid-November, Takauji offended the emperor by allotting land in Kozuke, the fief of Nitta Yoshisada, to one of his followers without permission from the court. Go-Daigo responded by labeling Takauji an "enemy of the throne" and, despite Takauji's loyal pronouncements, ordered his son, Takanaga, and Nitta Yoshisada to reclaim Kamakura. In December 1335 a punitive expedition marched out from Kyoto and defeated a blocking force commanded by Ashikaga Tadayoshi (Takauji's brother) in Mikawa province. The imperialists pressed on eastward, only to be savaged in

battle by Takauji himself in the Ashigara pass of the Hakone Mountains. A following battle in Suruga[30] sent Go-Daigo's army fleeing back westward, whence they had come, with Takauji in pursuit.

After a swift advance, Kyoto fell (albeit briefly) to Takauji's army on February 23, 1336. However, within days a counterattack by imperial forces forced him to retreat, first to Settsu and then to Harima. By the end of March he was in Kyushu. Here, throughout the late spring, he consolidated his power, defeating his only notable source of opposition in Kyushu, the Kikuchi clan, at Tadara-no-hama on April 15. The next month, having gathered men and materiel from Kyushu warlords, the Ashikaga army (under Takauji, Hosokawa Jozen, and Shoni Yorihisa) began to march on Kyoto again, part of it through western Honshu and the other slowly advancing via ship.

The Battle of Minatogawa

Nitta Yoshisada chose Minatogawa in Harima Province (near today's Kobe) to try and halt Takauji's northward movement, and pressed the other leading loyalist general, Kusunoki Masashige, to join him. Masashige, however, was less desirous of confronting Takauji's superior force in the open field, preferring instead to embark on a campaign of harassment until a better opportunity arose. He therefore advised Go-Daigo to leave Kyoto for the sanctuary of the heights of Mount Hiei, wherein the

terrain could be exploited for banditry against Takauji until such an opportunity arose.[31] Go-Daigo would have none of it, and determined to hold on to the capital. Instead, he ordered Masashige to reinforce Yoshisada, and the loyal retainer did as was bid, despite knowing that he was heavily disadvantaged.[32]

Yoshisada stood his 2,000 men on the east side of the Minatogawa estuary, at the point where it meets the sea. Opposite to him Masashige had barely 700, and these he deployed well forward. Takauji, meanwhile, had divided his army into three parts. The first, under Shoni Yorihisa,

Top: Kusunoki Masashige and his brother Masasue committed *seppuku* after being routed at the battle of Minatogawa (present-day Kobe). They were also joined by those Kusunoki retainers who had not already been killed. Masashige's last words were reported to have been, *"Shichisei hokoku!"* ("Would that I had seven lives to give for my country!"). *(via Clive Sinclaire)*

Above: Kusunoki Masashige prepares to fight for the emperor, attended by his standard bearers behind him. *(via Clive Sinclaire)*

was to assault against Yoshisada's front. The second, under Ashikaga Tadayoshi, was to await an advantageous moment to strike at Masahige. Meanwhile, a third force led by Hosokawa Jozen and Takauji himself would approach from the sea and land troops to Yoshisada's rear. This, it was reasoned, would cause a general confusion, which could then be exploited to maximum advantage.

The plan worked seamlessly. On June 5, seeing the approach of Shoni Yorihisa, Yoshisada hastily pulled back into a defensive position, leaving Masashige, in his forward position, isolated. Rapidly surrounded and outnumbered by Ashikaga Tadayoshi's force, Masashige nevertheless held out for over six hours, but finally was overwhelmed. The "horribly wounded"[33] Masashige, his brother Masasue, and his surviving followers committed suicide. Nitta Yoshisada, who had fled the field, was later killed at Minatogawa.

With this last defeat died the short-lived Kemmu Restoration. On July 6, Go-Daigo fled Kyoto to Mount Hiei, and in his place the puppet emperor Komyo (from the senior imperial family) was installed on the throne, and initiated a schism between two rival branches of the imperial family that lasted until 1392. Ultimately, the failure of the Kemmu Restoration confirmed that the authority of the warrior houses had become complete, as it was they who elevated Go-Daigo to power, sustained him as emperor, and who ultimately overthrew him. Henceforth, the imperial family was subsumed by the rule of the *shogunate*, until in 1868, over five centuries later, the Meiji Restoration succeeded in bringing *shogun* rule to an end.

For the Ashikaga family, the defeat of Go-Daigo marked a singular triumph. For the following two and a half centuries one of their number ruled as *shoguns*.[34] Whereas the Kamakura *bakufu* had existed in relative harmony with the imperial court, Ashikaga took over the last remnants of the imperial government. Indeed, there were many differences between this and previous *shogunate*s. As Kenneth Grossberg explains, "Unlike Minamoto no Yoritomo, the Muromachi *shogun* was to be more than a feudal lord, and unlike Hojo Yasutoki, more than a dictator bureaucrat."[35] While it is true that

Above: In his early life a modest landowner from Kawachi province, Kusunoki Masashige become an inspiring symbol of loyalty to the emperor and a hero in Meiji era legends. *(British Museum/Jo St Mart)*

under successive Ashikaga *shogunate*s, a degree of peace returned to Japan during which trade and culture flourished,[36] under its authority "warrior power and authority displaced and supplanted all but the last vestiges of rule by the imperial court."[37]

At the same time the country was ravaged by three bloody periods of warfare, the first of which began almost immediately, to be followed in quick succession by the

period of bitter and bloody dispute known as the *Namboku-cho-jidai*, during which time: "For more than sixty years the whole country was wasted by struggles between feudal barons of all degrees, espousing one cause or another, but always, save for a few conspicuous models of chivalry, striving to satisfy their personal ambitions and their hunger for domains."[38]

The events of this age are quite convoluted, so I have chosen to focus on those military actions that have been reasonably well documented. The first was a classic siege, which took place between January and April 1337 at Nitta Yoshisada's fortress at Kanagasaki. After two months of siege, Yoshisada's ally Uryu Tamotsu escaped to the fortress of Somayama, where he was joined soon after by Yoshisada himself. Although they hoped to launch a counterstrike to lift the siege, this never came, and the wretched occupants of the besieged castle, having run out of food and water, were forced to eat horseflesh to survive.[39] They held out for twenty days longer, but on April 7, Ko no Moroyasu, commander of the besieging army, broke through the walls and took the fortress. Prince Takanaga and Nitta Yoshiaki, son of Yoshisada, were forced to take their own lives. Prince Tsunenaga escaped, but was captured soon afterwards and killed as well.

Here one Kitabatake Akiie enters our story. In 1337 this important retainer of Go-Daigo, governor of the northern province of Mutsu, was ordered by Emperor Go-Daigo to come to the aid of his army to the south of Kyoto. During the slow advance south, his army was engaged by forces of the Northern Court in many battles, and was defeated on December 24 by Ashikaga Yoshiakira at Tonegawa (in Musashi). Continuing south, he occupied Kamakura, the capital of the Ashikaga *shogunate*, and then moved on Nara.

Early in 1338, Takauji was appointed *shogun*, marking formally the foundation of a new *bakufu*. So empowered, he immediately set his generals to work eradicating those who remained loyal to Go-Daigo. In Nara, while trying to rest and reorganize his forces, Kitabatake Akiie was attacked by Ko no Moronao and barely escaped to Kawachi Province. Then, after battling Ashikaga

ten year Onin War and finally by a ruinous age of civil war that has been given the name the Sengoku jidai or Warring States Period.

The Namboku-cho-jidai

Early in 1337, Go-Daigo hastily quit Mount Hiei and moved his entourage (and the symbolically powerful imperial regalia) to the Yoshino Mountains near to Nara. Here he established a *Nan-cho* (South Imperial Court) to rival the *Boku-cho* (North Imperial Court) of Ashikaga Takauji in Kyoto. Henceforth, until 1392, there were two centers of power in Japan. Together they presided over a

Tadayoshi near Sekigahara in Mino province in March, Akiie regrouped, only to be defeated again at Tennoji[40] (in Settsu province). Finally, in June his short life came to an end at the age of just twenty when he was finally defeated and killed at Ishizu (Iwami province).

In the face of these reversals, Nitta Yoshisada puzzled over ways to strike at the Ashikaga *bakufu*. He settled on an attack on the Kuromaru, (Black Fortress), a bastion of *kanrei* (Deputy)[41] Shiba Takatsune in Echizen province (present-day Nittazuka, Fukui, Fukui Prefecture). In August, Yoshisada led a force that included fifty mounted troops in an attack on the citadel.

Prewarned, Ashikaga Takauji had ordered Hosokawa Akiuji to the Kuromaru to assist Shiba Takatsune in the defense. Nearing the fortress, Akiuji ran straight into Yoshida's advancing army. In the confusion that followed, a contingent of *sohei* of the Heisen-ji monastery, originally part of Yoshisada's force, were induced by Takatsune's officers to abandon the attack. With his force so weakened, Yoshisada made a desperate attempt stop up the gap that had suddenly appeared in his formation. In so doing, Yoshisada was mortally wounded by an arrow.[42]

Although cowed, the Southern Court was as yet far from beaten. At the death on September 19, 1339, of Go-Daigo, a new incumbent was enthroned. Emperor Go-Murakami ordered the late Yoshisada's brother, Wakiya Yoshisuke, to lead another attack on Kuromaru. This time the assault was successful, and ended in Takatsune's surrender.

There was now a temporary lull in the fighting, during which time efforts to win support continued in earnest. In May of 1340, Go-Daigo's son, Prince Kanenaga, arrived on Kyushu on just such a mission.

The Battle of Shijo Nawate
We then travel eight years forward in the *Nanbokucho*,

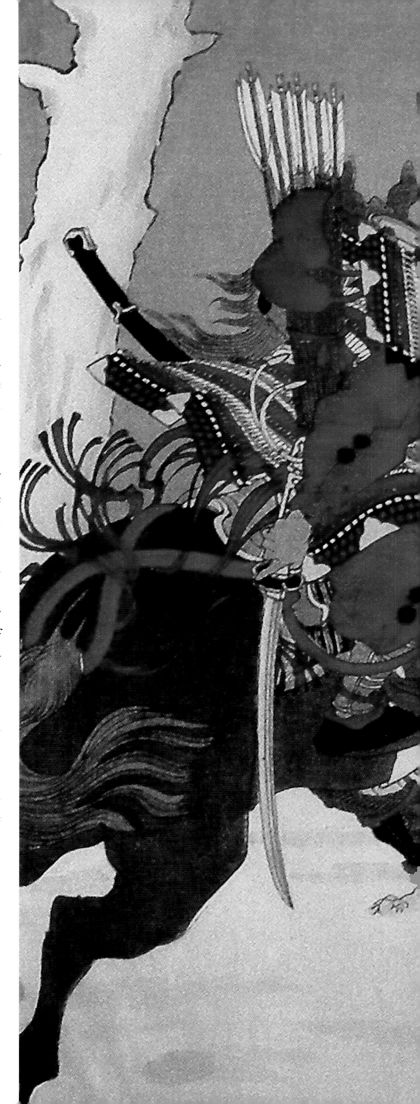

Right: Maeda Toshiie was utterly loyal to Toyotomi Hideyoshi and was named as one of the five regents—the council of Five Elders—responsible for keeping the realm in order while Toyotomi Hideyori came of age. Additionally, Maeda was also named as Hideyori's guardian, but he died within a year. *(British Museum/Jo St Mart)*

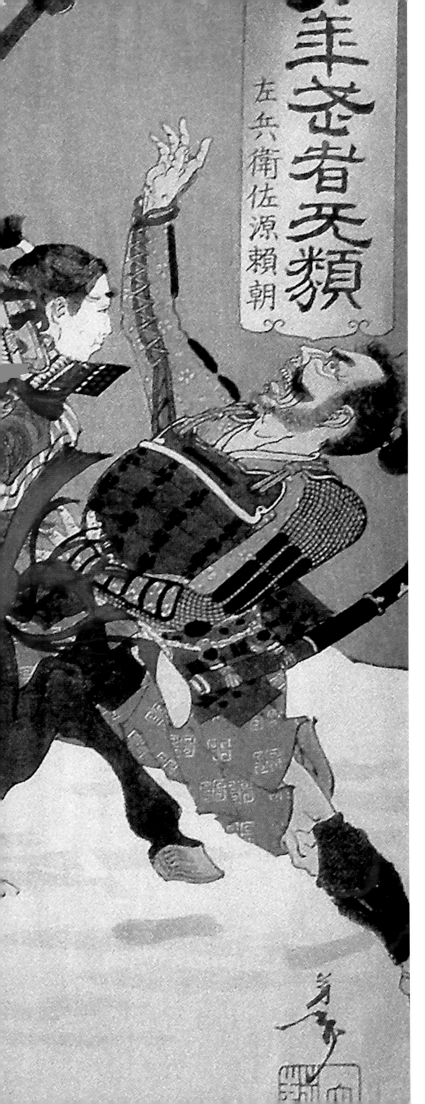

to 1348, before the next major clash of arms. This time it came at Yoshino itself, the very capital of the Southern Court, where an army from the Northern Court led by Kitabatake Chikafusa came to destroy the forces of loyalist Kusunoki Masatsura. Lacking the strength in numbers to withstand a prolonged siege of the emperor's Yoshino palace, Masatsura elected instead to march his whole force out to meet Chikafusa at Shijo Nawate, (in present-day Osaka). Chikafusa, meanwhile, led his force southwest towards Izumi, diverting some of the defenders away from the palace, and in short time the occupants fled. What is interesting is that the battle was again characterized by instances of single combat, the most famous being that in which Masatsura engaged the enemy commander Ko no Moroyasu, and, it is said, was about to take Ko's head when he was struck by an arrow. The 22-year-old Masatsura then committed *seppuku*.

It is not possible to describe here all of the actions that took place over the next four decades, but suffice to say the fortunes of the two courts continued to oscillate. Although the Northern Court was usually in a stronger position, the South succeeded in capturing Kyoto several times for short time periods. The capital suffered greatly during this time. In 1361, earthquakes and disease ravaged the populus, followed in 1362 by a drought that brought famine to the land. Then, in 1366, the first of a series of epidemics afflicted Kyoto (the city was badly affected again in 1373, 1374, and 1378). Finally, on December 16, 1392, Emperor Go-Kameyama abdicated. The union of the Northern and Southern Courts was achieved by the third Ashikaga *shogun,* Yoshimitsu, and the Namboku-cho Period was brought to an end.

The Onin War

Although history has generally been rather hard on the Ashikaga *bakufu,* Yoshimitsu appears to have been a genuinely effective ruler. As Kenneth A. Grossberg points out, "the more than three decades which span Yoshimitsu's public life witnessed Japan's first period of genuine political stability in over a century"[44] and continued to restore Kyoto to its "ancient primacy." However, despite the ostensible success in unifying the

Northern and Southern Courts by Yoshimitsu, and his achievement of a certain "political synthesis"[45] during the years of his reign, it is clear that the wars of the Namboku-cho had weakened the Ashikaga *bakufu* greatly. Although Yoshimitsu's Northern court maintained *de facto* rule over the court, by the end of the 14th century it was already demonstrating a number of grave failings. Chief among them was the fact that it had lost the backing of many powerful provincial families. Kenneth Grossberg points out that "Yoshimitsu's most urgent political problem at the time of his coming to power (was) how to bind the *shugo* close enough to the *bakufu* in Kyoto to guarantee at least their obedience and at best their cooperation."[46]

At the heart of the problem was land, or rather the lack of it. Under subsequent Muromachi[47] *shoguns* this problem, which had surfaced in the late 13th century, became critical, as the scarcity of new land grants with which to reward loyal supporters became a grave threat to stability. This was primarily because by the late 14th century there was an increasing scarcity of wild but workable land in mountainous Japan to open up to cultivation. After the fall of the Hojo, the *bakufu* had seized Hojo lands as well as those of all the *gokenin* who had fought with them for itself, instead of distributing among its own supporters. Collectively, the Ashikaga now directly controlled nearly one-quarter of the country. Building on that large holding, they attempted to launch punitive expeditions to confiscate land from insubordinate families who had fought for the emperor, as a way of assuaging the demands, but this was never an effective solution to the land issue.

The land crisis was made worse by a rise in the number of *shugo*,[48] which by the outbreak of the Onin War in 1467 was more than 250. The post of *shugo*, which is commonly translated as governor, was instituted by Minamoto no Yoritomo in 1185, as a means of extending shogunal powers over the land. As we have seen, these provincial governors had gradually become, to all intents and purposes, independent, and each maintained an army. Whereas previously most of these men had been in positions of authority, a new type of

Above: Hosokawa Katsumoto was in conflict with his father-in-law, Yamana Sozen, who resented the power he had as *kanrei* thus igniting the Onin War of 1467. This civil war started the *Sengoku jidai* (the Warring States Period). *(British Museum/Jo St Mart)*

shugo motivated solely by personal gain achieved prominence. When the *bakufu* tried to limit their landholdings, their armies, or the extent of their power, they entrenched within castles, consolidated their lands and men,[49] and stopped granting land (and thus power) as a reward for service. In this way *shugo* asserted their independence to the extent that they no longer sought the official imperial offices that had equated with power

Compounding this progressive dissolution of central authority was the attitude of the Ashikaga *shoguns* themselves. While it is true to say by the time Ashikaga Yoshimitsu, the position of *shogun* "had grown to become a princely figure of monarchical stature, possessing the trappings of power and legitimacy which we have come to recognize as the marks of early modern kingship"[51] it is also true that his heirs and successors grew too fond of luxurious courtly life and became fat and indolent, neglecting governance in favour of "…building ostentatious golden and silver pavilions, throwing lavish banquets, and composing flowery poetry."

This barbed invective is nowhere more apposite than in reference to the 8th Ashikaga *shogun*, Yoshimasa, who reigned for nearly a quarter of a century between 1449 and 1473. Under his reign we see the beginnings of a long decline culminating in civil war. That said, we should not attribute too much to Yoshimasa himself, as in marked contrast to his forebear, Yoshimitsu, this *shogun* clearly lacked the strength or will to impose his authority on the unruly elements in his realm. The situation clearly demanded a decisive leader, yet Yoshimasa was a mere boy almost accidentally engaged in the position of power, his youthful nature characterized to a large degree by impressionability. Accordingly, his mother and his close associates held great influence over his decisions, and he also permitted his wife to interfere in politics. His great fondness was for elaborate parties, and he preoccupied himself with building new temples and gardens; we could perhaps surmise that Yoshimasa sought refuge in these distractions, to compensate for his inability to administer to the affairs of the country.

Against this background of weak governance, the country spiraled towards into outright war. With no powerful central administration to adjudicate disputes, the *shugo* and *shugodai* squabbled over territory in localized conflicts. In 1467, tensions burst forth, and within a few years, practically every province in Japan was embroiled in a conflict we know as the Onin no Ran,[52] one of the most violent wars in its history, that was touched off by nothing more than a conflict between

in the Kamakura era. Power now was synonymous with control of land, tax collecting, and the *samurai*. Even the *bakufu* became irrelevant to *shugo*. By the middle of the fifteenth century, the only people who concerned themselves with the *bakufu* offices were those who actually held them. Complicating matters further was the fact that *shugo* were required to maintain residences in Kyoto,[50] and so they appointed relatives or retainers, called *shugodai*, to deputize for them in their home provinces. Over time the deputies themselves strove to assert their independence and challenge the authority of their nominal masters, creating another potential source of discord.

two families, the Hosokawa and the Yamana.[53]

At the time the two most powerful men in Kyoto were Yamana Sozen[54] and his son-in-law Hosokawa Katsumoto. The two men were very different. The Hosokawa family was long-established at court. Yamana Sozen, by contrast, was a *Tozama shugo* (outsider *shugo*), "who were not related to the Ashikaga by blood or house vassalage, were viewed as posing a special threat to *bakufu* authority and the stability of the central government."[55]

Although these two had long been facing-off, thus far neither had resorted to open warfare, instead occupying themselves in succession disputes of other warlords, notably between the Hatakeyama and Shiba families.

In 1464, Yoshimasa expressed his desire to resign the *shogunate*, so that he could dedicate himself to his cultural activities. Some commentators have suggested that administering to its upkeep interfered with his preferred life of relaxation. However, no children had so far been born between the *shogun* and his legal wife, Tomiko, so he consented instead to hand over the reins (after first adopting him as his legal heir) to his younger brother, Yoshimi. But in 1464 a legitimate heir, Yoshihisa, was born, and the matter of the succession was again deliberated by the powermongers. Like the *shogun*, *kanrei* Hosokawa Katsumoto wished for Yoshimi to succeed. However, Yamana Sozen, who resented the power Hosokawa exercised at court, took the birth of the *shogun*'s child as an opportunity to voice his dissent, and supported Yoshimasa's wife, Tomiko, in her bid to have the infant Yoshihisa made *shogun*. Concurrently, Hosokawa became embroiled in a dispute between two members of the Hatakeyama family over who would be appointed *kanrei* to the new *shogun*. Both Sozen and Katsumoto began to call for support from family relations and vassals, and before long the entire capital district of Yamashiro was congested with Yamana and Hosokawa supporters. Among those who rallied to Yamana Sozen was the powerful warlord Ouchi Masahiro, at the head of 20,000 troops. The prospect of civil war now loomed large, and it was clear that, in the event of a war in the capital, the *shogun* would be seen as powerless to stop it spreading to the provinces. In an

Above: Depicting an atmosphere of peace, calm, and prosperity, a *samurai* is shown eating rice while a woman serves sake from wooden container or *hishaku*. (The Art Archive/Okura Shukokan Museum Tokyo/Laurie Platt Winfrey)

attempt to prevent any further escalation he declared that the first to make war in the capital would be branded a rebel. Initially at least this was successful, and the two armies, roughly 80,000 strong, remained immobile. But within a few months, tensions had risen too far, and war became a foregone conclusion.

The *casus belli* came in February 1468 when a Hosokawa mansion in Kyoto was burned in an act of arson widely attributed to the Yamana. In reprisal, *samurai* acting for the Hosokawa attacked a Yamana storehouse. Amid mounting tensions, heightened by reports that a Yamana attack on the imperial palace was imminent, Hosokawa Katsumoto took Emperor Go-Tsuchimikado, the Cloistered Emperor Go-Hanazono, and their respective entourages into protective custody at shogunal residence at Muromachi. The situation quickly deteriorated, with each side making tit-for-tat attacks on

The battle for Shokokuji (on the north side of the imperial palace, in front of its north Imadegawa Gate) in October, in which Sozen himself led an attack on the Hosokawa positions inside a Buddhist monastery, typified the bloody carnage into which the fighting descended. In the aftermath, it was reported that eight carts were filled with enemy heads.

Throughout the fall those who had not already abandoned the city did so, even while more reinforcements for the warring factions flowed in. And all the while, as Kyoto was burning, Ashikaga Yoshimasa was lost in poetry readings and other cultural activities, and in planning the Ginkaku-ji, a Silver Pavilion to rival the Kinkaku-ji, the Golden Pavilion, that his grandfather, Ashikaga Yoshimitsu, had built.

As the war entered its second year, no superior, much less victor, had emerged between the two antagonists, and both were ensconced behind their barriers. There were small localized outbreaks of fighting, such as when Katsumoto brought in *trebuchets* and used them to fling rocks and exploding bombs into Yamana territory, but by early 1468 a welcome calm settled over Kyoto as both sides rested and faced each other off from across the trenches, assured of a protracted political and military fight. Although in Kyoto the two factions had fought to a stalemate early in the war, the violence had already spread to the rest of Japan. In Yamashiro Province, for example, two separate factions of the Hatakeyama clan fought each other to a standstill.

In Kyoto, Katsumoto initiated the political maneuverings with entreaties to the *shogun*, convincing him to castigate Sozen for fomenting rebellion, and thereby legitimize his own military actions—even though it was he who had made the first attack. He even persuaded Yoshimasa to make him the general of the official shogunal attacks on Yamana, but failed to grant him any tangible support. Then, in strange twist, Yoshimi, who was supported by Hosokawa, switched allegiances to Yamana (who supported his rival, Yoshihisa). The *shogun* promptly declared Yoshimi to be a rebel. After the *shogun*'s declaration some of Yamana's followers deserted, joining Katsumoto's "legal" cause, and

their opponents' property. A Yamana assault on the imperial palace was avenged at the end of May when Hosokawa supporters burned Yamana Isshiki's neighborhood and personal residence to the ground.

By the early summer, general fighting had erupted between the two camps. In short time many troops and civilians lay dead, and many buildings in the Northern district had been destroyed, either by the soldiers or by looters. Over the ensuing months scores more of the fine buildings were put to the torch, as fighting engulfed the city, and soon much of it had been devastated.

As the fighting wore on, the rival armies gradually established control over different sectors of the city, which they clung to tenaciously, defending them from lines of trenchworks criss-crossing the ruined city. Sozen's "Western Army" controlled western sections of Kyoto, and Katsumoto the east. The fighting was not spread to beyond the city limits. Katsumoto sent men onto the main thoroughfares outside, and into Sozen's home provinces, to prevent Yamana reinforcements from reaching the main battles.

Onin Ki

One of the primary sources of information on this period is the *Onin Ki*, a document written at least 20 (and possibly as much as 80) years after the conflict. It describes the causes and effects of the Onin War, the strategies employed by the antagonists, as well as its chief instigators, Yamana Sozen and Hosokawa Masamoto.

Though its author is unknown, his beliefs and philosophies are apparent throughout the text, as he relates the apparent futility of the war and the destruction it wrought on the capital. It remains an important work in part due to accounts of how the *Onin* War affected the city and its citizens:

"The capital which we believed would flourish for ten thousand years has now become a lair for the wolves. Even the North Field of Toji has fallen to ash …Lamenting the plight of the many fallen acolytes, Ii-o Hikorokusaemon-No-Jou read a passage:

'Now the city that you know
Has become an empty field,
From which the skylark rises
And your tears fall.'"

more switched sides as a result of the work of Katsumoto's emissaries to the provinces where Yamana and his allies drew their armies.

So, for much of 1468 the two forces engaged in stand-offs and limited sorties, both desiring to rebuild and to act only defensively. The time was spent in political, not military, conflict, until in 1469, the *shogun* named his son Yoshihisa, his heir. But Katsumoto, grown weary of battle, lacked the will to oppose the succession, and instead looked for a peaceful resolution to the dispute. Some limited peace was had, and a few years later, in 1473, both Katsumoto (who was forty-three years old) and Yamana (who was seventy years old) died. Even with the deaths of the instigators, the war dragged on, on a diminishing scale after 1475 when the various *daimyo* factions began to comply to a rare assertion of authority from the *shogun* to submit to his rule.

However, the fighting continued sporadically, as some stubbornly refused to give up. Finally, in 1477, some ten years after the fighting had begun, Ouchi Masahiro, the great champion of Ashikaga Yoshihisa's cause, also submitted to Yoshimasa and departed for home in

NOTES
1 Karl F. Friday *Samurai, Warfare and State in Early Medieval Japan* Routledge (2003) p.52
2 Terje Solum and Anders K. Rue *Saga of the Samurai: Takeda Nobutora The Unification of Kai* p.38, 50
3 Karl F. Friday *Samurai, Warfare and State in Early Medieval Japan* Routledge (2003) p.167
4 Karl F. Friday *Valorous butchers: the Art of War during the Golden Age of the Samurai* Japan Forum (1993) 5: 1; p.17
5 Numbering in thousands, rather than hundreds of troops. See Karl F. Friday *Samurai, Warfare and State in Early Medieval Japan* Routledge (2003) p.166
6 See Stephen Turnbull *War in Japan 1467-1615* Appendix *Trumpet Calls* for a description of how these were used.
7 This was the title of the post of the chiefs of the Kamakura shogunate in Kyoto.
8 It is important to note here that many modern scholars interpret this neither as a the achievement of total warrior dominance nor the establishment of feudalism in Japan. Instead they see the Kamakura period essentially as a period of power-sharing, as the institutions of the imperial aristocratic system remained in place, and were still extant when the Kamakura bakufu collapsed.
9 *The Taiheiki* Helen Craig McCullough trans. xxiv and xxxiii
10 The term *gokenin* was used to describe the landlords of privately owned (by the civil aristocracy and temples) rural estates. The term was

introduced under Minamoto no Yoritomo, as part of his efforts to cement his authority over provincial warriors. For a fuller explanation of this see Karl F. Friday *Samurai, Warfare and State in Early Medieval Japan* Routledge (2003) p.46-49 also The Taiheiki Helen Craig McCullough trans. xxxiii
11 Another effect of this, as Anthony Bryant points out is that 'there was also famine in the land, as farming had unavoidably been neglected during the invasions crisis' *Early Samurai AD200-1500* p.25
12 This position, like that of the *shogun*, had become merely titular.(*The Taiheiki* Helen Craig McCullough trans. xxxvi)
13 The Taiheiki Helen Craig McCullough trans. xxxiii
14 *The Taiheiki* Helen Craig McCullough trans. xxxviii
15 *The Clear Mirror: A Chronicle of the Japanese Court during the Kamakura Period (1185-1333)*. Translated by George W. Perkins p.177
16 The imperial Regalia of Japan (Sanshu no Jingi), also known as the Three Sacred Treasures, consisted of the sword, Kusanagi (or possibly a replica of the original), the jewel or necklace of jewels, Yasakani no magatama and the mirror Yata no kagami. Also known as the Three Sacred Treasures of Japan, the regalia represent the three primary virtues: valor (the sword), wisdom (the mirror), and benevolence (the jewel).
17 Karl F. Friday *Samurai, Warfare and the State in Early Medieval Japan* p.126

18 *The Taiheiki* Helen Craig McCullough trans. p.70-74
19 *The Taiheiki* Helen Craig McCullough trans.p.105
20 *The Taiheiki* Helen Craig McCullough trans. p.85-91
21 *The Taiheiki* Helen Craig McCullough trans. p.89
22 As related by Kanazawa uma-no-suke in (*The Taiheiki* Helen Craig McCullough trans.) p.183
23 The Taiheiki Helen Craig McCullough Chapter 7
24 *The Taiheiki* Helen Craig McCullough p.197
25 Terje Solum and Anders K. Rue *Takeda Rises to Power: The Kai Takeda (1130-1467)* p.24
26 *The Taiheiki* Helen Craig McCullough p181-190
27 Terje Solum and Anders K. Rue *Takeda Rises to Power: The Kai Takeda (1130-1467)* p.23
28 *The Taiheiki* Helen Craig McCullough trans. xliv
29 *The Taiheiki* Helen Craig McCullough trans. p.240
30 *The Taiheiki* Helen Craig McCullough trans. p.274-281
31 This is the popular version as given in the Taiheiki. Another version in a contemporary account, the Baisho Ron, has it that Kusunoki tried to persuade Go-Daigo to have Nitta Yoshisada killed, and then to make his peace with Takauji. The truth is probably somewhere between the two.
32 By this act of loyalty to the throne, Kusunoki Masahige established a much-heralded reputation,

Yamaguchi with his troops. In a final act of defiance he burnt down the area of Kyoto surrounding his mansion.

So the eleven-year-long Onin War ended, not because one side achieved victory, but because both sides simply did not have the strength to continue any more. Most of the city had already been reduced to ashes, and neither the Yamana clan nor the Hosokawa clan had achieved its aims, save for killing numbers of each other.

In the aftermath of the war, with the soldiers gone Kyoto was beset by mobs of looters who descended on the city, taking anything of value. Several years would pass before peace could be restored.[56]

Another effect of the Onin War was that it removed all pretense of a national government backed by legitimacy flowing from the emperor via the title of "*shogun.*" The *shogun*, who had demonstrated such a remarkably *laissez faire* attitude towards the war,[57] must be seen as at least partly culpable, for his indifference advanced the breakdown of authority. From this point forward, for all practical purposes, the Hosokawa family held the reins of power, making mere puppets of the Ashikaga *shogun*s. When Yoshimi's son Yoshitane was

made *shogun* in 1490, the Hosokawa *kanrei* drove him from power in 1493 and declared another Ashikaga, Yoshizumi, to be *shogun*.

But the chaos had an effect that went far beyond the confines of Kyoto, insomuch as it was the catalyst for the cataclysmic events that came after. Triggered by the fighting and lawlessness in Kyoto, violence spread into the countryside, auguring a 150-year period of warfare and bloodshed that consumed the entire country. This a tumultuous era in Japanese history is known to us as the Sengoku jidai or "Era of the Country at War."

During this time powerful *daimyo* directly ruled over personal fiefdoms, known as *han*, and battled each other to extend their landholdings. This in effect then became a mass power-struggle between the various houses to dominate the whole of Japan.

at a time when most acted self-interestedly, that endures to this day.

33 Anthony J Bryant *Early Samurai AD200-1500* p.27

34 The period of governance by the Muromachi or Ashikaga shogunate, which was officially established in 1338 by Ashikaga Takauji, ended only in 1573, when Oda Nobunaga drove the 15th and last *shogun* Ashikaga Yoshiaki out of Kyoto.

35 Kenneth A. Grossberg *From Feudal Chieftain to Secular Monarch: The Development of Shogunal Power in Early Muromachi Japan* Monumenta Nipponica 31: 1; p.29

36 Anthony Bryant *Early Samurai AD200-1500* p. 7

37 Karl F. Friday *Samurai, Warfare and the State in Early Medieval Japan* Routledge (2003) p.168

38 George Sansom *A History of Japan 1334-1615* p.348

39 For Buddhists, this was close to the worst disgrace one could face; eating horseflesh was believed to break one's karma, forcing them to be reborn in the next life as an animal or something worse.

40 Both Sekigahara and Tennoji were later witness to more famous battles

41 The post of kanrei was created in 1362 by Ashikaga Yoshiakira. His function was "to unify channels of communication between the *shogun* and the various Bakufu organs". Kenneth A. Grossberg *From Feudal Chieftain to Secular Monarch: The Development of Shogunal Power in Early Muromachi* Japan Monumenta Nipponica 31: 1; p.31

42 Chapter 20 of the Taiheiki chronicles the events leading to the death of Yoshisada at Kuromaru. It states that an arrow wounded his horse, making it unable to jump over a ditch. It fell and trapped Yoshisada's left leg. An arrow in the flurry struck him between the brows, and he drew his sword and slit his throat. The resemblance to accounts of the death of Minamoto no Yoshinaka as described in the Heike Monogatari has led to questions about whether the account is factual.

43 Son of the late Kusunoki Masashige.

44 Kenneth A. Grossberg *From Feudal Chieftain to Secular Monarch: The Development of Shogunal Power in Early Muromachi Japan* Monumenta Nipponica 31: 1; p.29

45 Kenneth A. Grossberg *From Feudal Chieftain to Secular Monarch: The Development of Shogunal Power in Early Muromachi Japan* Monumenta Nipponica 31: 1; p.29

46 Kenneth A. Grossberg *From Feudal Chieftain to Secular Monarch: The Development of Shogunal Power in Early Muromachi Japan* Monumenta Nipponica 31: 1; p.40

47 Yoshimitsu moved the shogunal residence from Sanjo Bomon-dai to the Kitanokoji Muromachi district of Kyoto, closer to the imperial palace. Henceforth the period is commonly referred to as the Muromachi.

48 See John Whitney Hall *Foundations of the Modern Japanese Daimyo* The Journal of Asian Studies 20: 3; pp.317-329, in which he traces the institutional origins of the daimyo.

49 Increasingly, private armies of bushi lived as one, in the residences of their lords and masters, and with everything provided by them. This allowed the shugo to exercise greater control over their vassals and dissuade them from seditious plotting.

50 This requirement was formalized under the Tokugawa shogunate as the *sankin kotai*.

51 Kenneth A. Grossberg *From Feudal Chieftain to Secular Monarch: The Development of Shogunal Power in Early Muromachi Japan* Monumenta Nipponica 31: 1; p.29

52 Easily the best book in English on this critical event is H. Paul Varley's work *The Onin War* (1966) Columbia University Press

53 The Yamana had long been a thorn in side, rebelling against *shogun* Ashikaga Yoshimitsu in 1391 (The Meitoku rebellion). The rebellion was crushed by the Ouchi clan

54 Sozen was a Buddhist monk who went by the nickname Red Monk. Katsumoto was *kanrei* (the Deputy to the *Shogun*).

55 Kenneth A. Grossberg *From Feudal Chieftain to Secular Monarch: The Development of Shogunal Power in Early Muromachi Japan* Monumenta Nipponica 31: 1; p.40

56 Mary Elizabeth Berry describes the destruction wrought on the city during the Onin War in graphic terms in her book *The Culture of Civil War in Kyoto*

57 Even when the war broke out, it is said that Yoshimasa was calmly drinking.

JAPAN AT WAR

Japan emerged from the Onin War divided, a ripe bed onto which the seeds of further conflict, once scattered, could flourish. These seeds were sown at once by several established and emergent groups who, hungry for power, embarked on a long protracted struggle for domination—the Sengoku jidai[1]—which persisted for nearly a century. In the first fifty years of this tumultuous time feudal Japan disintegrated as a consequence of multifarious events in which, variously, power was lost and won, alliances were broken and others forged, and territories from the northern tip of Honshu to southern Kyushu were conquered and others surrendered. During this time countless battles were fought between innumerable enemies for a myriad of reasons—Stephen

Turnbull's forces of *fission*—and by the 1550s these disputes had become a struggle for control of the country as a whole. Collectively, these would eventually serve to deplete the strength of the majority of the warrior families to such an extent that the first of three great *daimyo*, or forces of *fusion*, of the Sengoku Period—Oda Nobunaga—was able to occupy the capital Kyoto and assert his authority over the land as the first feudal unifier. Under his successors, Toyotomi Hideyoshi, and Tokugawa Ieyasu, unification of the country under a military government was completed.

Before looking in more detail at those events, it is appropriate to discuss the key military and social trends of the period. In the military sphere, three developments

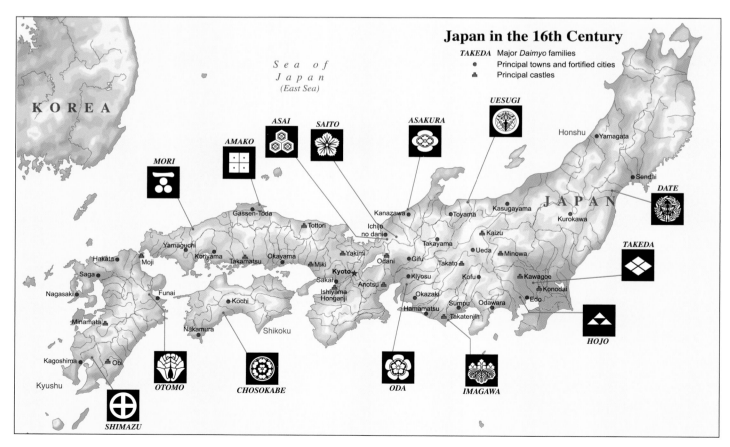

渡水湖伏之馬左智明

in particular are most interesting. The first was the increasing number of *ashigaru* (foot soldiers) in the armies of the *daimyo*, the second was the type of weapons that *ashigaru* used, and the third was the change in the way that cavalry operated.[2]

First deployed in large numbers (and with limited effect) during the preceding Onin War, during the early years of the Sengoku jidai, the *daimyo* came to rely heavily on *ashigaru*. These men were initially armed with pikes of varying lengths, and when properly martialed they proved to be extremely effective. Their usefulness increased dramatically when they were armed with bows, which they could fire from behind protective palisades, and even more so with the introduction in the early years of the 16th century (probably in around 1510) of firearms, in the form of Chinese, and later Portuguese, *arquebus* (matchlocks) that the Japanese called *teppo*.[3] Even the famed commander Takeda Shingen, whose cavalry was perhaps the most formidable of any army, reportedly addressed this order to his retainers: "Hereafter guns will be the most important (weapons). Therefore, decrease the number of spears and have your most capable men carry guns. Furthermore, when you assemble your soldiers, test their marksmanship and order that the selection of (gunners) be in accordance with the results (of the test)."[4]

Although initially these weapons were used only sporadically in battle by small numbers of gunners, and their impact on warfare was limited, Japanese commanders (notably Oda Nobunaga) later developed tactics that made more effective use of the weapon, and by the end of the 16th century it had assumed great importance in the Japanese arsenal. As Delmer M. Brown writes, "The introduction of the Portuguese *arquebus* and the subsequent widespread manufacture of firearms soon led to radical developments in military techniques."[5] These developments included widescale deployment of *teppo*-equipped foot soldiers on the battlefield from the mid-16th century, which proved to be highly effective against cavalry, most notably at Nagashino in 1575. As Brown goes on to point out, "By the time of Nobunaga's death in 1582 probably one-third of the soldiers in the armies of most of the leading military barons were gunners."[6]

Early Japanese Firearms

Reports vary as to when and how firearms were introduced to Japan, but it is believed that, early in the 16th century, two of three Portuguese adventurers who had become stranded on an island off the southern coast of Kyushu carried and hunted with hand-held firearms. These were arquebuses—muzzle-loaded matchlock smoothbore weapons, the predecessors of rifles and other longarm firearms. The local *daimyo* was said to be so impressed with the guns that he bought them and eventually had a local swordsmith copy them.

Soon guns (*teppo*) were being produced and used throughout Japan. According to author Clive Sinclaire, guns quickly became the deciding factor in a number of important battles. Men who were trained in their use were generally lower-ranking *ashiguru* (foot soldiers), rather than *samurai*, and it was quickly realized that the latter could easily be dispatched by the former, their social inferiors.

Above: Matchlock guns of various styles and sizes used in Japaan during the 18th century. Over the previous two centuries firearms had became so important that they had a major effect on military training and techniques. By the time of the Battle of Sekigahara in 1600 it is estimated that some 80,000 guns were taken to the field. (*via Clive Sinclaire*)

Of course, the *samurai* cavalryman did not disappear from the battlefield. Instead he foresook his traditional bow and arrow and adopted new weapons, notably various types of "shock" weapons (spears and glaives).[7] But, although cavalry was still widely employed in the latter part of the Sengoku jidai, the year 1575 ultimately marked its zenith. Even with developments in armor, with the necessarily thicker *cuirass*[8] to protect against musket fire, no longer would mounted soldiers dominate the battlefield. Thus, in the Sengoku jidai we see a further move away from the kind of close-quarters fighting that had characterized previous conflicts, towards longer–range engagements.

There was proliferation in other areas too, particularly castle-building. During the 16th century a great profusion of "castles" sprang up over Japan, as a means of projecting or retaining power over clan domains. As we shall see, a great number of the battles fought during this time were contests for possession of these fortresses, which out of necessity grew in scale and complexity over the simple structures used in previous centuries.[9] And this, in turn, prompted the evolution of new siege tactics and weapons.

In socio-political terms, although the Sengoku jidai gave rise to a number of important phenomena, including the *ikko-ikki* bands and an emerging merchant class, those developments that impacted on the governing power structure are our primary concern. Our focus is on the *daimyo*, since it is these men whose names and actions dominate the Sengoku jidai.

The late John Whitney Hall traced the evolution of the *daimyo* to the late Kamakura Period, at which time there emerged *shugo*, the first of four *daimyo* types who became the new political masters of Japan, "each building successively on the institutions of the previous, and embracing larger and more effective areas of hegemony."[10] These *shugo* were appointed as "military governors" by the Ashikaga *shogun* to administer the provinces, and "were in effect the institutional forerunners of the later *daimyo*."[11] As Hall pointed out, "Of all the institutional products of the Ashikaga period, the *daimyo* were without doubt he most significant."[12] However, as we have seen, the *shugo* were increasingly occupied with matters of politics at the capital, and they came increasingly to delegate responsibility for administering their estates to deputies called *shugodai*. Slowly these *shugodai* had begun to supplant their masters as the arbiters of power in the provinces.

The disastrous Onin War served only to accelerate the demise of the *shugo* families, and likewise the central authority of the troubled Ashikaga *shogunate*. Thus, throughout Japan, between 1467 and 1530, a new group of families rose to fill the power vacuum thus created. In the course of this power shift, established clans such as the Takeda and the Imagawa, who had ruled under the authority of both the Kamakura and Muromachi *bakufu*, were able to expand their spheres of influence. And many others—among them the Hojo and Asakura—rose from relative obscurity to prominence.

Two key figures are often advanced as the archetypal *sengoku daimyo*. The first is Hojo Soun, whose rise began in the 1490s, fitting conveniently with Hall's demarcation between the *sengoku daimyo* and earlier *shugo-daimyo*. Less commonly cited is Asakura Toshikage, who in 1479 overthrew his former patrons at the Kofukuji to cement his control over Echizen. During the Onin War, Toshikage had initially supported the Yamana

Below: A detail from a panel showing the siege of Osaka Castle, November 1614–January 1615. *(Werner Forman/Corbis)*

Toshikage Jushichikajo (House Code of Toshikage)

Interestingly, Toshikage was the author of one of the earliest *samurai* house codes, the *Toshikage Jushichikajo*, by which he exercised control over his vassals:

Do not give a command post or an administrative position to anyone who lacks ability, even if his family has served the Asakura family for generations.

Post intelligence agents (*metsuke*) in both near and distant provinces, even if the world may be at peace. In so doing you can spy on the conditions of these domains without interruption.

Do not excessively covet swords and daggers made by famous masters. Even if you own a sword or dagger worth 10,000 pieces (*hiki*, equivalent of 10 *mon*), it can be overcome by 100 spears each worth 100 pieces. Therefore, use the 10,000 pieces to procure 100 spears, and arm 100 men with them. You can in this manner defend yourself in time of war.

Those retainers who lack special talent or positions, but who are steadfast, must be treated with compassion and understanding. Those who are effeminate may still be used as attendants or messengers if their demeanor is outstanding, and they must not be dismissed lightly. However, if they lack both [steadfastness and good deportment], then it is useless to retain them.

Regrettable is the practice of selecting an auspicious day or considering a lucky direction in order to win a battle or take a castle, and even shift the time and date accordingly. No matter how auspicious the day may be, if you set sail your boat in a storm or confront a great host alone, your effort will come to naught. No matter how inauspicious the day may be, if you can discern between truth and falsehood, prepare for the orthodox and surprise attacks secretly, be flexible in all situations, and depend on a good stratagem, then your victory is assured.

Do not permit any castle other than that of the Asakura to be built in this province. Move all high-ranking retainers without exception to Ichijo-ga-tani (the Asakura Castle). Permit their deputies (*Daikan*) and lower officials (*gesu* or *shitazukasa*) to remain in their districts and villages [to manage their estates].

Above: Hojo Ujitsuna took Edo Castle, which was under the control of Uesugi Tomoki—beginning the rivalry between the Hojo and the Uesugi families. *(British Museum/Jo St Mart)*

but switched his loyalties to the Hosokawa in 1471, a move that was coupled with a break from the Shiba *shugo* family. In 1472 he defeated the Echizen Kai, and by this act became ruler of the province in all but name. The battle at Kofukuji was really an instrument by which to quash the last challenge to his authority, and thereinafter his family went uncontested in Echizen.

Toshikage can be seen as the first of a new class known as the *nari agari mono*, or upstarts, itself part of a social phenomenon known as *gekokujo* (literally "the lower topple the higher").[13] Instances of this are a notable feature of the first years of the Sengoku Period. These men were lower-ranking retainers of the traditional aristocracy, who broke out from within the rigid social strata and in some instances ascended to positions of considerable power. On these grounds Toshikage is sometimes regarded as the first independent *daimyo* of the Sengoku age.

Some scholars, however, reserve that title for another man, Hojo Soun. He features strongly in the events of the early Sengoku, and his story is absorbing. Born Ise Shinkuro, his early life is something of a mystery, but

approval and military assistance of the Imagawa and establishing that he would be welcomed by the local *samurai*. He took Horigoe Castle in 1493 and banished Ashikaga Chachamaru, the Lord of Izu, who fled to Kai and sought refuge with Takeda Nobutsuna. Soun then established a strong military base at Nirayama, and went on to subdue all of Izu Province.

Hojo thereafter established himself as an independent *daimyo* and, little by little, expanded his fief, taking Odawara[19] from the Omori "without provocation and by means of trickery"[20] in 1495, and then Sagami Province itself. Three years later he invaded Kai Province in 1498 and clashed with the Takeda clan, who evidently planned to assist the exiled Chachamaru in retaking Izu. This scheme was cut short when Soun forced him to commit suicide. In 1504 Soun invaded Musashi, taking advantage of the dissensions within the Uesugi, and thereafter fought a long series of campaigns to further his gains.

Above: Statue of Hojo Soun outside Odawara station in Japan. Odawara Castle was the center of the Hojo family's domains until it was taken by Toyotomi Hideyoshi. *(British Museum/Jo St Mart)*

most sources[14] agree that he rose from relatively humble origins to the position of a low-ranking *samurai*,[15] and through fortuitous family connections climbed to great heights on the social and political ladders.

After studying under the monks at Daitokuji in Kyoto,[16] Soun may have been a *ronin* before he entered the service of Imagawa Yoshimi in 1468, during the Onin War, and made his mark by intervening on the behalf of Imagawa Ujichika[17] during a interfamily succession dispute when the latter's cousin, Oshika Norimitsu, tried to usurp him. Soun disposed of Norimitsu and as a reward Ujichika gave him Kokokuji Castle[18] (in Suruga Province), with the remit to use this as a base from which to defend the Imagawa's eastern borders.

Steadily, Soun increased his following and influence, and when in 1491 neighboring Izu Province was troubled by a feud over succession rights, Soun used the act as a pretext for an invasion, having first secured both the

Above: Asakura Yoshikage was a weak leader who lost the support of his followers and then was forced to commit *seppuku*. *(British Museum/Jo St Mart)*

Above: Hosokawa Katsumoto was in conflict with his father-in-law, Yamana Sozen, who resented the power he had as *kanrei*, thus igniting the Onin War of 1467. This civil war started the Sengoku jidai (the Warring States Period). *(British Museum/Jo St Mart)*

In 1512 Soun went to war with the Miura of eastern Sagami, capturing Kamakura[21] and, in 1513, 1514, and 1516, crushing attempts by the Miura to recapture lost territories in. In 1518, at the age of eighty-six, Soun handed full control of the family to his son Ujitsuna; he died the following year.

Building on the accomplishments of Soun, the Hojo clan remained a major power in the Kanto region until its subjugation by Toyotomi Hideyoshi late in the Sengoku Period.[22] Carl Steenstrup concludes that, "As a historical figure, Soun unquestionably occupies an important place. The start of his campaigns in 1491 ushers in the heyday of the sengoku warlords."

The Hojo and Asakura were just two of many "new" noble houses that came to prominence in the Sengoku jidai, supplanting the established order through guile and force. Other prominent examples include the dislodgment of the Hosokawa by the Miyoshi, the Shiba by the Oda, and the Toki by the Saito.

By contrast, the fortunes of many of the older *shugo* families went into terminal decline. "Only in rare instances, such as the Shimazu, Otomo or Date, did *shugo* families manage to perpetuate their power to become daimyo at a later age."[23]

So to the fortunes of some of the great houses, notably the Hosokawa. In the late 15th century a succession of Ashikaga *shoguns* had been controlled by the powerful Hosokawa *kanrei*. But, beginning with the assassination in 1507 of Masamoto, we see a gradual decline in the fortunes of the Hosokawa clan, endemic of a process that was being repeated elsewhere in Japan. After Masamoto's death, the clan became divided and was weakened by internecine fighting. Eventually, they were forced to flee the city when it was attacked by Oda Nobunaga.

Another remarkable social development was taking place in the early Sengoku jidai, as the monks of the

Buddhist Jodo Shinshu or "True Pure Land" sect began to assert political power by uniting *monto* (believer) farmers, monks, and priests in armed bands known as *ikki*. Through acts of resistance and rebellion these came to challenge the rule of the *daimyo* in several provinces[24] and would even challenge the might of Oda Nobunaga for a decade.

The Jodo Shinshu, which followed Amida Buddha's teachings, was centered on the Honganji temple[25] in Kyoto and formed numerous *ikki* from 1457.[26] In 1485, the *ikki* of Yamashiro had grown sufficiently powerful to drive the clan armies out of province and the following year set up a form of government there.

In Kaga, the domain of *daimyo* Togashi Masachika, there was perhaps the most remarkable instance of this phenomenon.[27] The Togashi had lost Kaga in 1447 to two vassal families, the Motoori and Yamagawa. During the Onin War, Masachika, an ally of the Hosokawa, procured the support of Kaga's *ikko-ikki*, and with the help of Asakura Toshikage reclaimed Kaga by defeating his younger brother Kochiyo in 1473. However, relations between Masachika and the *ikko-ikki* soon deteriorated,

descending into a series of violent, but ultimately unsuccessful uprisings. In 1487 Masachika was called away to Omi by the *shogun* Ashikaga Yoshihisa to give battle to Rokkaku Takayori.[28] He led an army out of Kaga and in his absence an estimated 100,000 to 200,000 *ikko-ikki* (including many priests, but against the will of the Honganji[29]) revolted once again, this time drawing on support from Togashi house members. Despite some initial victories following his return, Masachika was forced to draw back behind his castle walls and to commit suicide. The *ikko-ikki* established Kaga as *hyakusho mochi no kuni*, or "country of the farmers." They built a fortified castle-cathedral along the Yodo River for their headquarters, and remained independent for nearly 100 years.[30]

Despite innumerable fascinating sagas in this landscape of political turmoil, our focus is on the great battles, which, because of their proliferation, must be

---

Below: Hosokawa Tadaoki (at center) was the son of Hosokawa Fujitaka. He fought his first battle at the tender age of fifteen under Oda Nobunaga. *(British Museum/Jo St Mart)*

outlined with some brevity. I have chosen to do so geographically and chronologically, focusing on central, western, and northern Japan in turn, as invariably clans tended to fight their neighbors for territory.

Above: The final battle of Taira no Masakado. He had rebelled against the government, which made him a hero to local peoples, but after a price was put on his head he was killed by his cousin Sadamori and Fujiwara no Hidesato at the Battle of Kojima. *(British Museum/Jo St Mart)*

Western Japan

Our first focus is on western Japan, including Kyushu, the ancient seat of the Yamato emperors, mountainous Shikoku, and the western provinces of Honshu.[31] In Kyushu, one of the most powerful families was the Otomo, a position similar to that held by the Ouchi family centered at Yamaguchi in Suo on eastern Honshu. In building Yamaguchi, the Ouchi clan imitated the city planning of Kyoto and accumulated great financial power through cultural imports from the continent and trade with Korea and the Ming Dynasty in China. As a result, Yamaguchi came to be known as the "Kyoto of the West," and the distinct "Ouchi Culture" flourished.

These two powerful families had a traditional rivalry, and it was perhaps inevitable that they would clash. The Otomo had been central to the efforts against the Mongol invasions of Japan in 1274 and 1281, and had been a major backer of the Ashikaga *shogunate*. So too had the Ouchi, playing a particularly influential role in the Nanboku-cho Wars against the Imperial Court.

In 1501 tensions between these two erupted into a war, the zenith of which was the Battle of Uma-ga-take in Buzen, in northern Kyushu, and which culminated in a victory for the Otomo. Over the course of a thousand years the Otomo had become one of the most durable of the old Shugo clans, having numerous feuds with other local clans over the next five decades, and clashing at various points with the Shôni, Tawara, and Tachibana.

But it was the Ouchi who made the greatest territorial gains, under the ambitious leadership of Ouchi Yoshioki. In 1508 Ouchi Yoshioki marched on Kyoto to oust *shogun* Yoshizumi and restore the deposed *shogun* Ashikaga Yoshitane to the throne, and for this was named deputy *kanrei*. Yoshioki remained in the capital for nearly a decade, defeating (with Rokkaku Sadayori) an attempt by a resurgent Hosokawa Masakata to topple the *shogun* at the Battle of Funaokayama in 1511. Under his stewardship some order returned to the capital, but in 1518 Yoshioki was forced to return to Yamaguchi after a series of raids by Amako Tsunehisa on his outposts in Aki province. Under Tsunehisa's leadership the Amako clan had become powerful in Izumo, and ambitious.

In 1521 a formal peace treaty was signed between the two clans but this lasted for but one year, for in 1522 Tsunehisa struck again at the Ouchi in Aki, demanding that Môri Motonari[32] move on Kagamiyama Castle. Motonari, formerly an ally of the Ouchi, complied while Tsunehisa attempted to bring down Kanayama Castle.

However, Tsunehisa's campaign of conquest failed and he withdrew in 1524, clashing with the Ouchi again in 1527 over control of Bingo province.

At the same time, neighboring Bizen witnessed another example of the *gekokujo* phenomenon, when in 1522 the Akamatsu clan lost control over Mimasaka and Bizen to the Urakami, their former vassals. The Akamatsu, which grew powerful in the Muromachi period, had been in decline for the best part of a century, and with this development their power was eclipsed.

Ouchi Yoshioki (1477–1528)

Ouchi Yoshioki was an early Sengoku-era *daimyo* in Suo, Nagato and Iwami, and *kanrei* to *shogun* Ashika Yoshitane. Since the 14th century, the Ouchi clan had become a major power in western Honshu, from where they controlled trade with the continent. Yoshioki maintained efforts to increase the power and influence of the clan, bringing him into conflict with the Kyushu clans, notably the Otomo of Bungo and the Amako of Izumo. In 1508 Yoshioki led an army to Kyoto to restore the recently deposed *shogun*, Ashikaga Yoshitane. He settled in Kyoto and resided there for the next ten years. In 1511 (with Hosokawa Takakuni) he defeated a resurgent challenge to the *shogunate* by Hosokawa Masataka and Hosokawa Sumimoto at Funaokayama, north of Kyoto. In 1518 Yoshioki faced off the ambitions of the Amako, beginning a rivalry between himself and Amako Tsunehisa that would endure until he died.

Another of the "western" families that became prominent in the early 16th century was the Sue. We first hear of them in August 1523, when Sue Yorifusa, who was a senior retainer of the Ouchi clan, fought with Tomoda Yorifuji at Tomoda in Aki. This marked the beginning of a rise in fortunes of the Sue, which was to reach its zenith under Yorifusa's son Harukata over the following three decades.[33] The following year, in July, Ouchi Yoshioki captured Sakurao Castle, also in Aki, and forced Tomoda Yorifuji to submit to his rule. This campaign of expansion continued in 1525, when Yoshioki made further territorial gains in the province. Aki, an old province comprising the western part of

present-day Hiroshima Prefecture, and its immediate environs, were the scene of many battles during the Sengoku Period.

Of course, the Sengoku jidai was characterized not only by inter-clan disputes, but also interfamilial conflict. An example of this arose in the Satsuma *han*, which spread over Satsuma, Osumi, and Hyoga provinces. It was ruled over by a *daimyo* of the Shimazu clan, and it was for this title that discord developed within the family, when in 1526 Shimazu Katsuhisa, the current lord, faced a challenge by Shimazu Sanehisa, the lord of Izumi Castle. Seeking to establish himself as an independent power, Sanehisa marched against the *daimyo*, forcing him

Above: Ouchi Yoshioki in the thick of battle. *(British Museum/ Jo St Mart)*

to seek refuge in Bungo Province; the deposed Katsuhisa then proposed the appointment of his eldest son, Shimazu Takahisa, of the Mimasaka branch of the Shimazu, as the head of the clan. This was accepted by Sanehisa, and a period of peaceful coexistence ensued. But after more than a decade had passed, things were to come to a head again.

In the interim Katsuhisa, who retained control over much land, made efforts to promote the Iriki-In clan, whose lands bordered those of the Shimazu. Among the grants that he bestowed on a favored retainer, Iriki-In Shigetomo, was Sanehisa's fort at Momotsugi. On October 9, 1539, Shigetomo took the fort under cover of darkness.[34] This event served to greatly increase Shigetomo's reputation, earning him the respect of the *daimyo* Shimazu Takahisa. During the following year, Shigetomo overcame many forts, including those at Hirasa, Kuma no sho, Miyasato, Tazaki, and Takea, gaining further prominence within Satsuma for his clan. During the year to follow, however, the relationship between Shigetomo and Shimazu Takahisa began to sour as rumors that Shigetomo was plotting a rebellion against Takahisa took hold.

As yet, no major battles had been fought in the western provinces. Soon, however, all that was to change. In the ten years since the Amako had fought with the Ouchi in Bingo Province, the aging Tsunehisa had stepped down and passed leadership of the clan to Haruhisa. Under Haruhisa, the Amako had been steadily making territorial gains, reaching as far west as Harima in 1538. Then, in 1540, he once again invaded the Môri lands of Aki Province with an army of 20,000, forcing Môri Motonari to retreat within the walls of his castle at Koriyama.

Sue Harukata (1521–1555)

Son of a famous general, Sue Harukata became head of the Sue clan when aged just eighteen and was also a senior retainer of the Ouicho clan. A friend of Ouchi Yoshitaka, Harukata conducted the campaign against the Amagos and was responsible for the relief of Koriyama Castle in 1540.

In 1541 Harukata took part in the attack on Izumo, but it was unsuccessful. In 1551 Harukata and Otomo Sorin led a coup deposing Yoshitaka and forcing him to commit *seppuku*. In 1554 Yoshimi Masayori and Môri Motonari rebelled, twice defeating Harukata— Oshikibata (1554), Miyajima (1555)— leaving him no alternative but to commit suicide.

Haruhisa determined, once and for all, to rid himself of the Môri, the traditional enemy of the Amako. He torched Yoshida, the castle town, but persistent attempts to dislodge Môri Motonari and his 8,000 defenders from Koriyama itself were frustrated. Haruhisa prepared for a

Below: Sue Harukata (at center left) in battle. In the Western provinces he was known as *Saigoku-muso no Samuraidaisho* ("*samurai* general without peer"). *(British Museum/Jo St Mart)*

Môri Motonari (1497–1571)

Môri Motonari lived through a period known as the "Epoch of a Warring Country." His clan lived in the west Chugoku region and Motonari, through a mixture of deviousness and inspired battlefield leadership, raised them from a subordinate position to one of pre-eminence.

Motonari was the third son of a minor *daimyo* and in 1516, aged only eighteen, he conducted a skillful defensive campaign against a superior force of invaders. This so impressed Amago Tsunehisa, a neighboring *daimyo*, that he offered the promising young man his daughter in marriage. Such alliances came at a price, and in 1522 Tsunehisa duly called for Motomari's aid in attacking Kagamiyama Castle;

Tsunehisa was held up but Motonari was successful, gaining much credit.

The Môri chief died the following year and Motonari was appointed guardian to his successor, a young boy. This new *daimyo* soon died also and when, after a brief struggle, Motonari became chief, there were rumors, never substantiated, that he had a hand in both deaths.

Now secure at home, Motonari allied himself with first one regional clan and then another. Then, in 1540, the region was invaded by Amako Haruhisa; Motonari held Koriyama Castle for four months until relieved in early 1541. The following year Motonari, now allied with Ouchi Yoshitaka, invaded Izumo, but it was an unsuccessful campaign and they were forced to withdraw. Despite this,

Motonari expanded his power, but when, in 1554, he fell out with Sue Harukata, the latter invaded with some 30,000 men. Although outnumbered two-to-one, Motonari defeated the invaders and in 1555 scored a masterful victory at Miyajima, making him the most powerful lord in western Japan.

In 1566 Motonari defeated his only remaining opponent, Yoshihisha, who was banished to a monastery. Thus, when Motonari died at the age of seventy-four, he was one of the greatest warlords of his time.

Above: As well as being a successful warrior and strategist, Motonari (above left) was an influential patron of the arts and a significant poet.
(British Museum/Jo St Mart)

lengthy winter siege, bringing up fresh men and supplies, but found his trains harassed by small night-time raiding parties that ventured out from the castle. In November, an army under Sue Harukata was sent by the Ouchi to try and relieve Koriyama. With the addition of these extra troops, Motonari was emboldened to launch a coordinated attack on on Haruhisa's besiegers, inflicting heavy casualties and causing him to retreat. This victory, and the death of Tsunehisa the following year, would encourage the Môri and Ouchi to invade the Amako's Izumo Province in 1542.

The First Battle of Gassen-Toda

As mentioned, the victory at Koriyama and death of the former Amako *daimyo*, Tsunehisa, was interpreted by the Ouchi and Môri as a sign of weakness and an opportunity for advancement of their ambitions. So, in the summer of 1541, Ouchi Yoshitaka led a joint 30,000-strong army into Izumo and Iwami, to confront an Amako army half as strong. But their advance into Izumo toward the Amago citadel of Gassen-Toda proceeded at a dawdling pace, and by the time they had gained the fortress it was January, and much of the momentum had

been lost. The allied force invested the castle for the best part of a year, until in January 1543 they fell back in disarray. Motonari himself was nearly captured in the retreat, and Yoshitaka lost his adopted son Ouchi Harumochi along with large number of troops.

Thereafter, Yoshitaka paid little attention to his military, preferring to devote his energies instead to cultivating the arts and culture of Yamaguchi. Consequently, his retainers became divided; one faction led by Sagara Taketo supported retrenchment, while another led by Sue Harukata strove for continued expansion. Some years later, in 1551, Sue Harataka overthrew Yoshitaka and became the controlling influence over the Ouchi clan through a puppet *daimyo*, Ouchi Yoshinaga.

Battle of Miyajima

This was all a precursor to a major battle between the loyal Ouchi ally Môri Motonari and Sue Harukata at Miyajima in Aki in October 1555. On June 1 the previous year Motonari had defeated Harukata at

Below: In time Môri Motonari defeated his enemies and controlled the whole of Chugoku. *(via Clive Sinclaire)*

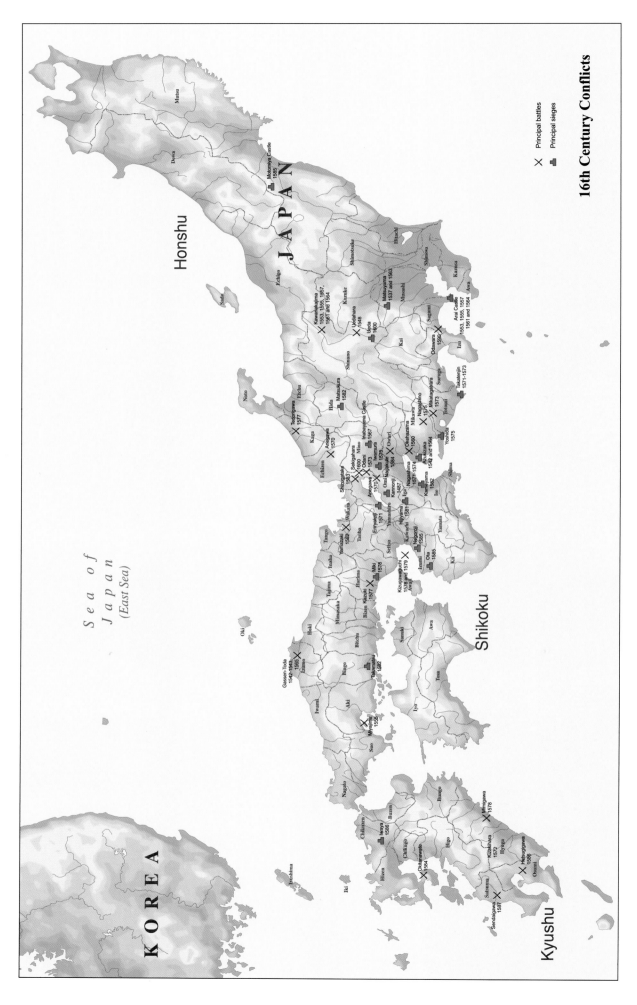

16th Century Conflicts

✕ Principal battles
🏯 Principal sieges

Sea of Japan (East Sea)

KOREA

Tsushima

Iki

JAPAN

Honshu

Shikoku

Kyushu

Mutsu

Dewa

Echigo

Sado

Noto

Etchu

Hida

Kaga

Echizen

Wakasa

Tango

Tajima

Inaba

Harima

Mimasaka

Hoki

Bitchu

Bizen

Izumo

Iwami

Aki

Suo

Nagato

Buzen

Chikuzen

Hizen

Chikugo

Higo

Bungo

Hyuga

Satsuma

Osumi

Iyo

Tosa

Awa

Sanuki

Kii

Izumi

Yamato

Ise

Shima

Iga

Omi

Mino

Owari

Mikawa

Totomi

Suruga

Kai

Izu

Sagami

Musashi

Shimosa

Kazusa

Awa

Hitachi

Shimotsuke

Kozuke

Shinano

Settsu

Kawachi

Yamashiro

Tamba

Gassen-Toda
1542-1543,
1565

Miyajima
1555

Okitanawate
1584

Iwaya
1586

Kizakihara
1572

Mimigawa
1578

Hetsugigawa
1586

Sendaigawa
1587

Takamatsu
1582

Yamazaki
1582

Iwasaki
1582

Kozuki
1577

Miki
1578

Eiryakuji
1571

Kizugawaguchi
1576 and 1579

Awaji

Nagashima
1571-1574

Ota
1585

Negoroji
1585

Hijiyama
1581

Kannonji
1487

Kameyama
1562

Atsukizaka
1542 and 1564

Anegawa
1570

Shizugatake
1583

Sekigahara
1600

Odani
1573

Ono

Wemmura

Okehazama
1560

Nagakute
1584

Ishibayama Castle

Yoshida
1575

Nagashino
1575

Mikatagahara
1573

Takatenjin
1571-1573

Teduorigawa
1577

Matsukura
1582

Kawanakajima
1553, 1555, 1557,
1561 and 1564

Uedahara
1546

Ueda
1600

Matsuyama
1537 and 1563

Arai Castle
1553, 1555, 1557,
1561 and 1564

Odawara
1590

Mozuriya Castle
1585

Oshikihata. He then ordered the construction of a fort on Miyajima (also known as Itskushima) as part of a ploy to draw Sue into a trap.[35] Knowing such information would likely find its way back to Harukata's camp, Motonari made strong indications that Miyajima would be abandoned. The ruse worked, and Sue occupied Miyajima.

Meanwhile, the second phase of Motonari's scheme was being executed. This required first that the army capture Sakarao, a fort on the mainland that was an essential link for Sue's army on the island. With this achieved, Motonari waited for a thunderstorm to begin raging overhead, and used this as cover to sail stealthily across the strait to the island.[36] Once landed, Motonari and his sons, Takamoto, Kikkawa Motoharu, and Kobayakawa Takakage, regrouped and launched a devastating attack at dawn that overwhelmed the Sue army. Both Sue Harukata and Sue Nagafusa died, Harukata by his own hand.

The Second Battle of Gassan-Toda

The death of the Amako *daimyo* Haruhisa in 1562 presaged a long decline in the fortunes of the clan, from which it would never again rise. This presented Môri Motonari, whose rise in the western provinces had begun at the Battle of Miyajima, with a prospect to exploit. In 1564, with an army of 25,000, he undertook a campaign to wrest all of Izumo from the new Amako *daimyo*, Yoshihisa. Although his initial attempts to take the key citadel at Gassan-Toda failed, he was able to capture several outlying Amako forts in an effort to isolate the stronghold. Shiraga, the key post in these outer defenses, fell in late 1564 despite Yoshihisa's efforts to break the siege.

Motonari then resumed his efforts against Gassan-Toda in September 1565, and by the end of the year, with dwindling supplies and morale among the defenders of the castle, victory was assured. In January the following year Yoshihisa surrendered the castle and was exiled. This was another milestone in Motonari's ultimately triumphant quest to gain control over the entire Chugoku area

Battle of Kizakihara

In southern Kyushu, the Shimazu had traditionally enjoyed dominance in Osumi Province. They had a long-term rival in the Ito clan of Hyuga; nearly a hundred years previously Shimazu Takahisa had won a victory over the Ito at Obi (1485). In 1572, Ito Yoshisuke began determined efforts to increase Ito land assets. To this end he first captured Obi, one of the eight districts of Hyuga and the focus of much fighting between the Ito and Shimazu, after which he consolidated his hold over southern Hyuga. Yoshisuke then began advancing into Osumi, all the while fomenting an insurrection against the Shimazu among the border clans. Takahisa quickly subdued these threats and prepared for a deciding confrontation with Yoshisuke. They met at Kizaki Plain, on the Osumi-Hyuga border. In the event the day was won by the Shimazu, and the Ito were routed. In 1576 Takahisa defeated the Ito again at Takabaru, and within two years Yoshisuke had abandoned his lands and fled to the refuge of the Otomo.

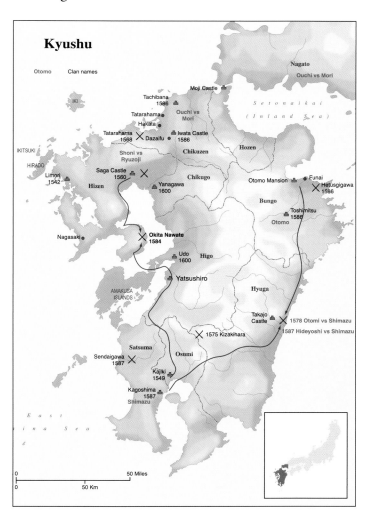

The Battle of Mimigawa

The emergence of the Shimazu as a power in southern Kyushi did not go unheeded in other quarters, particularly among the Otomo clan. Along with the Shoni and the Shimazu, the Otomo had, since the Yamato Period, been one of the major clans of Kyushu, and the only one with the strength to check the ambitions of their newly powerful neighbors.

With the ultimate goal of recapturing lands taken earlier from the Ito family and crushing the Shimazu, in 1578 Otomo Sorin and his son Yoshimune marched a 50,000-strong host into Hyuga. While the Otomo general Tawara Chikataka was sent with the bulk of the army to besiege Shimazu Iehisa in Taka Castle, the remainder of the force pressed on into Hyuga. Over the ensuing weeks, at Taka Castle, Iehisa led a heroic defense against the much more powerful Otomo army, allowing his brother Yoshihisa time to assemble a relief force, which he then marched to Sadowara. Concurrently, his brother Yoshihiro was bringing an army north on a different line of march, and had already seen off an advance Otomo force, when he razed the Otomo fort at Matsuyama. From Sadowara, Yoshihisa pressed on towards Taka, where he linked up with the rest of the Shimazu clan. On December 10, 1578, the huge Otomo and Shimazu armies clashed at Mimigawa, near to Taka Castle.[37] Tawara Chikataka led the fighting with a spirited frontal attack, which the Otomo barely contained. Iehisa then joined the melee, sallying his men out of the castle and into the enemy's rear positions. The Otomo were quickly routed, losing thousands of men[38] and presaging their decline as a significant force in Kyushu.

Central Japan

We turn at this point to the battles of the central provinces, those east of Mimasaka, Inaba, and Bizen, and bordered in the north by Dewa and Mutsu.[39] This delimitation includes of course the capital, Kyoto, which had been so ravaged during the Onin War and for many years after remained in a parlous state of chaos. As touched on at the beginning of this chapter, under the

Above: Sasa Narimasa (at front left) at the first battle of Azukizaka, 1542. In later battles he was given command of arquebus troops thanks to his skill in gunnery tactics. *(British Museum/Jo St Mart)*

Ashikaga *shogun* Yoshizumi, the Asakura family rose to prominence in the province of Echizen. In 1503, Sadakage ascended to the position of *daimyo* and soon faced a challenge to his authority from a faction of Asakura retainers. This was quashed with the help of his uncle, Norikage, who was perhaps the greatest of the family warriors and the source of many famous sayings.[40]

After proving his loyalty to the *daimyo*, Norikage proved fundamental to the consolidation and expansion of the Asakura's power in Echizen and its neighboring provinces. In 1506 he fought the first of many battles

in 1509 with the Battle of Ichiburi, where he defeated Uesugi Sadanori, and subsequently at Nishihama, where he was besieged by warriors loyal to Uesugi Funayoshi. Ultimately, the siege failed and Funayoshi was killed. Tamekage continued to acquire territory and power, defeating Funayoshi's successor as *shugo*, Uesugi Akisada, in league with Hojo Soun, whose name we have already heard. Together, within a few years, these two had brought about the complete collapse of the Uesugi clan. In later years, having established a position of power within Echigo, Tamekage was forced to confront both the rebellious *ji-samurai*[41] within Echigo and the growing power of the *ikko-ikki* in the *Hokuriku*, (literally North Land Region).

In 1531 the nominal Shugo family, the Togashi, had been finally driven from Kaga by the *ikko-ikki*, and the latter assumed the dominant political position. The *ikko* began to assert influence over the common people in other provinces, notably neighboring Etchu, and to increase hostility to the ruling *daimyo*. Those *daimyo* who opposed the spread of teachings that emanated from the Honganji suffered rioting or even armed attacks.

By 1536 these provocations had become a serious threat to Nagao Tamekage, prompting him to raise an army, which in December he led out from the castle of Kasugayama and marched westward, towards Kaga. At Sendanno in Etchu, he met the *ikko-ikki* army, under a little-known figure called Enami Kazuyori. The victory he won over the Nagao that day was one of the Kaga *ikko*'s greatest triumphs, presaging a rise in their power that was checked only through the intervention of Oda Nobunaga some decades later. For the Nagao, the defeat at Sendanno, which saw the death of Tamekage and many other Nagao clan warriors, spelled the beginning of a long period of internal conflict. Leadership of the clan fell to Tamekage's eldest son, Harukage, but his weak rule was troubled by power struggles that eventually toppled him in favor of his younger brother, Kagetora, in 1547. Once in power Kagetora (who went by a number of names in his lifetime, the last of which was Uesugi Kenshin[42]) started on a long and difficult effort to repair the deep and bitter divisions within the clan.

with the *ikko-ikki* of Kaga (of whom we heard in the opening of this chapter), at Kuzuryugawa, which is in present-day Fukui.

In nearby Echigo, we see the personification of the *nari-agari mono*, or "upstarts," for which the Sengoku jidai is noted. Here the Nagao had traditionally served as retainers of the Uesugi, and between 1500 and 1505, while holding the position of *shugo dai* (deputy) to Uesugi Funayoshi, *shugo* of Echigo Province, Nagao Tamekage led *daimyo* Yamanouchi Uesugi's forces to victory against the Ogigayatsu Uesugi in a series of conflicts.

From this point on, Tamekage sought to break away from servitude and establish himself independently. He fought a number of battles with the Uesugi, culminating

Two clans that were the principal rivals to the Nagao and to Kagetora were the Hojo (whose story we left off in 1518 with the succession of Ujitsuna) and the Takeda, in particular Takeda Shingen, who, together with Kagetora were perhaps the greatest rivalry of the Sengoku jidai.

The Siege of Arai Castle

In 1516, Hojo Soun was at the pinnacle of his success, gained as we have seen through a good measure of guile and wit. The final chapter in his military career came in 1516 at the siege of Arai Castle, in Sagami Province.

Some years earlier, Yoshiatsu, the head of the rival Miura clan, and his son, Yoshimoto, had formed an alliance with the Ogigayatsu branch of the Uesugi to oppose the further Hojo expansion in Sagami. But, upon commencing their advance into Hojo territory, Yoshiatsu's army faltered, having made only minor inroads, and failed even to take the forts on the outer defensive line. Further problems for the allied camp came in the form of unrest within the Uesugi (already documented), which served to divert them from the campaign. Consequently, the Hojo were able to bring the full force of their army to bear, seize the initiative, and turn the Miura. By September 1512 they had pushed Yoshiatsu back to Okazaki Castle, a keystone in his defenses on the Miura Peninsula.

Soon, however, he was forced to quit Okazaki and retreat to Arai, a castle held by his son Yoshimoto. With the Hojo diminishing his outer cordon, Yoshiatsu's position was by now badly compromised. His forces were helpless to prevent Soun picking off his remaining outer forts. Soon they were reduced to only Arai, where Soun allowed the besieged Miura to slowly wilt for almost three years. Then, in 1516, with the enemy near starvation, Soun launched a decisive attack. After a brave defense, but facing imminent defeat, Yoshiatsu took the only course considered for a man of his stature and, together with his son, committed suicide. It is suggested in some accounts that Yoshimoto actually cut off his own head to achieve this end; however unlikely this seems, *samurai* everywhere were awed by the tale.

A year before he died Soun passed over control to his son, Ujitsuna,[43] who was to continue his father's quest to gain control of the Kanto, and make the Hojo capital Odawara "the commercial and intellectual capital of the plain."[44] Under Ujitsuna the Hojo clan approached the pinnacle of its struggle for power.[45] But, over the course of this irresistible rise, the Hojo began to make dangerous and powerful enemies, eager to halt further expansion. Among them were former allies such as the Satomi and Ashikaga, the Uesugi and, eventually, the Imagawa and Takeda. One of the first steps in Ujitsuna's quest was in 1524, when he attacked and captured Edo Castle in Musashi[46] from Uesugi Tomoki. The latter had endeavored to take the initiative in defending the castle[47] by marching his troops out to meet the Hojo army in battle. However, Ujitsuna, "a gifted strategist,"[48] simply circled around behind him, and took the castle with the connivance of Ota Suketada, the castle keeper, who betrayed the Uesugi to the Hojo.

This act proved the catalyst for a bitter feud between the Hojo and Uesugi families, part of a seventeen-year struggle for control of the Kanto region.[49] In retaliation for the attack on Edo, two years later Satomi Sanetaka of Awa Province landed troops at Kamakura and, before retiring, burned much of the town, including the Tsurugaoka Hachiman Shrine. In 1530 Hojo and Uesugi clashed again at Ozawahara in Musashi. This was the first battle in which Ujitsuna's son Ujiyasu, then just a boy of fifteen years,[50] had command (later he assumed complete control of the clan). Some four years later the climactic battle of the long-running spat between these two clans, and for which Ujiyasu has become rightly famous, took place at Kawagoe in Musashi.

In 1537, Tomoki, of the Ogigayatsu branch of the Uesugi clan, died and was succeeded by Tomosada. Ujitsuna promptly attacked Tomosada's domain and captured Kawagoe Castle.[51] The Uesugi and Ashikaga viewed this development with alarm, and determined to

---

Left: Miura Yoshiatsu took refuge in the city of Arai, but his allies had deserted him and after a long siege the city fell in 1516. Yoshiatsu had little option but to commit *seppuku. (British Museum/Jo St Mart)*

Above: Murakami Yoshikiyo (at right) fighting Takeda Shingen, aka "The Tiger of Kai." *(British Museum/Jo St Mart)*

try and prevent further Hojo expansion into the Kanto. An alliance between two branches of the Uesugi (the Yamaouchi and Ogigayatsu) under Uesugi Tomosada and Uesugi Norimasa, respectively, together with Ashikaga Haruuji, was formed to try and retake Edo from the Hojo. As part of this plan, in October 1544 a combined force besieged Hojo Tsunashige at Kawagoe.

Though two earlier attempts to retake the castle had failed, the allies were encouraged by an alliance between the Takeda and Imagawa against the Hojo, which they felt would present sufficient threat to prevent the despatch of a relief force from Ujiyasu. Throughout the winter and into the early spring Tsunashige's 3,000 defenders held off a much mightier[52] attacking force, but faced likely starvation. However, in May, Ujiyasu secured a treaty with the Imagawa that allowed him to focus his full efforts on Kawagoe. But, having failed to find a peaceful resolution to the dispute with the Uesugi, Ujiyasu led an 8,000-strong army to Kawagoe to try and relieve the siege. Once in the vicinity he infiltrated a *samurai* past the Uesugi positions to inform his brother of the *status quo*, and put his *ninja* to work gathering information about his enemy's disposition.

Using this intelligence, and working in union with the castle defenders, he launched a night attack on the Uesugi headquarters, fomenting total surprise, confusion, and panic in their ranks. The besieging army, although numerically much stronger, was routed, not least because, under Ujiyasu's orders, his army was not bulked down by heavy armor, and was ordered not to waste precious time in the inevitable search for trophy heads.[53] This battle was a blow struck to the Uesugi fortunes, from which they did not recover until Uesugi Kenshin, who had been adopted into the family line, rose to achieve greatness a decade after.

In the early 16th century, the Hojo had a valuable ally in the Kanto region[54] in the form of the Imagawa clan.[55] But in 1536 Imagawa Ujiteru died without having produced an heir, and a succession dispute erupted between Imagawa Yoshimoto[56] and his elder brother, Genko Etan. The *Hanagura no ran*, as this was dubbed, embroiled both Hojo Ujitsuna and Takeda Nobutora of Kai province. With the military assistance of the former, Yoshimoto eventually overcame his brother, and secured control of the clan.

However, in late 1538, while he was occupied with assisting his neighbor, Ujitsuna found himself exposed to a sudden attack by the Satomi and Ashikaga in Musashi. In November Satomi Yoshitaka and Ashikaga Yoshiaki led 10,000 men to attack the Hojo outposts in Musashi. Ujitsuna hastily assembled an army of 20,000 from Izu and Sagami, and gathered them at Edo before advancing out to meet the enemy at Konodai in Shimosa (located in and around the northern part of modern Chiba Prefecture). The Satomi and Ashikaga were quickly defeated, and Yoshiaki was killed. In the aftermath of the battle the Hojo chased the Satomi back onto the Boso Peninsula (which forms the eastern edge of modern Tokyo Bay), their territorial stronghold.

Neighboring Kai bore witness to the rise of another of the great *daimyo* families, the Takeda. Originally a

Above: Portrait of Takeda Shingen. *(wikipedia.com via Jo St Mart)*

Takeda Shingen (1521–1573)

One of the foremost *daimyo* of his time, this warrior was originally named Takeda Katsuchiyo, but this was later changed to Takeda Harunobu and finally, in 1559, to Takeda Shingen. He eventually ruled Shinano and Kai Provinces, and during his fifty-two years achieved considerable success as a military leader.

Shingen was the eldest son of Takeda Nobutora, *daimyo* of Kai, but on realizing that his father was grooming his younger brother, Nobushige, as his successor, Shingen carried out a successful coup in 1541 and sent his father into permanent exile.

Immediately threatened by a coalition of *daimyos* Shingen attacked first, defeating them at the Battle of Sezawa (April 1542) and following through with an advance into southern Shinano. In a four-year campaign he won a series of victories, his only setback being at the Battle of Uedahara (the first in history in which firearms were used), in which Shingen was wounded and several of his commanders were killed. Recovering quickly, Shingen eventually defeated the Murakami army at Toishi Castle in 1551 and by 1553 most of Shinano was under his control, although he did not hold it completely until 1564.

In 1568 he commenced a campaign against the Hojo in Sagami and Suruga, and by 1570 Shingen was the only *daimyo* with either the strength or the ability to challenge Oda Nobunaga in his relentless subjugation of Japan. After crushing the Imagawa, in November 1572 Shingen moved against Tokugawa Ieyasu, a Nobunaga ally, capturing Futamata. Shingen then won a minor victory over a combined Oda Nobunaga army at the battle of Mikatagahara (January 1573) but only a few months later he died in his camp after a life which, as with so many of his contemporaries, had been devoted to almost constant campaigning.

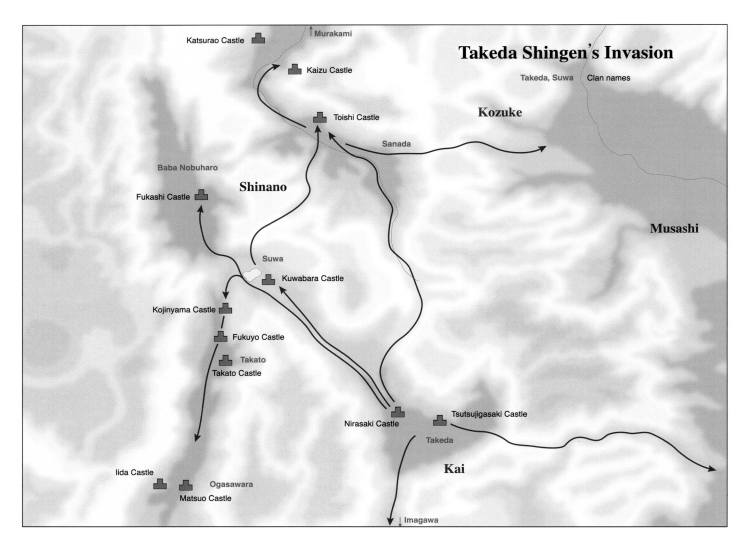

branch of the Minamoto, along with a number of other families, they aided their cousin Minamoto no Yoritomo against the Taira clan in the Genpei War. Later, Takeda Nobumitsu helped the Hojo during the Shokyu War and in reward received the governorship of Aki province.

At the start of the Sengoku Period, the Takeda were *shugo* of Kai, Aki, and Wakasa provinces. In 1415, they helped to suppress the rebellion of Uesugi Zenshu, and through this an animosity developed between the Uesugi and Takeda families, which would last roughly 150 years.

After succeeding his father Nobumasa as head of the clan in 1507,[57] Takeda Nobutora defeated a challenge to his authority from his uncle Nobushige.[58] Over the course of the next decade he fought against the Oi,[59] the Imagawa,[60] and the Imai, and in 1519 established the Takeda clan stronghold at Tsutsujigaseki in Fuchu. In the following year he moved to crush those families in Kai who had thus far refused to pay him homage. During the 1520s he challenged the Hojo domain of Sagami, and in

1528 launched a failed and unpopular[61] invasion of Shinano, which was under the Suwa clan.

In 1531, following further clashes with the Hojo the previous year, Nobutora defeated a coalition of *daimyo* in neighboring Shinano province, including the Suwa, Imai, and Hiraga, at Kawarabe.[62] "The hunger for more land" soon brought Nobutora into conflict, on his southern borders with the Imagawa, the Hojo in the southeast, the Uesugi in the east, and Suwa in the north. In 1535[63] the Imagawa and Hojo launched an invasion of Kai, reprieved by the timely intervention of Uesugi Tomoki against Sagami. That September Nobutora made peace with the Suwa, and after the death of Imagawa Ujiteru he achieved peace with that clan through the marriage of his eldest daughter to Imagawa Yoshimoto,[64] enraging Hojo Ujitsuna and prompting him to attack Suruga.

With his southern borders secure, Nobutora turned his attentions to Shinano, opting to advance via Saku, the domain of Hiraga Genshin. At his side[65] was his fifteen-year-old son Takeda Harunobu (later Shingen), taking part in his first engagement (*ujin*). He would become the greatest of the Takeda commanders.

In November 1536 Nobutora moved into Saku, surrounding the Hiraga fortress of Un no kuchi[66] with 8,000 men. But the resistance proved unexpectedly stiff and, after thirty-four days, all attempts to seize the fortress failed. As winter set in, bringing snow and cold,

Harunobu resigned himself to failure and deided to withdraw. Some accounts have it that, during the withdrawal, Shingen (who was acting as the rearguard) undertook a sudden *volte-face*, and led his men in a renewed assault on the castle garrison. Catching them

Below: Shimazu Tadatsune (the fearless *daimyo* of Satsuma) called Sanada Yukimura (at left) the "number one warrior in Japan." Others called him "a hero who may appear once in a hundred years," and "Crimson demon of war." *(British Museum/Jo St Mart)*

unprepared, the defenders were overcome and Genshin was killed, presaging the destruction of his family early the next year. Whatever the truth of the matter, this was Takeda Shingen's first major victory in battle (Un no Kuchi) and the birth of the legend surrounding him.

In June 1541, Shingen overthrew his father in Kai, and sent him into exile in Suruga. There are several theories for why he did this, explored in much more depth by Terje Solum. To my mind the most likely is that he wanted to prevent power of the clan passing to his brother Nobushige.[67] Whatever the reason, Shingen was now head of the clan, and of Kai, still reeling from a series of natural disasters that had brought hardship and famine to the province. Shingen therefore embarked upon several civil projects aimed at restoring the infrastructure.

Shingen returned to military endeavors during the next year. In April he defeated an alliance of Shinano warlords, including Ogasawara Nagatoki,[68] Suwa Yorishige, Murakami Yoshikiyo,[69] and Kiso Yoshiyasu, at Sezawa[70] in Shinano, beginning a campaign into southern Shinano that would occupy him for some years and which encompassed many battles and sieges. In September 1544 he overcame Fujisawa Yorichika[71] in Ina-Matsushima,[72] and the following spring took his main castle, Fukuyo. Between August and September 1545 Shingen intervened twice on the behalf of the Imagawa, fighting the Hojo in Suruga,[73] before securing a peace between the two. He then returned to his relentless campaign of conquest in Shinano.

On the plains of Odaihara, in Saku, in 1546, while concurrently investing Shiga castle, Shingen met and defeated a relief force dispatched by Uesugi Norimasa (led by Kanai Hidekage). Using some 500[74] heads that his *samurai* had taken in the battle, Harunobu mounted a macabre display outside the castle, designed to bring about the surrender of the occupants, under Kasahara Kiyoshige. Although he had to wait until 1547, the tactic worked, and the garrision surrendered.

But the Takeda commander had little opportunity to rejoice at another victory, for in early 1548 his ambition was to face a temporary setback. Murakami Yoshikiyo, perhaps the most formidable of Shingen's enemies in

Above: Obata Toramori fighting for Takeda Shingen. *(Jo St Mart)*

Shinano, moved on Uedahara in the north of Shinano.[75] Shingen quickly assembled an army of 7,000, including those that had taken Shiga, and headed north through the snow-bound Daimon Pass to face the threat. The opposing forces met at Uedahara, on the western bank of the Chikuma River, on February 14. Itagaki Nobukata, one of Harunobu's best commanders, led the initial foray into Yoshikiyo's ranks. However, the charge was repelled, and the Takeda troops were forced to retire having lost many of their number, including Nobutaka himself.

Perhaps the best-documented aspect of this engagement was that, in subsequent exchanges, Murakami deployed fifty *ashigaru* armed with Chinese

the Murakami's Toishi (1550–51)[78] and Katsurao castles (1553), the Kiso's Fukushima and Kannomine in 1554, and finally the Ogasawara stronghold of Matsuo (1554), all of which resulted in Takeda victories.

The Takeda were by now the undisputed masters over most of Shinano. Murakami Yoshiharu and Ogasawara Nagatoki[79] were expelled, and subsequently turned to the Uesugi of Echigo for help.[80] Here was the starting point for an epic series of battles, beginning in 1553 and destined to last for more than a decade, between Takeda Shingen[81] and his great rival Uesugi Kenshin.[82] These bloody contests are among the most celebrated in Japanese history.

Kawanakajima—The First Battle [83]

The plain of Kawanakajima, then in the north of Shinano Province, lies in the Northern Japanese Alps, between the Sai River to the north and the Chikuma River to the south, and with mountains to the west. In the mid-16th century, this plain formed the natural border between Uesugi Kenshin's domain of Echigo, and Takeda Shingen's domain of Kai.

The first of five battles fought between these two at Kawanakajima took place in April of 1553,[84] when Shingen launched an exploratory raid into the southern end of the Kawanakajima plain, marching 5,000 men along the banks of the Chikuma River. They penetrated some way before the vangard encountered the Uesugi army at Zenkoji, not far from the Uesugi camp at Obasute. Shingen's forces disengaged, and Uesugi pursued them to Katsurao, which had recently been taken from the Murakami by Takeda Nobushige and was held by Oso Genpachi. The castle fell on April 23, and the following day Shingen made the decision to pull back to his Tsutsujigasaki, the Takeda stronghold in Kai. He spent the rest of the summer preparing for another effort against the Uesugi, retaking the Chiisagata district from Murakami Yoshikiyo in August, before advancing to Fuse in the southern part of the Kawanakajima Plain. In response Kenshin marched his 8,000-strong coalition army[85] onto the plain and, until mid-September, the two engaged in a series of small skirmishes, none of which

arquebuses,[76] to give fire support for his bowmen. What effect these weapons had on the outcome of the battle is not clear, but about 700 of Takeda's men were killed, among them Itagaki Nobutaka and two other generals, Amari Torayasu and Hajikano Den'emon. Shingen himself suffered a spear wound to his side.

Soon after the loss of Uedahara, Shingen had an opportunity to avenge their defeat with a victory over Ogasawara Nagatoki at Shirojiritoge.[77] Leading a small contingent of horsemen, Shingen approached an Ogasawara encampment under cover of night. At dawn, while the Ogasawara lay slumbering and defenseless, he sprang his attack. Without armor or weapons the Ogasawara troops could not put up much of a fight, and Shingen soon overran the camp. He followed this with sieges of the Ogasawara stronghold at Fukashi in 1549,

was decisive. Five days after a battle at Fuse on September 15, Kenshin withdrew. Shingen followed suit early the next month.

The Second Battle

Two years later, Shingen returned to Kawanakajima in another attempt to bring the Uesugi to battle. Advancing with 5,000 men across the plain as far as the banks of the Sai River (for this reason the second battle is sometimes also known as the Battle of Saigawa), he made camp on a strategic hill to the south of the river, known as the Otsuka. Uesugi Kenshin had chosen the Shiroyama just east of the Zenko-ji temple to locate his 8,000 men, knowing that this would provide him with a commanding view of the plain. However, a few miles to the west lay the Asahiyama fortress of the Kurita clan, allies of the Takeda, and from this position their commander, Kurita Kakuju, could menace the Uesugi right flank. Recognizing the significance of this position, prior to the battle Takeda sent 3,000 of his own men with some 300 guns to aid in the defense of the fortress. These men would witness the fiercest fighting of the campaign.

As expected, Kenshin ordered a number of attacks against the Asahiyama fortress, but this and all that followed were beaten back. After some deliberation, Shingen marched his army down to the banks of the Sai, intending to cross at the first chance. However, Kenshin checked this move by moving his own army off Shiroyama and into position on the opposite bank. Stalemated, each waiting for the other to make a move, the armies entrenched, and from August to November the two great warlords had to satisfy themselves with facing off across the river. Some small scale skirmishing did occur, but there was no large-scale clash of arms. After months of this protracted and futile posturing, both leaders simply upped and withdrew to deal with more pressing matters in their home provinces.

The Third Battle

In 1557, emboldened by his mounting power in the Kanto, Shingen launched an audacious strike deep into Uesugi territory, across the Sai River at the mountain fortress of Katsurayama. From here Shingen could look over Zenkoji, Kenshin's most important stronghold and where his army was based. However, Kenshin refused to be drawn and declined to fight. Shingen then attempted another provocation by taking Iiyama Castle, which lay to the northeast of the Zenkoji, and thus press Kenshin

Uesugi Kenshin (1530–1578)

An outstanding military commander, Uesugi Kenshin was the fourth son of Nagao Tamekage, a warlord who was killed fighting against the *ikko-ikki* in Etchu. In the subsequent succession dispute between his older brothers, the youthful Kenshin was sent to Rizen temple, and remained there until 1544.

The successful brother, Harukage, proved unpopular and some of his father's courtiers conspired to depose him and install Kenshin in his stead. There was no overnight coup and Kenshin had to conduct a four-year campaign before prevailing in 1547. He then sought to consolidate his power and by 1551 was on the verge of success, but was challenged by Takeda Shingen.

The rivalry between these two became legendary and they fought numerous battles against each other, although both also fought other opponents. In 1560, for example, Kenshin sought to regain control of the Kanto from the Hojo, a campaign culminating in the siege of Odawara Castle in Sagami Province (June 1561). At the end of that year he took Matsuyama Castle, only to lose it again two years later. It was at this time that he received the title of *Kanto-kanrei* from the *shogun* Ashikaga Yoshiteru.

Although Kenshin's territorial ambitions were limited he inevitably clashed with Oda Nobunaga when he seized some territory in the Hokuriku region that both he and Nobunaga considered within their spheres of influence. Nobunaga sent an army against Kenshin, but despite being at a numerical disadvantage, the latter triumphed at the Tedorigawa (November 1577), forcing Nobunaga to withdraw.

During the winter of 1577-1578, Kenshin prepared for a major expedition against Nobunaga, but his health deteriorated rapidly and he died in April 1578, possibly from excessive drinking. There was no legitimate male heir and his two adopted sons then commenced a long and ruinous power struggle, considerably weakening the clan.

on two flanks. This seems to have finally stirred Kenshin into action, for he now led a substantial army out of Zenkoji. Counterattacking in force, he forced Shingen to withdraw, and the Takeda pulled back to the safety of the south.

The Fourth Battle

The fourth and penultimate battle, and also the only one that saw significant combat,[86] came some four years later.[87] This time it was Kenshin who sought to gain the advantage, leading an army of 18,000 out of Katsurayama in September 1561, with the determined purpose of destroying Takeda Shingen. Leaving a garrison to defend Zenkoji, he moved into a position on Saijoyama, a mountain some way to the west of Shingen's castle at Kaizu. Had he known that the castle was defended at his time by a skeleton force of barely 150 *samurai*, it is likely he would have pressed his advantage immediately. However, he delayed, and through a system of *noroshi-da* (signal fires),[88] the castellan of the castle, Kosaka Danjo Masanobu, was able to pass a warning to

Shingen, who was about eighty miles away at Tsutsujigasaki fortress in Kofu.

In response, Shingen marched out of Kofu at the head of 16,000 men, reinforced by 4,000 more as he marched through Shinano Province.

Approaching the familiar environs of Kawanakajima, he chose cautiously to approach Kaizu along on the west bank of the Chikuma River, using the water as a natural barrier between him and Kenshin's army on the Saijoyama. Kenshin sat tight, past experience of and respect for his enemy telling him that victory would require the element of surprise. Shingen entered Kaizu unmolested.

Consulting with his strategists, Takeda concieved a clever plan to defeat his enemy. Under this Kosaka Danjo Masanobu left Kaizu with 8,000 men, and on the night of September 9/10 advanced up Saijoyama under cover of night with the task of driving Kenshin's army down to the plain. Here Shingen, with another 8,000 men, would be waiting to slaughter them. However, Kosaka's approach was compromised and, informed of his approach, during the night Kenshin calmly[89] and safely led his men off Saijoyama via its western slopes. So, as dawn broke, Shingen's men found himself confronting an army not in chaotic retreat, but preparing to charge at him. The first wave[90] of attacks was led by Kakizaki Kageie, at the head of his mounted *samurai*, and this was followed by another and another. While the Takeda formation held firm, the ranks were slowly but surely becoming depleted.

What occurred next is another of those legendary incidents in *samurai* history, no doubt colorfully embellished over the centuries by storytellers, yet it is worth hearing all the same. Spying a weakness in the line, Kenshin and a small troop of cavalry forced a way through to the rear of the Takeda positions and, still mounted, burst into Shingen's *honjin*[91] (field headquarters). Kenshin immediately set about Shingen with his sword. The latter parried as best he could with his signaling fan, and apparently held Kenshin off with this long enough for one of his retainers to spear Kenshin's mount and drive him off. This would have been the only time that the great rivals ever came face to face, which makes the story all the more intriguing.

Meanwhile, the Takeda troops stood firm in the face of persistent attacks on the line. Slowly, the main Uesugi force was pushed back towards the Chikumigawa.

Kosaka's force had by this time reached the top of Saijoyama and, finding the Uesugi position gone from there, hurried down the mountain on the predicted line of retreat. After first fighting through the 3,000 Uesugi warriors defending the ford on the Chikuma, Kosaka's force attacked the retreating Uesugi from the rear, forcing them to retreat. No attempt was made to prevent this withdrawal, first to Zenkoji, and then to Echigo Province, but perhaps this can be explained by the enormous casualties suffered by the Takeda, estimated at nearly two-thirds of their number. Among them were many of Takeda Shingen's leading generals, including his younger brother Takeda Nobushige and great uncle Murozumi

Above: Takeda Shingen defends himself with his *Gumpai-wichiwa* (fan) when attacked by Uesuji Kenshin during the Fourth Battle of Kawanakajima. *(via Clive Sinclaire)*

Left: Takeda Nobushige was killed at the Fourth Battle of Kawanakajima (1561), fighting *samurai* belonging to Uesugi general Kakizaki Kageie. His head was recovered by Yamadera Nobuaki, a Takeda family retainer, who was also said to have killed his master's killer. *(British Museum/Jo St Mart)*

Torasada. For the Uesugi the cost was even higher, with losses of fully three-quarters of their fighting strength, among them Shida Yoshitoki and Shoda Sadataka.

The Fifth Battle

In September 1564, Takeda Shingen decided to try once more to defeat Uesugi Kenshin at Kawanakajima. After advancing into the plain, he set up camp on a hill called Shiozaki. Kenshin duly responded by placing his army across the Sai River. For two months the armies sat and looked at each other across the water, engaging in some light skirmishing of little consequence, and then withdrew yet again. This was the last time the two commanders would meet in battle, since thereafter both increasingly became preoccupied with other, less formidable rivals in the Kanto.

For Shingen such a rival was Hojo Ujiyasu, whose story we left after his victory over the Uesugi at Kawagoe in 1545. That triumph against great odds gave way to a period of comparative peace, in which Hojo Ujiyasu expanded the Hojo territory, which now covered five provinces, and managed and maintained what his father and grandfather had held.[92] However, his unceasing territorial ambitions faced many potential obstacles. To the west lay the domains of the powerful Takeda and the Imagawa clans, leaving Kozuke to the north and the eastern Kanto provinces as the only feasible areas for expansion. But others, including Uesugi Kenshin and Takeda Shingen, also eyed the Kozuke lands, and Ujiyasu had to settle amicably on partition.

So it was to the east that he turned, towards the provinces of Awa and Shimosa. This was the domain of the Satomi, a formidable enemy, whose power base was on the Boso Peninsula. Satomi Yoshitaka, who had been severely defeated at the first battle of Konodai, had resisted an earlier attempt by Hojo Ujitsuna to push into Awa in 1540, and all attempts for two decades thereafter. During this time he consolidated his position largely free from harassment, as his enemies concentrated their efforts elsewhere.

In 1560, the land-hungry Hojo again began to threaten his domain, prompting Yoshitaka to call for the support of Uesugi Kenshin, who led an attack into the Kanto and assuaged the threat.

Then, in 1564, after many years of retrenchment, Yoshitaka felt sufficiently emboldened to take the initiative against the Hojo[93] with a move into neighboring Musashi.[94] The focus was again Konodai Castle, but this time it was his son Yoshihiro who led the 8,000-strong Satomi army. Initially at least, he was successful, siezing the castle and forcing the Hojo to withdraw. Hojo Ujiyasu then launched a powerful counterstrike with as many as 20,000 men under his command, catching Yoshitaka off his guard. Acknowledging that he could not attempt to contain such an overwhelming number, Yoshihiro made the appearance of a withdrawal, in an attempt to lure his enemy into a trap. Ujiyasu, however, was not so easily

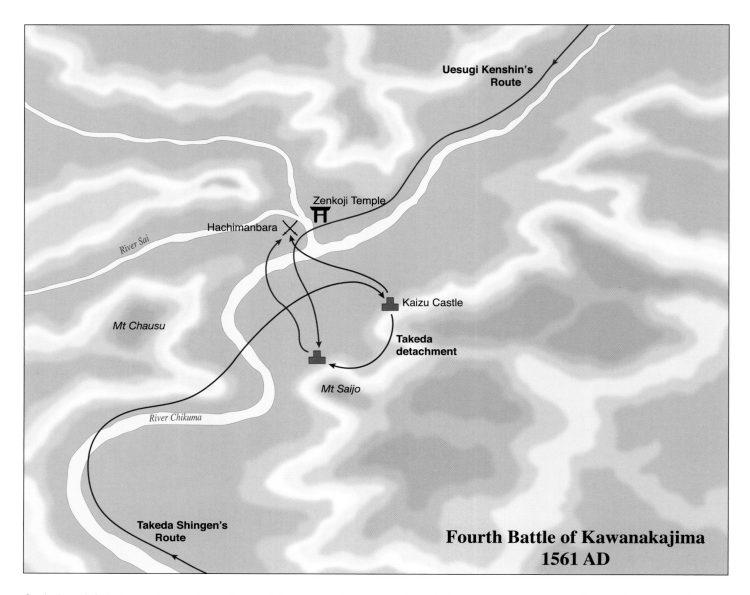

Fourth Battle of Kawanakajima
1561 AD

fooled and failed to take the bait. Instead, he ordered his son Ujimasa to lead a small force to attack the Satomi rear. Now surrounded, in the ensuing battle large numbers of the Satomi fell and Yoshihiro was forced to flee, having endured the sight of his son Chokuro being slain by the Hojo retainer Matsuda Yasuyoshi.

The defeat at Konodai spelled the end for the Satomi clan, for thereafter their power ebbed and, although they were a troublesome thorn in the side for the Hojo for years to come, they were in a greatly weakened state.

Across the Uraga-suido (Uraga Channel) from the Boso Peninsula is the Miura Peninsula, which at that time was the easternmost point of Sagami, governed from Odawara Castle. From 1495 onward, five generations of the Hojo had held this strategically important castle and the province, which bordered with Izu, Kai, Musashi, and Suruga.

In 1569, after a temporary alliance between the two clans had collapsed, Takeda Shingen made the latest in a long series of attempts to take the castle from the Hojo.[95] Seemingly undaunted by the strength of the *yamashiro* (mountain-top castle) defenses, Shingen invaded Sagami with a 10,000-strong army, first laying siege to the neighboring fortress at Hachigata before moving on Takiyama.

Having failed to take either, Takeda moved on to Odawara. Surrounded by moats with water on the low side, dry ditches on the hillside, and with banks, walls and cliffs located all around, the castle proved equally impenetrable. Despite effecting some damage to the outer works, Shingen was forced to retreat after only three days. He was pursued by Hojo Ujiteru and his brother Hojo Ujiyasu, and was ambushed at the Mimasetoge Pass. In the battle that ensued the Takeda vanguard had to fight furiously to avoid being overrun. Takeda Shingen then led up the main body and ordered an attack by the famous "red fire unit." This body of mounted troops, the name of which was derived from Shingen's slogan *furinkazan*,[96] was commanded by his friend and general Yamagata Masakage. He had outfitted his cavalry in bright red armor and, opening any attack, their appearance and ferocity spread fear, confusion, and panic in the enemy ranks. At Mimasetoge, they seem to have had just such an effect, for the Hojo turned and fled the field. Imminent defeat was thus turned to victory. With the Hojo retreating en masse to the north, the Takeda could return safely to Kai to lick their wounds and make good the loss of some 900 dead.

It is interesting to note, as Stephen Turnbull has done, that while both of these men "possessed the military resources to begin the unification of Japan…geographical factors meant that they had to concentrate instead on maintaining their own territories against their neighbors."[97]

Perhaps appropriately in this age of disorder, the process by which Japan was to be forcibly united under one leader after these many years of fighting began not with Takeda or Hojo, but a fairly minor *daimyo* in central Japan. The coast of the Tokaido, encompassing Totomi, Mikawa, Owari, and Suruga, was in the mid-16th century the domain of four families, the most powerful of which was the Imagawa, and to a much lesser degree the Oda. However, the name of this latter clan was shortly to assume great signficance under Oda Nobunaga,[98] a man fundamental to the unification of Japan in the later Sengoku jidai.

His father, Nobuhide, had presided over a long period of hostilities with the Imagawa, who were gradually extending their influence westward from Suruga. They had annexed Totomi following a war with the controlling Shiba family, and threatened Mikawa. The Oda had their power base in Owari, and Nobuhide correctly judged these territorial ambitions as a threat to

---

Below: Son of Oda Nobuhide, Oda Nobunaga is considered one of the three unifiers of Japan, and one of the greatest of 16th century *samurai*. *(The Art Archive/Kobe Municipal Museum/Laurie Platt Winfrey)*

Above: Oda Nobunaga and (mounted) Yamanouchi Kazutoyo, who fought at the battle of Nagashino in 1575. After Nobunaga's death, Yamanouchi became a vassal of Toyotomi Hideyoshi, and fought for Tokugawa Ieyasu at Sekigahara. He died in 1605. *(via Clive Sinclaire)*

his own domain. At Azukizaka in 1542 the two clashed, with Nobuhide emerging as the victor over Imagawa Yoshimoto. However, despite this defeat, Yoshimoto continued to expand into Mikawa. Nobuhide made determined efforts to prevent the province from coming under Imagawa influence, taking certain strongpoints in Mikawa, including Yasuyoshi Castle, but by 1548 the ruling Matsudaira family had, effectively, become Imagawa retainers.

Unrest then broke out in Mikawa when a family retainer, Toda Yasumitsu, rebelled and declared his support for the rival Oda clan. With the Matsudaira preoccupied with quashing Yasumitsu's rebellion,

Nobuhide seized his opportunity to strike. At the head of an army of some 4,000 men he marched on Okazaki, the Matsudaira capital. Matsudaira Hirotada, the young *daimyo*, dispatched envoys to the Imagawa for assistance,[99] and from Suruga presently came Taigen Sessai, Yoshimoto's uncle, with an army. To meet this, Nobuhide led an army out of Anjo, a Mikawa castle that had been taken in 1541 from the Matsudaira.

Nobuhide met the waiting Sessai on the old battlefield at Azukizawa, a location chosen by Sessai with the purpose of springing an ambush on his opponent. This achieved, general fighting broke out and the battle was fought to a furious conclusion. In the event, Nobuhide was defeated and his army was sent on its way back to Owari, thus avenging the defeat of six years previous.

Nobuhide died the next year, and in the aftermath Sessai retook Anjo.

In the twelve years that passed before the two met again, at Okezahama, the Oda clan witnessed two events of major significance. In 1551, after the death of Nobuhide, a bitter power struggle erupted within the many factions of his clan. By progressively eliminating opposition,[100] his impetuous and ruthless eldest son Nobunaga emerged in 1559 as the undisputed leader of the family. As an aside, in 1558 Nobunaga's path crossed for the first time with one Matsudaira Takechiyo—the future Tokugawa Ieyasu[101]—who at the time, as vassal to Imagawa Yoshimoto, was also beginning to make his mark on the political landscape of 16th century Japan. Takechiyo was part of an army that attacked Terabe Castle in Mikawa, after the man charged with its defense, Suzuki Shigeteru, declared for Nobunaga. With the castle under siege, Nobunaga sent a relief force but this was driven off through to the efforts of Takechiyo. Then, in 1559, at the siege of Odaka, he pulled off a remarkable victory against all odds.

Ieyasu was also to play a key role in the events that unfolded before the climactic Battle of Okehazama, marking the emergence of the second of the three great "unifiers" of Japan.

Battle of Okehazama

In 1560, Imagawa Yoshimoto, buoyed by recent victories, decided to attempt a decisive move west, vanquish the Oda and any others who stood in his path, and occupy Kyoto.[102] Assembling a powerful host of 25,000 men, in June Yoshimoto began his advance along the Tokaido coast. Upon gaining Owari Province, he attacked and burned the Oda frontier fortresses of Washizu and Marune.[103]

The destruction of Washizu and Marune set the stage for a much larger clash of arms between the Oda and Imagawa, and their respective warlords Nobunaga and Yoshitomo, at Okezahama. The commanders of the besieged forts, Sakuma Morishige and Oda Genba, had managed to get off letters of warning to Nobunaga in his Kiyosu stronghold. His retainers vacillated over what course of action to take. To some it seemed logical, given the great numerical superiority of Imagawa's army, to adopt a defensive posture, or even to capitulate. Oda Nobunaga, however, to surprise of his retainers, had no such qualms and resolved to sally out and meet his adversary in the field.

After hastily gathering an army perhaps 2,000 strong (and thus outnumbered by twelve to one), he marched out of Kiyosu. Meanwhile, Yoshimoto's army had advanced along the narrow coastal corridor that is today the Tokaido trunk route, and upon arriving in a wooded gorge known as Dengaku-hazama, near Okehazama, made camp. Informed of these movements by his scouts, Oda Nobunaga positioned his own forces at the nearby Zensho-ji temple.

Imagawa Yoshimoto (1519–1560)

Imagawa Yoshimoto, the third son of Imagawa Ujichika, seemed destined for a monastic life, spending many of his first twenty-five years in a Buddhist temple. A dispute over the family succession then broke out and the clan split into two, one party favoring Yoshimoto, the other his elder half-brother (by a concubine), Genko Etan. Forsaking the monastic life (to which he never returned), Yoshimoto defeated and killed his rival during the *Hanakura-no-ran* (Hanakura disturbances).

Yoshimoto then sought to influence the neighboring Takeda clan, played a key role in Takeda Shingen's *coup d'état* in 1540, and then married the latter's sister. His flank now secure, Yoshimoto then began an Imagawa expansion westwards, bringing him into conflict with the Oda clan, with whom he fought on several occasions. In 1544, Yoshimoto, still allied with the Takeda, marched against the Hojo clan, but achieved little. Despite this, by the late 1550s he controlled a wide area including Suruga, Totomi, and Mikawa, and felt sufficiently secure to take on the challenge posed by Oda Nobunaga, who he considered to be an upstart. In June 1560 Yoshimoto advanced towards Kyoto, but his army was heavily defeated by a much smaller force at Okezahama, during which Yoshimoto himself was slain. Thereafter the Imagawa rapidly lost power and influence, eventually becoming no more than officials in the service of the Tokugawa clan.

Acknowledging that a frontal assault would likely end in a rout, Nobunaga opted instead to use a time-worn deception against his enemy. A small party was placed at the temple with a great show of banners, to give the illusion of a much larger force, and detract from the movement of his main force on a circuitous route through the wooded hills.

In the Imagawa camp no one was prepared for the imminent attack. The march in the summer heat had fatigued the troops, and most were taking the chance to recuperate with drink, as soldiers are wont to do. On June 19, taking advantage of the enemy's unpreparedness, and a sudden thunderstorm, Nobunaga moved into his final position, before launching a lightning attack into the Imagawa encampment. The Imagawa warriors fled in panic, leaving their commander undefended. Emerging from his tent to investigate the source of the commotion, Yoshimoto was quickly cut down,[104] along with almost every other Imagawa commander. Nobunaga, against seemingly insurmountable odds, had achieved a complete victory. This was to be the first step in his quest for unification. For the Imagawa, any hopes of taking Kyoto were shattered, and within years the clan itself would be destroyed. By contrast, through this victor, Nobunaga was suddenly elevated to "the first rank of *samurai* commanders"[105] and thereby attracted many of the former Imagawa vassals (including Tokugawa Ieyasu) to his side. Remarkably, it would be Nobunaga who took Kyoto some eight years hence.

The Mino Campaign

But before a move on the capital could even be considered, Nobunaga had to secure his own powerbase. To that end he began preparations for a campaign of conquest in Mino, bordering Owari to the north. One year after his victory at Okehazama, an opportunity presented itself when the *daimyo*, Saito Yoshitatsu, died. In previous years Mino had been wracked by internal conflict, beginning in 1542 when Saito Dosan had overthrown the ruling Toki clan and seized control of the province. His wife was of the Toki family, and her son, Yoshitatsu, was adopted by Dosan. However, the latter disinherited Yoshitatsu in favor of another son, Nagatatsu, thus provoking a civil war. In May 1556 Yoshitatsu led an army to the Nagaragawa, defeated and killed Dosan, and therafter assumed control of Mino.

Oda Nobunaga (1534–1582)

Odu Nobunaga, eldest son of a minor *samurai*, showed little inclination to rule properly when he succeeded his father. It was so bad that his mentor committed suicide to make him see sense and Nobunaga made a complete *volte face,* setting himself the astonishingly ambitious goal of unifying Japan.

Nobinaga first eliminated domestic rivalry, which included having his younger brother (who was, in fact, plotting against him) murdered, and by 1559 Nobunaga was in firm control. After some initial setbacks he won a major victory over a powerful army led by Imagawa Yoshimoto at Okezahama. He then went from strength to strength,

starting in 1561 with an alliance with Matsudaira Motoyasu (later Tokugawa Ieyasu), thus ending long-standing hostility between their two clans. Next came a campaign against the Saito lasting for six years, culminating in their defeat at Inabayama Castle in 1567.

A major stepping stone was the elimination of the powerful and influential thousand-year-old Mount Hiei monastery, which was razed to the ground and every last monk was killed. Nobinaga was quite ruthless and some years later set fire to a fortress in which over 20,000 people died.

Nobinaga was one of the first Japanese to welcome Europeans and

was so fascinated by Christianity that he was baptized. He also saw the value of firearms, devising tactics, both offensive and defensive, for their use.

Despite his many successes he was one of many Japanese to lose their lives through treachery, in this case at the hands of a hitherto trusted general, Akechi Mitsuhide. Nobinaga had made a jest at a banquet that caused Mitsuhide to lose face. His revenge was to turn on his leader, surrounding him in a temple, where Nobinaga had no alternative but to commit suicide. He was just forty-eight years old.

Above: Imagawa Yoshimoto in battle. (*via Clive Sinclaire*)

Below: Imagawa Yoshimoto is said to have shaved his eyebrows and blackened his teeth in the fashion of a Kyoto noble. (*British Museum/Jo St Mart*)

When Yoshitatsu died five years later, Nobunaga responded immediately, leading an army northwest from Owari into the Saito domain. To counter the aggressors, Tatsuoki, Yoshitatsu's teenage heir, marched out of the capital Sunomata (in present-day Gifu Prefecture) at the head of an army. This was quickly defeated at Moribe by Nobunaga, who marched on and took possession of Sunomata itself. A week later, at Jushijo, a few miles north of Sunomata, the Saito sprung an ambush on a contingent of Oda troops. In response, Nobunaga rushed out from Sunomata and defeated the Saito in a brief night battle. After fighting a few more small actions and taking a further two Saito forts, Nobunaga returned to Owari Province.

Nobunaga had not done with Mino yet. In 1563 he built the castle at Komaki in Mikawa (in present-day Aichi) to which he relocated for the commencement of a campaign in Mino. In the meantime, by convincing Saito retainers[106] to switch their allegiance, Nobunaga weakened the Saito clan significantly. Mounting a final attack in 1567, Nobunaga captured Inabayama Castle, and changed the name of both the castle and the surrounding town to Gifu. Tatsuoki was sent into exile, and thereafter the Saito clan withered and died.

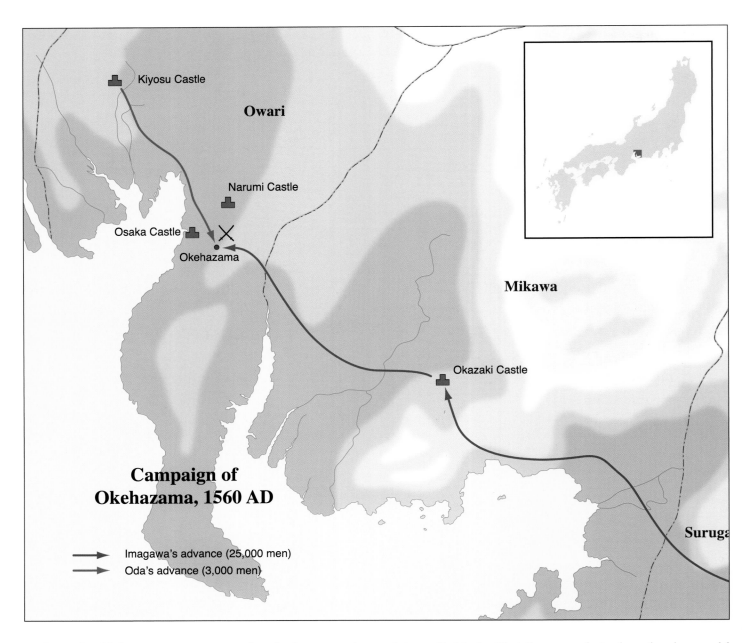

Kiyosu Castle

Owari

Narumi Castle

Osaka Castle

╳

Okehazama

Mikawa

Okazaki Castle

Campaign of Okehazama, 1560 AD

→ Imagawa's advance (25,000 men)
→ Oda's advance (3,000 men)

Suruga

In 1568, Nobunaga was presented with the excuse he had been seeking to march on the capital. That year he received an illustrious visitor from Kyoto at Gifu Castle. This was Ashikaga Yoshiaki, the brother of the thirteenth *shogun* of the Ashikaga *shogunate*, Yoshiteru, who had been murdered and replaced by a puppet *shogun,* Ashikaga Yoshihide. Yoshiakai petitioned to Nobunaga to embark on a campaign toward Kyoto, overthrow the usurper, and install him as the new *shogun*. Eyeing an opportunity to enter the imperial capital under the banner of legitimacy, Nobunaga consented to the pleas, and began to plan his campaign.

To enter Settsu, and move on Kyoto, Nobunaga would have to pass through Omi, and in his path stood the Rokkaku clan, of southern Omi. The incumbent

daimyo, Rokkaku Yoshikata, made it clear that he would not consent to recognize Yoshiaki as *shogun*. Nobunaga answered his obstinacy by launching a rapid attack on a series of Rokkaku castles in Omi, forcing out the Rokkaku clan.[107] Charging Tokugawa Ieyasu with guarding his lines of communication, he entered Kyoto and forced the controlling Miyoshi clan out of the city. Ashikaga Yoshiaki was subsequently installed as the fifteenth *shogun* of the Ashikaga *shogunate*, albeit as a puppet of Nobunaga, and would soon begin to chafe under the yoke. Through this daring and quite unexpected feat, the upstart Nobunaga had usurped all of the other *daimyo*,[108] and it was perhaps inevitable that a response would be forthcoming from them.

Battle of Anegawa

Nevertheless, with Kyoto now firmly in his grasp, Nobunaga sought to captilize on his success, and next turn his attentions to conquering the rest of Omi, and Echizen. Such a move would bring him into conflict with the Asakura clan, historically superior to their Owari neighbors, and contemptuous of the Oda's growing power and influence. Around 1570 *daimyo* Asakura Yoshikage entered into a conspiracy hatched by *shogun* Ashikaga Yoshiaki to move against the domineering Nobunaga, whose persistent interferences he wished to be rid of. Once Nobunaga got wind of the plot, he launched a pre-emptive attack on Yoshikage. This, however, brought him into conflict with Asai Nagamasa, who chose to honor his long-standing alliance with the Asakura, broke a more recent pact with the Oda, and sent out an expedition to pressure the Oda army from the rear. Nobunaga quickly repositioned his troops, curtailing the pressing threat posed by the Asai army and, in union with Tokugawa Ieyasu's 8,000 troops, moved on Nagamasa's Odani Castle.

Answering Nagamasa's pleas for support, Asakura Yoshikage dispatched an army from Echizen. Nobunaga, who was at that time reducing the Asai stronghold at Yokoyama, turned to meet this force, and drew up positions on the southern bank of the Anegawa (Ane) River.

The scene was now set for a clash of arms between two mighty armies, one of 28,000 and the other 20,000. On the morning of July 30, 1570, the two armies locked horns in "blazing summer sunshine across the bed of the Anegawa River."[109] Nobunaga held the right flank against the Asai, while on the left the Tokugawa were opposed by Asakura. Despite their disadvantage in numbers, it soon appeared that Asai Nagamasa's men were gaining the upper hand. On Nobunaga's flank Ieyasu had bottled up the Asakura, allowing him to attack the exposed flank of the Asai. The allies were left with little option but to retreat, leaving a thousand of their men dead on the battlefield, along with a number of commanders. However, the day proved to be something of a Phyrric victory, as the fighting had so enervated his men that Nobunaga was compelled to withdrew from the area, relieving the pressure on Odani.

One of the most noteworthy aspects of the action at Odani, perhaps even overshadowing its military significance, is the presence of Toyotomi Hideyoshi[110] as a leader of Oda troops. Little is known about his life prior to 1570. Born into a lowly peasant family, and over fourteen years in Nobunaga's service, he had risen from the rank of a humble sandal bearer to become one of the most important Oda commanders. With Nobunaga and Tokugawa Ieyasu, he was the last of the triumvirate of Sengoku era unifiers to achieve prominence.

Asakura Yoshikage (1533–73)

Asakura Yoshikage was a Sengoku-era *daimyo*, court regent, and aesthete from Echizen. He assumed leadership of the clan from his father, Asakura Takakage, in 1548. At that time Echizen was endangered by *ikko-ikki* uprisings in neighboring Kaga, but Yoshikage was able to build a relatively secure position in the territories centering on his stronghold at Ichijodani.

But away from the cosseted world of Ichijodani, life was not always so tranquil. Beginning in 1565, Yoshikage became embroiled in a plot that would eventually cost him his life. The *shogun*, Yoshiteru, was assassinated and Yoshikage shortly received call to arms from Yoshiteru's brother and successor, Yoshiaki. Yoshikage vacillated over his course of action, so Yoshiaki appealed instead to Oda Nobunaga, and with his assistance, was installed as the 15th Ashikaga *shogun* in 1568.

Yoshiaki soon grew restive under Nobunaga, however, and began to solicit from various *daimyo* support for a scheme to expel Nobunaga. Fearing Yoshikage might answer Yoshiaki's call, Nobunaga pre-emptively invaded Echizen.

The Asai of Omi promptly raised an army to alleviate the pressure on Yoshikage, but this army was defeated at the Battle of Ane River, prompting Yoshikage to seek a firmer alliance with the Asai. But Nobunaga quickly destroyed the fledgling coalition at the Asai stonghold at Odani Castle. Yoshikage escaped and returned to Ichijodani, but was betrayed there by his cousin, Kageaki, and forced to commit *seppuku*.

Although this was the last time he engaged either Asai or Asakura in battle, Nobunaga now faced off against two groups that would prove to be among the most obstinate opponents to his authority, the *ikko-ikki* militant Buddhist sects, and intransigent warrior monks (*sohei*) headquarted at Mount Hiei. Wary of the *ikki*'s growing power,[111] he had engaged them at Ogie Castle in 1569, but the *ikki* emerged victorious from that battle, in which Nobunaga's brother Nobuoki was killed.

Thus, in the early summer of 1570, Nobunaga began a decade-long effort, known as the Ishiyama Hongan-ji War, against the extensive network of *ikko-ikki* fortifications, temples, and communities. The most important of these was the cathedral fortress of Ishiyama Hongan-ji, which once stood on what is today the site of Osaka Castle. In August 1570, Oda Nobunaga marched out of his castle in Gifu with 30,000 troops, and laid siege to Ishiyama. As part of his plan to reduce the citadel, he ringed it with a series of purpose-built forts. On September 12, the *ikko-ikki* launched a nightime attack and destroyed several of these forts, forcing a partial withdrawal of the Oda army. While Oda himself turned his attention to the sieges of the Nagashima fortress, which stood defiant on the border between his own province of Owari and neighboring Ise, elements of his army remained camped outside the Hongan-ji, blocking supplies to the fortress in an attempt to starve out its defenders.

Siege of Enryakuji

A few months after their defeat at Anegawa, the Asai and Asakura avenged their loss with a minor victory over an Oda army near Otsu, an action that saw the deaths of Môri Yoshinari and Oda Nobuharu (one of Nobunaga's younger brothers). Seeking further retribution against Nobunaga, they next arranged an alliance with the powerful *sohei* of the Mii-dera temple at the base of Mount Hiei.[112] At the summit of Mount Hiei was the vast and influential Enryaku-ji temple complex, which together with the other temples was a potential threat to Nobunaga's lines of communication north of Kyoto.[113] Beginning on September 29, 1571, Nobunaga moved to

Above: Tokugawa Ieyasu was renowned for taking the heads of his opponents. *(via Clive Sinclaire)*

eradicate the threat, in a most brutal way. Starting with the town of Sakamoto at the foot of the mountain, Nobunaga's army of 30,000 moved towards Enryakuji at the summit, destroying everything in its path. Much of Mii-dera was razed, as the warrior monks could do little against Nobunaga's large and highly trained *samurai* army.[114] Following these attacks, the monks were granted a reprieve, and rebuilt their temples once more. The standing army of warrior monks would never be reconstituted.

Sieges of Nagashima

Beginning in 1571, and executed concurrently with the siege of the Ishiyama Hongan-ji, Nobunaga laid siege three times over a four-year period to the complex of fortresses controlled by the *ikko-ikki* and surrounding the fortified monastery at their Ganshoji and Nagashima. These fortresses were situated in naturally difficult terrain on a swampy delta,[115] at the point where three rivers converge, to the southeast of the modern-day city of Nagoya.

The first siege began on May 16, 1571, when troops led by Sakuma Nobumori and Shibata Katsuie launched an attack from Tsushima, to the northeast of Nagashima. As the defenders laid down fire, the Nobumori/Katsuie troops attempted to ford the shallow but broad river delta separating them from the *ikki* fortresses, but many of their horses quickly became mired in the soft mud of the "maze of reed beds and creeks."[116] As a further hindrance, the defenders had strung ropes across the waterways, which ensnared the horses' legs. Then, in the final act of the clearly carefully crafted defense plan, the defenders opened a dike and let the pent-up waters inundate the battlefield. Many more *samurai* were lost in the deluge, and the attack quickly developed into a fiasco. With a number of Oda generals dead and Shibata himself badly injured, the attack was halted and the survivors withdrew to safety.

Two years later, in July 1573, Nobunaga returned to try again. Bolstered by his success at Mount Hiei, he brought a considerable force, which included a good number of his favored *teppo*.[117] Nobunaga ordered his commanders Sakuma Nobumori and Hashiba Hideyoshi (later to be known as Toyotomi Hideyoshi) to mount a diversionary force attack from the west, while he himself assaulted from the front under the covering fire of the gunners.

But just as battle was joined, the clouds opened, releasing a torrential downpour on his army. Instantly the *teppo*, a powder-fired weapon notoriously sensitive to rain, was rendered ineffective, and Nobunaga found himself in a badly compromised, defensive position. Seizing their chance the *ikko-ikki* troops counter-attacked. They too fielded many *teppo*, but had wisely protected them during the storm. As soon as the the skies cleared, the *ikki* began to release volleys of fire at the defenseless Oda troops, narrowly missing Nobunaga himself with one of their bullets. He fell back, and made a half-hearted attempt to return to the attack, but was eventually forced to retreat.

The diversionary force, meanwhile, had enjoyed rather more success, capturing Yata, the southernmost of the Nagashima fortresses. However, their efforts were in vain, for they were forced to withdraw in the face of a counterattack by *ikki* troops.

In 1574, Oda Nobunaga launched his third and final attack on Nagashima. This time he brought up the ships of the *Kumano Suigun* under a gifted naval captain, Kuki Yoshitaka.[118] Yoshitaka's ships blockaded the sea entrances to Nagashima and opened a bombardment of the area, using cannon and fire arrows,[119] (an elementary form of rocket), against the *ikki*'s wooden watchtowers. This facilitated Nobunaga's capture of two key outer forts, Nakae and Yanagashima, which guarded the western approaches to the complex.

The defenders were gradually forced back into Ganshoji and Nagashima, but to all intents and purposes they were now isolated from outside sources of food, water, and other supplies. In the late summer, Nobunaga completed the final element of his cordon, a wooden wall from one outer fort to another. He then threw up a large wooden palisade around the fortresses and then set it aflame. All those inside perished in the conflagration,[120] final proof, if any were needed, of Nobunaga's driving and ruthless ambition.

Battle of Futamata

By 1572, perhaps due in part to the machinations of Yoshiaki, the Oda were engaged in struggles on many fronts—with the Asai and Asakura, the Takeda, and the Miyoshi. While we have focused much attention on the ventures of the Oda, it is important to remember that in the mid-1570s Nobunaga was but one of a number of powerful *daimyo* who harbored the same aspirations to conquer Japan. Takeda Shingen was just such a man. To date he had survived two plots to overthrow him, and was now perhaps the only *daimyo* with the necessary power and tactical skill to stop Oda Nobunaga.

Sieges of Taketenjin

Although he had previously enjoyed cordial relations with Tokugawa Ieyasu, forming a mutual agreement for control of the remaining Imagawa lands in Totomi and fighting in union against Yoshimoto's heir, Ujizane, the covenant was quickly broken, as Shingen realized that possession of the Tokugawa domain was crucial to his ambitions.[121] Once the threat of the Imagawa had been dispelled, Shingen determined on a move against his erstwhile ally, and take Totomi. The Takatenjin fortress was an important Tokugawa stronghold in that province and a natural target for Shingen. Beginning in 1571, he laid the first of series of sieges to reduce the castle. This first attempt ended in failure, as his efforts could make no impression on the defenses. In 1573, control of the clan passed to his son Katsuyori, and the following year, at a time when the Tokugawa were in a still-weakened state and their ally Oda Nobunaga was engaged against the *ikko-ikki*, Katsuyori mounted a second siege. Requests for reinforcement from the castle commander, Ogasawara Ujisuke, met with rebuff, and he capitulated. The capture of Taketenjin was a great loss for the Tokugawa clan, for many had considered it impregnable.[122] To further the displeasure and shame of his family, the Takeda rewarded Ujisuke lands at Omosu in Suruga province as a reward.

Battle of Mikatagahara

In late 1572 Shingen marched south from Shinano into Mikawa at the head of an army. He first invested Futamata, a cliff-top fortress overlooking the Tenryo River, planning to use this as a forward base for a move against Ieyasu's stronghold at Hamamatsu. Charging his son Katsuyori with the task of bringing it down, Shingen then pulled back to await developments. Katsuyori

Above: *Teppo ashigaru* (gun foot soldiers) aiming firearms, one with a support as used to help take the weight and/or to give a stable firing position particularly for use aboard ships. *(via Jo St. Mart)*

accomplished a quick submission by the simple and familiar expedient of denying the defenders water. His attention was drawn to the fact that the castle drew its water from the river using buckets lowered into the river on ropes from a tower. This he destroyed with unmanned rafts floated down the river. Denied their crucial water supply, the garrison had little option but to surrender.

them form up in a broad line facing the enemy. Late in the afternoon, with snow falling softly, he gave the order to fire. Shingen countered by unleashing Yamagata Masakage's famous "red devil brigade" of cavalry that scattered the Oda front line. Masakage's cavalry was then pulled back and a new set of horsemen led by Takeda Katsuyori and Obata Masamori initiated a fresh charge. Despite some valiant efforts by Ieyasu's officers, the Takeda cavalry began to press around his flanks.

With additional pressure from the main body of the Takeda army bearing on him, Ieyasu was forced to signal a retreat. Scurrying back to Hamamatsu with a small band of horsemen, Ieyasu now had to hastily engineer an elaborate ruse to prevent the fort from falling to the enemy. He employed a tactic popular at that time, which was to lure the enemy into a fort by making it appear abandoned. Once inside the walls carefully concealed troops would spring out, secure the gates, and slaughter the intruders. This is precisely what Ieyasu now did, except that he had no troops to conceal, since they were scattered along the line of retreat.

Baba Nobuharu and Yamagata Masakage, leading the pursuers, knew this game well and, on gaining the castle and seeing its open gates, balked at going inside. Without realizing it they had been the victim of an audacious double bluff, one that was quite possibly Ieyasu's salvation.[124] The two commanders elected to make camp for the night, and in the darkness they were attacked by a small Tokugawa force. Falling back, the Takeda were driven into a ravine,[125] where they were set upon and slain in droves. Those who survived the slaughter withdrew at first light.

The Death of Takeda Shingen

Shortly after this campaign, at the zenith of his power, the great Takeda leader, Shingen, the sole remaining *daimyo* with the military strength and confidence to challenge the might of Nobunaga and his allies, finally succumbed to what seems to have been a long-standing illness. According to the *Koyo Gunkan*,[126] in spring, while investing Ieyasu's Noda Castle, "On the 11th day of the 4th month around 1pm, Lord Shingen's condition took

In January 1573, with Futamata secured, Shingen returned to Mikawa with a body of 28,000 troops for a move against Hamamatsu. To oppose him, Tokugawa Ieyasu had fewer than half this number—8,000 of his own men reinforced by 3,000 sent by Oda Nobunaga.[123] Given this, defense would have perhaps been a wiser strategy, but underdogs had triumphed before, and Ieyasu boldly marched out to challenge the invaders.

On January 25, 1573, the two confronted each other on the Mikata Plain (Mikatagahara) just to the north of the Hamamatsu. To make full use of his *teppo*, Ieyasu had

a turn for the worst. His pulse became extremely rapid. On the night of the 12th, approximately 9pm, he developed an abscess/rash in his mouth, and 5 or 6 of his teeth fell out. He gradually weakened." Takeda died in May, not as popularly reported from a sniper's bullet, but some unconfirmed internal illness. The clan was robbed of their greatest leader, and even Uesugi Kenshin is reported to have wept on hearing the news.

Battle of Odani

In the late summer, the indubitably vital Oda Nobunaga moved to eliminate the niggling threat of the Asai clan in Omi, and their stronghold at Odani. Four times previously Odani had been the focus of fighting, and in this instance Nobunaga took 30,000 men to the castle, which was held by Atsuji Sadahide. The first Oda attack broke through the outer defenses, but further Oda efforts stalled in the face of solid resistance. Adding further difficulty, Asakura Yoshikage brought an army of 20,000 men from Echizen to nearby Otake Castle to threaten Nobunaga's flank. Although there was some indeterminate skirmishing, culminating in a sneak attack on the Oda camp at night, Yoshikage failed to press his advantage and Nobunaga wisely retreated. However, later that year Nobunaga had more success, and subsequently gave Toyotomi Hideyoshi a fief in the north of the province.

Battle of Nagashino

Despite the loss of their guiding light, the Takeda, now led by Katsuyori, continued to make gains against the Oda and Tokugawa. In March 1574 Katsuyori led an army into Mino Province and surrounded Akechi Castle. Nobunaga hastily dispatched a relief force under his eldest son Nobutada and Ikeda Nobuteru, but this arrived too late, as Akechi's commander had already surrendered. All roads now led to a more decisive clash of arms between the Takeda and their rivals. That event was not long in the coming and emerged as a key turning point in the course of the Sengoku jidai, an epochally significant clash of arms at Nagashino in Mikawa that would decide once and for all who would be master of

Tokaido. For this reason, Nagashino ranks alongside Sekigahara as the most famous and celebrated of all *samurai* battles.

In the late spring of 1575 Takeda Katsuyori embarked on a campaign to drive through Totomi and Mikawa and seize Kyoto, a crucial stepping-stone in his personal quest for supreme authority. Prior to marching out on May 30, Katsuyori had been machinating with certain of the Tokugawa officials, and one of these offered to open the gates of Okazaki Castle, Ieyasu's capital, to the Takeda army. This was a significant coup, for taking Okazaki would isolate Ieyasu from his ally Nobunaga and allow Katsuyori to destroy the Tokugawa with ease.

With half his army currently fighting to the north against the Uesugi clan, Katsuyori departed Shinano with only approximately 15,000 men. Furthermore, the treachery within the Tokugawa camp had by now been exposed and the traitor executed. With the element of

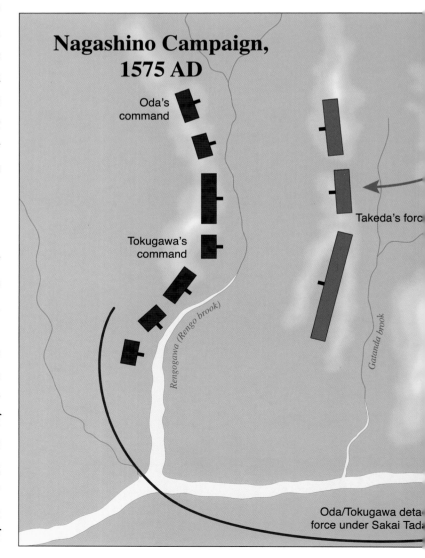

148

surprise denied him, Katsuyori elected to bypass Okazaki and invest Yoshida Castle to the south. Anticipating just such a move, the Tokugawa had reinforced the castle with 6,000 men; Katsuyori had no desire to see his campaign mired in a prolonged siege against a strong garrison, and therefore moved up the Toyokawa River toward Nagashino Castle, where he arrived on June 14.

Nagashino Castle was a small fortification, originally in the possession of the Suganuma family and taken from them by Tokugawa Ieyasu some two years previously. The castle garrison numbered barely 500 men. Katsuyori opened his attack on June 17, and for the ensuing five days made concerted efforts to bring down the castle. This cost him many casualties and certainly influenced a decision to change strategy, to try and starve the defenders out instead.

With the besieged garrison facing the grim prospect of a slow death from hunger, one of their number, a young

samurai named Torii Sune'emon, undertook a dangerous but vital mission, slipping through the enemy lines to convey an appeal for help to Nobunaga and Ieyasu, who were at Okazaki deciding on a course of action. Secure with a promise that help was on its way, Sune'emon set out back towards Nagashino to bring the good news to the castle occupants. But before he could recross the lines he was captured by the Takeda. Katsuyori promised him, as an alternative to being killed, clemency in return for an act of betrayal, which would have him passing word to the garrison that no relief could be expected. But when he was paraded in front of the castle walls, Sune'emon shouted instead words of encouragement and conveyed Nobunaga's pledge of help. For this brave act of defiance he was put to death.

Faced with the impending arrival of the Oda and Ieyasu armies from Okazaki, Katsuyori overruled his more reticent commanders and resolved to meet the enemy in the field. That opportunity quickly presented itself; by the 27th Nobunaga's army was halted about three miles southwest of Nagashino Castle at a place called Shitaragahara.

The terrain in this area precluded easy maneuver, being bounded and crossed by rivers and with wooded areas obstructing a clear line of sight. On the night of June 27/28 it rained heavily on the battlefield, and muddied the ground underfoot; the next day dawned hot and humid, and as the armies went about their preparations the hellish prospect of battling against men and heat alike in the cloying earth must have troubled many troops.

Although estimates vary of the relative strength of the opposing armies, most sources agree on a figure of about 38,000[127] for the combined Oda/Tokugawa army (30,000 and about 8,000, respectively). This total included about 1,000 *teppo*,[128] commanded by seven members of Nobunaga's personal bodyguard. Against them, the Takeda had 15,000 soldiers, one-third of whom were mounted. Importantly, the Takeda had their best commanders with the forward cavalry units, and it was these that generally bore the brunt of the first attacks.

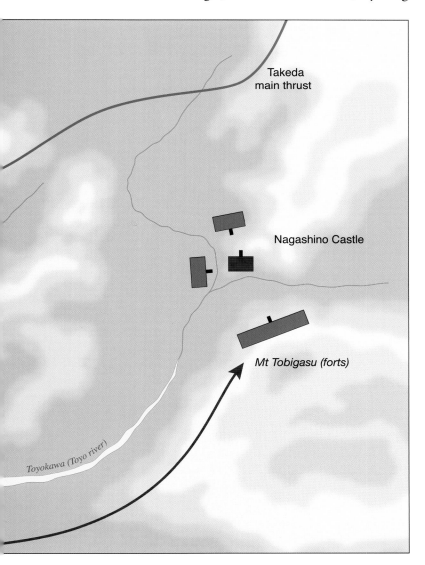

Takeda main thrust

Nagashino Castle

Mt Tobigasu (forts)

Toyokawa (Toyo river)

The duel between the mounted troops and gunners would emerge as the key facet of this battle. Nobunaga had already correctly assessed that before he could destroy the Takeda, he first had to defeat their cavalry. Furthermore, by this time "The more astute military barons (had) discovered that when using firearms the advantage lay with the army which could remain on the defensive behind breastworks."[129] Therefore, as part of his preparations, Nobunaga had a loose, zig-zagging palisade thrown up on hills facing the Takeda camps, fifty yards behind the natural obstacle of the Rengo, a small stream bisecting Shitaragahara.

The palisade was designed to provide some protection for Oda's *teppo* against the Takeda cavalry,[130] and had numerous breaks to allow free movement of counterattacking troops. Furthermore, it was sufficiently high to prevent a horse jumping it, while its position complicated movement on the already difficult terrain.

Fifty yards behind this fence, Nobunaga placed three ranks of *teppo*.

The remainder he formed in a line running north to south from Mount Gambo down to the Toyokawa River, a total distance of about a mile and a quarter.

Prior to the main battle, Nobunaga had "sent out small forces to make surprise raids on the enemy rear and to feint frontal attacks…and these tactics caused Takeda to order his center to move against Nobunaga's breastworks.[131]

For his part, Katsuyori had left 3,000 men to maintain the siege of Nagashino, and moved up four groups of 3,000 men, where they now stood poised at a woodline 200-400 yards away from the Oda across Shitaragahara. He planned to use three groups for the initial attack, and hold one in reserve.

At 6:00 AM, Katsuyori signalled for the attack to begin, and the three forward units charged out of the woodline at the Oda lines. However, on gaining the steep river banks the attack began to lose momentum, as the cavalry struggled across. The Oda *teppo-taisho* (gunnery commanders) exploited the fatal delay and ordered their men to begin laying down controlled volley fire,[132] each rank of gunners firing in rotation.[133] Fusillades of lead swept

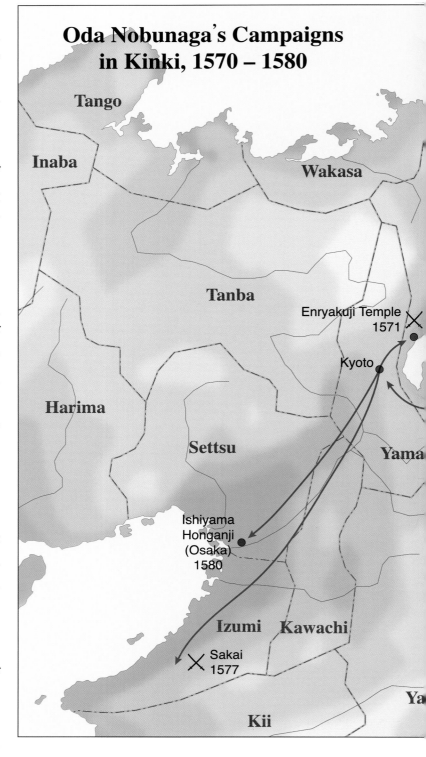

through the Takeda horsemen, killing a great number in their saddles; those few who managed to exploit the breaks in the palisade were quickly set upon by *ashigaru*.

Meanwhile, a force of 3,000 men was sent to the Takeda rear to attack the besiegers of Nagashino Castle. The Oda troops scored a quick victory and relieved the castle garrison. At Shitaragahara, neither side was able to gain the upper hand, and the battle surged and ebbed in much the same way for three hours, with successive waves

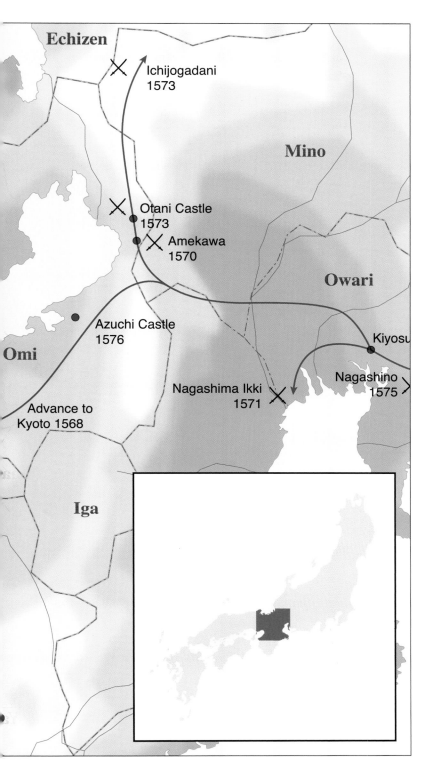

Ichijogadani
1573

Otani Castle
1573

Amekawa
1570

Azuchi Castle
1576

Kiyosu

Nagashino
1575

Nagashima Ikki
1571

Advance to
Kyoto 1568

and the battle broke down into individual combats as the Oda *samurai* came out from the behind the palisade to engage their attackers. At about 1:00 PM, after a full seven hours of relentless fighting, the Takeda began to retreat. Nobunaga ordered a pursuit and, despite the valiant attempts of Katsuyori's generals to fight a rearguard action, many of their *samurai* were overtaken and cut down.

Katsuyori hastily withdrew back towards his home provinces. In one day of fighting he had lost a third of his army, including many high-ranking commanders.[134] One salvation was that the forces that had been fighting in the north were present to cover Katsuyori's withdrawal, and therefore Nobunaga's pursuers broke off pursuit at the border. Nobunaga's casualties were by contrast comparatively light, at 6,000, and Takeda had been removed as a contender for power. Indeed, Nagashino was the high-water mark for the Takeda; after their mauling their power began to wane.

Siege of Iwamura

Standing in glaring contrast, the Oda's fortunes were firmly in the ascendant. With his eastern flank facing Mikawa secured, Oda Nobunaga could now consolidate his power around Kyoto. To this end he sent Shibata Katsuie and Maeda Toshiie to Echizen and Kaga and began to lay plans for a conquest of the western provinces. At the same time he moved to take other Takeda holdings. One of these was Iwamura Castle, in southeast Mino province (located in modern-day Gifu Prefecture). Akiyama Nobumoto had captured Iwamura for the Takeda in February 1572, during the latter's push into Totomi Province, the campaign that had culminated in the Battle of Mikatagahara.

Nobutomo was subsequently entrusted with its defense and it was he who faced Oda Nobutada, eldest son of Nobunaga, when he invested the castle in 1575 with a substantial army of 30,000. The Takeda clan, still reeling from the blow dealt them at Nagashino, could do little to oppose them, and sent no relief. Iwamura fell in December. Nobutomo was captured and executed and the castle was then given to Toyotomi Hideyoshi.

of Takeda cavalry charging forward, only to be repulsed by Oda gunfire. In mid-morning, on the northern flank, the outermost Oda unit suddenly fell back, allowing the Takeda to rush into the breach, only to be hit in the flank by another Oda unit. On the southern flank fierce hand-to-hand fighting was raging.

At this point Katsuyori committed his reserves and personal bodyguard to the battle, and they took the lead in the charge at the Oda lines. But this too was stopped,

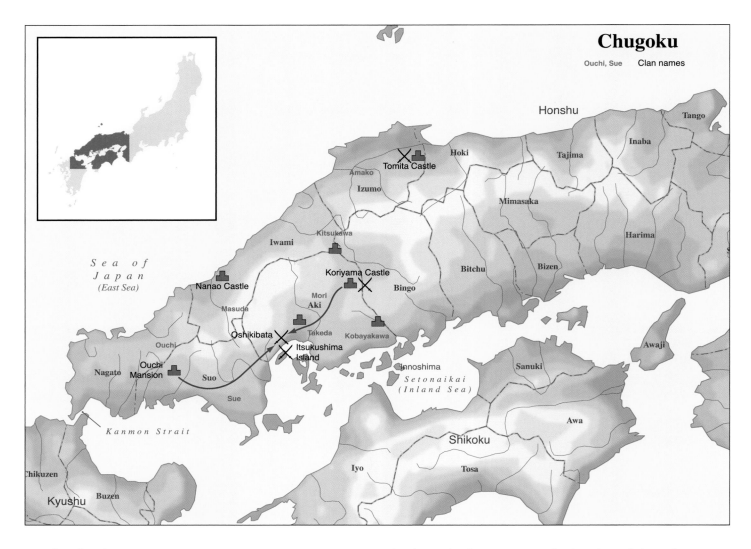

Chugoku

Ouchi, Sue   Clan names

Battle of Tedorigawa

With the successful recapture of Iwamura, Nobunaga reclaimed all of Mino Province. Cresting a wave of unprecedented success, he now faced a test that nearly proved to be his undoing. This came from the Hokuriku, where Uesugi Kenshin had made significant territorial gains since the final battle of Kawanakajima in 1571. In the year 1576, with his traditional enemies, Takeda Shingen and Hojo Ujiyasu, dead, Kenshin began to consider further expansion, and the possibility of mounting a challenge to Nobunaga. An opportunity presented itself in 1577, when Hatakeyama Yoshinori, one of the lords of Noto Province (modern-day Ishikawa) was overthrown and killed by one of his retainers, Cho Shigetsura, seemingly because the latter had declared for Oda Nobunaga. Kenshin was quick to take advantage of the ensuing unrest. He invaded Noto, seized Nanao from Yoshitaka, the new head of the Hatakeyama, and besieged Cho in Anamizu Castle. Shigetsura was put to

death, and after securing the loyalty of the other Noto warriors, Kenshin moved into Kaga. From here he was within striking distance of Nobunaga and Kyoto.

Recognizing the threat that this development posed, Nobunaga marched an army up to Echizen, where he linked up with his generals, Shibata Katsuie and Maeda Toshiie. Their joint command numbered about 50,000 men. Kenshin had gathered his army at Matsuo Castle, near the Tedori River in Kaga, and across from which Nobunaga now arrayed his forces. With large numbers of *teppo* and cannon[135] at his disposal it seemed likely that Nobunaga would content himself with engaging the enemy at long range, in a protracted siege that Kenshin was unlikely to endure. Thus, the wily Kenshin elected to try and beat his enemy another way, by tempting him into launching an attack. To carry this off Kenshin divided his forces, dispatching a small force to move further up the river and thus appearing to weaken his defenses.

Nobunaga fell for the ruse; believing that he had been gifted a perfect opportunity to attack, at night he ordered his forces across the river against Matsuo. Kenshin chose this moment to spring his trap. The river's floodgates were suddenly opened, releasing a great deluge of water into the channel. Against the sudden torrent the Oda attack broke down. Uesugi's forward units were able to repel the attackers, while inflicting heavy casualties, and forcing them to withdraw back towards Omi.

The defeat at Tedorigawa caused a major crisis in confidence in the Oda camp. Consequently, Nobunaga, in a state of deep shock, halted his operations in Noto, Kaga, and Etchu Province areas. But at this opportune moment, with his forces preparing to march on Kyoto, and the Oda camp in paralysis, Uesugi Kenshin died (most likely of complications relating to his great fondness for drink). As some have speculated, had Kenshin begun his march on Kyoto earlier, the outcome may have been very different.

Battle of Kozuki

Such conjecture aside, by December of that year Nobunaga had recovered his shaken confidence and taken up the banner of unification again. His generals Toyotomi Hideyoshi and Akechi Mitsuhide now began bring pressure to bear on the provinces in the Chugoku and Kanto regions, in advance of a move against western Honshu, Shikoku, and Kyushu.[136]

In the Chugoku, Nobunaga still faced a powerful opponent in the Môri clan, which under Môri Motonari had succeeded in subjugating first Aki and then its neighboring provinces, until by 1575 he controlled virtually the entire region. The Môri clan then chose to throw its weight behind another Nobunaga enemy, the *ikko-ikki*, besieged in the Ishiyama Honganji in Settsu. In August 1576 Oda Nobunaga had enlisted Kuki Yoshitaka to set up a blockade of Osaka Bay and disrupt the fortress's supply lines, but in a resultant battle[137] off Kizugawaguchi against a superior Môri fleet, the Oda blockade was lifted. The Môri were now able to provision the complex by sea and, consequently, in 1577, Oda Nobunaga ordered Hashiba (Toyotomi) Hideyoshi to expand into Chugoku

to dilodge the troublesome clan. For this campaign, the Oda were supported by a force under Amako Katsuhisa, who through this union with Nogunaga sought to re-establish the Amako family as a power in western Japan.

As the Oda pressed forward into Harima, they came up on Kozuki Castle, a Môri stronghold at that time under the control of Akamatsu Masanori. In December, after he had refused all demands to yield, Oda set his troops against Kozuki's outer defenses. Later that month, the Ukita clan sent a relief force in an attempt to break the siege, but this was intercepted and defeated in a bitter fight. With the relief force driven off, Hideyoshi again demanded the surrender of the castle. The demand was again rebuffed, and so Hideyoshi ordered the castle to be taken. He eventually succeeded at a great cost to both sides, including an estimated 1,000 of the castle garrison. Masanori committed suicide, and Kozuki was entrusted to the Amako. Over the next few years, possession oscillated between different owners. In 1578 the castle was captured by the Ukita, only for it to be regained by the Amako and then lost shortly after to the Môri.

Siege of Miki[138]

Another flashpoint in the struggle against the Môri was Miki Castle, also in Harima, and a crucial link in the supply chain to the embattled defenders of Ishiyama Honganji in neighboring Settsu. Miki was at that time under the command of Bessho Nagaharu, who previously had been an ally of Nobunaga. The Môri were determined not to lose Miki, so for two years the castle was provisioned by sea under the protection of the powerful Môri fleet, while Bessho grimly held out.

In 1578, Kuki Yoshitaka returned with a fleet for another effort to take the waters at the entrance to Osaka Bay, the outcome of which was the second Battle of Kizugawaguchi.[139] Facing a fleet of 600 Môri ships, Yoshitaka fielded six recently constructed and advanced "battleships" (*o-adakebune*)[140] armored with iron and equipped with cannon, in addition to a combination of small (*kobaya*), medium (*sekibune*), and large (*adakebune*) craft. The introduction of these technologies seems to have swung the balance, for several of the Môri vessels were burned and sunk, and Yoshitaka's fleet ultimately emerged triumphant.[141]

Then, in 1580, with Môri fortunes in terminal decline, Toyotomi Hideyoshi invested Miki with a force of 7,000 men, beginning with the forts on its outer perimeter. The Môri supply effort had long since ceased, and with the defenders in a weakened state, Hideyoshi was finally able to blockade the castle from all sides. Accepting that further resistance was futile, Nagaharu agreed to surrender the castle. Although he, his brother Tomoyuki, and their retainer Goto Motokuni were all forced to commit *seppuku*, the remaining members of the garrison were spared. Partly as a consequence of the loss of Miki, Nobunaga was now able to conclude the long siege of the Honganji. A blockade was quickly enforced, the supply lines were broken, and without means to continue their brave defense the defenders of Honganji capitulated.

Siege of Matsukura

Following the death of Uesugi Kenshin in 1578, the

Below: Toyotomi Hideyoshi, one of the greatest *samurai* leaders, whose reign is named after his castle in Kyoto, Momoyama. *(via Clive Sinclaire)*

Uesugi domain descended into a year-long civil war, known as the *Otate no Ran*. Taking advantage of the Uesugi's feud, Shibata Katsuie, who was by this time master of Echizen,[142] embarked on a course to conquer the Uesugi and ultimately the entire Hokuriku region. With Sassa Narimasa, another of Oda Nobunaga's allies in the Hokuriku Region, he began a drive for the borders of Echigo. By 1581 they had Toyama Castle and were entrenched in Etchu, and from there set about eliminating local Uesugi and the remnants of *ikko-ikki* resistance in Kaga. Shibata Katsuie finally succeeded in taking their last strongholds at Torigoe and Futoge in early 1582, following which "300 men of the ikko-ikki were crucified."[143]

Uesugi Kagekatsu immediately recognized the mounting threat to his domain, and forthwith reinforced Uozu Castle with a number of his important retainers. In May 1582, the Oda attacked both this and Matsukura Castle. After a bitter struggle, in the first week of June Uozu fell and the Uesugi were thereby expunged as a force in Etchu.

The Siege of Takamatsu

In 1582 Hideyoshi launched an expedition to the Chugoku region, as part of his efforts to subjugate the

Above: Toyotomi Hideyoshi is said to have been born the son of a foot soldier—but is seen as a great hero who ushered in a golden age. *(via Clive Sinclaire)*

western provinces (detailed below). In April, he invaded Bitchu Province and moved to dislodge the Môri clan from Takamatsu Castle, considered by the latter as vital to the defense of Bitchu and Bingo, and thus Aki. The castle was originally built by the Mimura family, and controlled by their vassals, the Ishikawa family; both these families had been eliminated by the Môri when they took Bitchu province and Takamatsu in 1575. The Môri had entrusted the castle to their vassal Shimizu Muneharu, a close relative of the Ishikawa, and after a month of siege he showed no inclination to give up his charge.

Hideyoshi now presented Muneharu with tempting terms for surrender, offering him Bitchu Province as a reward for capitulation. Muneharu refused, and so, acting on the advice of his chief lieutenant, Kuroda Yoshitaka, Hideyoshi employed a clever strategy to weaken the stubborn Muneharu, and hasten his surrender. Near to the low-lying castle runs the Ashimori River; by diverting its waters with dykes, his engineers were able to inundate the castle.[144] Hideyoshi also constructed towers on barges, from which his arquebusiers could pour down fire on the defenders, who themselves were unhindered by the flooding. The battle very soon escalated, with

reinforcements for the defense from the Môri, and also Kikkawa and Kobayakawa clans. Faced with the prospect of a tough and lengthy struggle, Hideyoshi sent his own request for reinforcements to Nobunaga, a seemingly innocent enough request from a general to his commander-in-chief, but with momentous consequences.

The Assassination of Oda Nobunaga

In 1582, Oda Nobunaga was at the pinnacle of his power and enjoying an uninterrupted period of success. Toyotomi Hideyoshi was reducing the Môri clan; Niwa Nagahide was preparing for an invasion of Shikoku; Takigawa Kazumasu was observing the Hojo clan from Kozuke and Shinano Provinces; and Shibata Katsuie was already installed in Echigo Province, the former domain of the Uesugi clan. Thus, after nearly a century-and-a-half of political instability and warfare, Japan seemed to be on the verge of unification under one man. Nothing, it seemed, could interrupt the realization of his ambition. But at this juncture a startling and unexpected series of

Above: Kuroda Yoshitaka was a *daimyo* of the late Sengoku Period through to the early Edo Period. He was the chief strategist under Toyotomi Hideyoshi. *(British Museum/Jo St Mart)*

events now served to upset this state of affairs, which would act as a catalyst for renewed and bloody power struggles between Nobunaga's most important commanders, Toyotomi Hideyoshi, Tokugawa Ieyasu and Shibata Katsuiie, and Akechi Mitsuhide.

Events unfolded rapidly during Toyotomi Hideyoshi's siege of Takamatsu Castle in 1582. Nobunaga received a request for assistance from Hideyoshi, and quickly despatched reinforcements[145] under Akechi Mitsuhide to the west. Planning to follow Mitsuhide to Takamatsu, Nobunaga was *en route* when he elected to rest for the night at Honno-ji temple in Kyoto. With him were only a few dozen personal servants and bodyguards. Seizing on Nobunaga's perilously vulnerable situation, Akechi Mitsuhide wheeled round his army and marched it back

towards Kyoto, where at dawn on June 20 he surrounded Honno-ji and then put it to the torch. Nobunaga recognized that his small band had little option but to surrender. Instead, he committed *seppuku* together with his son and heir, Nobutada.[146] Thus, the first of the three great unifiers of Japan met with his end.

Battle of Yamazaki

There were predictably speedy attempts to fill the vacuum created by Nobunaga's untimely death. The usurper, Mitsuhide, immediately began to try to cement his position by convincing Oda vassals to recognize him as the new master of former Oda territories.[147] He also began sending entreaties to the imperial court to legitimize his position and win acceptance.

Upon recieving the news of the *coup d'etat*, Toyotomi Hideyoshi agreed an immediate peace treaty with the Môri,[148] mindful to keep Nobunaga's death a secret. He then led his troops on a forced march towards Kyoto, maintaining an exhausting pace of 20 to 30 miles each day.[149] In Sakai he met up with Niwa Nagahide and Oda Nobutaka, and less than two weeks after the coup had toppled Nobunaga, Hideyoshi's army was nearing Kyoto.

Akechi Mitsuhide controlled two castles, Shoryuji and Yodo, in an area called Yamazaki (in present-day Kyoto Prefecture), but only a relatively small army with which to take on the might of the allied force. Attempts to bolster this with troops recruited locally were unsuccessful, and so too was an appeal to Hosokawa Fujitaka. Mitsuhide quickly realized that his odds against the allied force were better on an open field of battle than bottled up inside his fortresses. Mitsuhide therefore moved south of Shoryuji, to Yamazaki, to confront the advancing enemy. Anchoring his right wing on the Yodo river and the left on a wooded peak called Tennozan, he had perhaps assumed this locale would prevent easy maneuver.

Hideyoshi, who was now in the vicinity, concluded that by gaining Tennozan, he could control the road to Kyoto. While he himself moved out to Yamazaki with the bulk of the allied army, a detachment under Nakagawa Kiyohide was sent to secure Tennozan. At Yamazaki, Mitsuhide waited with his forces behind the narrow Enmyoji-gawa.

During the night of July 1/2 his camp was infiltrated by Hideyoshi's *ninja*, who carried out acts of arson and spread fear and confusion. On the following morning, Hideyoshi's men began to form up across the Enmyoji-gawa from the Akechi camp. Meanwhile, Mitsuhide sent a detachment across the river against the allied positions established on Tennozan, but the Akechi troops were driven back under a hail of fire from Hideyoshi's *teppo*. Hideyoshi now ordered his own right flank to cross the river, and into Mitsuhide's front lines. The left wing was then thrown in, with additional support from atop Tennozan, and together they made short work of the Akechi troops. Those who were not slaughtered fled back in the direction of Shoryuji. Mitsuhide himself fled

Toyotomi Hideyoshi (1537–1598)

Toyotomi Hideyoshi was born in a small village where his father, a former *ashigaru*, owned a small farm. Well known locally as a cheeky boy with a monkey-like face, Hideyoshi refused to follow his father and, instead, secured a job as *betto* (groom) to no less a person than Oda Nobunaga. The latter was so impressed that he encouraged the youngster to become a proper soldier, which Hideyoshi did with enthusiasm, rising rapidly, until by 1582 he was commanding an army.

He was on campaign when he heard of Nobunaga's assassination and immediately made peace with his opponent before marching home. There he found and defeated the assassin Mitsuhide's army, although the latter escaped, only to meet an ignominious death at the hands of bandits.

Hideyoshi now took charge and gradually brought Nobunaga's former followers under his flag, either by negotiation or by defeating them in battle. Following the Battle of Sizugatake (1583) his only remaining opponent was Tokugawa Ieyasu. After fighting each other to a draw at Nagatuke (1584) they became firm friends, Ieyasu marrying Hideyoshi's sister.

Hideoshi then became an excellent administrator and was considered to be the leading Japanese of his time. After his death he was declared a *Shinto* deity, being given the name *Hokoku* (wealth of the nation).

Hideyoshi's legacy can be seen in many aspects of Japanese society. He introduced a class structure, imposed restrictions on travel between provinces, banned weapons for farmers, and conducted surveys of land and production that formed the basis for systematic taxation. He also influenced the culture of Japan, particularly the tea ceremony. In the political sphere, he set up a governmental system that balanced out the most powerful *daimyo*. He was given the title *taiko* (from which the modern word tycoon is derived) and died in 1598.

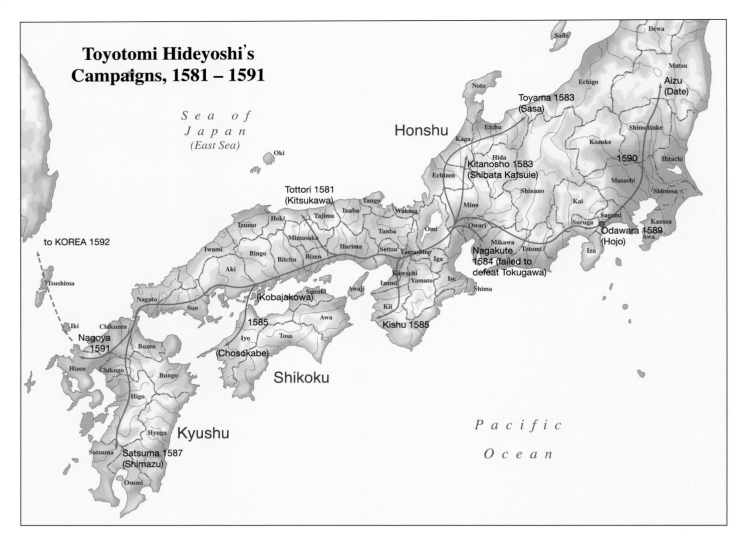

Toyotomi Hideyoshi's Campaigns, 1581 – 1591

towards Sakamoto, but was captured and put to death by bandits in the town of Ogurusu, thus bringing and end to his brief and inglorious reign. His head was cut off and presented in front of Nobunaga's grave. The rest of the Akechi army, now under his cousin Akechi Mitsuharu, fought and were defeated by the pursuing Hori Hidemasa, a Toyotomi ally, at Uchidehama.

While the defeat of the Akechi avenged the death of Oda Nobunaga, it also created a power struggle that would soon draw the Toyotomi, Shibata Katsuiie, and Tokugawa Ieyasu into open conflict.

At the time of Nobunaga's death in late 1582, Tokugawa Ieyasu was near Osaka. He journeyed back to Mikawa, avoiding Akechi troops that were trying to find and kill him. One week after he arrived in Mikawa, Ieyasu's army marched out to avenge Mitsuhide. But they were too late, for Hideyoshi had already defeated the Akechi at Yamazaki. Shibata Katsuiie was tied up battling the Uesugi in Etchu, and like Ieyasu was thus denied the

opportunity to make a quick response to the incident at Honno-ji.

Hideyoshi's quick thinking in the aftermath was critical, for it elevated him to the first rank of Nobunaga's retainers. This must have further rankled with Shibata who, as Sadler points out, had been Nobunaga's long-term ally, and now found himself in a position of inferiority to Hideyoshi, a mere vassal who had risen from the ranks.

The two potential flashpoints that arose after the death of Nobunaga were, first, the awkward and potentially divisive question of the succession, and, second, the partitioning of former Oda lands. The power vacuum provided ample opportunity for land grabs. Hideyoshi Ieyasu, who as "…lord of five provinces (was) in a fine strategic position for profiting by any other favorable circumstances that might arise,"[150] promptly invaded Kai and took control. When Hojo Ujimasa responded by sending his much larger army into Shinano and then into Kai province, Ieyasu brokered a settlement that left him with both these provinces, while the Hojo took control of Kazusa Province.

In the summer the main power brokers met at Kiyosu to debate the matter of the succession. There were two clear contenders, each with his supporters. Hideyoshi and Nobunaga's second son Nobukatsu declared for Nobunaga's infant grandson, Samboshi,[151] and Shibata for the other candidate, Nobunaga's third son, Nobutaka. At the same gathering, the various interested parties resolved the partitioning over former Oda lands, with Hideyoshi taking Yamashiro, Tamba, and Kwatchi, while Katsuie had Echizen and the northern part of Omi. But the question over who should succeed went unanswered, and around each contender gathered a faction of supporters.

Neither of the two other powerful clans, the Uesugi or Tokugawa, could be drawn into declaring their allegiance, perhaps biding time for events to unfold. Yet by the time that fighting broke out in December 1582,

both Katsuie and Hideyoshi had gathered substantial support.

In the first significant action, Nobutaka was easily defeated when he made an ill-judged attempt to attack in winter from Echizen. In the early spring of 1583 Hideyoshi moved on Ise, and subsequently Katsuie dispatched his son Shibata Katsutoyo into northern Omi to reduce Hideyoshi's forward outposts there. After some months of maneuvering, the Shibata ally Sakuma Morimasa had taken Hideyoshi's Iwasakiyama and was attempting to capture Shizugatake, in Omi Province, near Lake Biwa, when he was suddenly surprised by Hideyoshi and soundly defeated.[152] Katsuie committed suicide in Echizen when news of the defeat reached him.

Battles of Komaki and Nagakute

By 1584, Nobukatsu's relationship with Hideyoshi had soured, and he began seeking an alliance with the Tokugawa Ieyasu. Although he had thus far watched this succession struggle from the sidelines, Ieyasu now chose to take up Nobukatsu's cause. It is difficult to gauge if

Below: Tokugawa Ieyasu (at center left) at the Battle of Sekigahara in 1600. *(British Museum/Jo St Mart)*

this was a calculated move by Ieyasu to test the resolve of Hideyoshi and draw him into the field, brought on by feelings of enmity, or something besides. Although his motive is unclear, Ieyasu nonetheless risked possible annihilation by leading an army into Owari province, where he established a position at Komaki. Hideyoshi responded by promptly marching his own an army into Owari, marking the start of what would come to be known as the Komaki Campaign.

The two sides postured and skirmished around Komaki, where each had built extensive defensive works,[153] before engaging at the only battle of real significance during this short war, at Nagakute, in present-day Aichi. After months of unproductive marches and maneuvering, a stalemate had developed at Komaki, which Hideyoshi sought to break by dispatching Ikeda Nobuteru with 12,000 men around the Tokugawa army, at Mikawa. However, the local farmers reported these movements to Ieyasu, and he hastily led a 9,000-strong army out to intercept them. In the event, the Ikeda army was quickly chased off. When Hideyoshi learned of the defeat at his headquarters, he led out an army to attack the Tokugawa, but Ieyasu elected to avoid contact and ultimately returned to Komaki.

Oda Nobukatsu subsequently made his peace with Hideyoshi, at a stroke removing the cause of conflict between Ieyasu and Hideyoshi. Without a cause for further fighting, Ieyasu went to Osaka the following spring and reconciled himself with Hideyoshi. Nonetheless, the Komaki Campaign had made Hideyoshi wary of Ieyasu, and henceforth, with the exception of the Odawara Campaign in 1590, the Tokugawa took no further part in Hideyoshi's campaigns.

The Western Campaign

In the year 1582, the western provinces saw the first facets of the great drive to reunify Japan. These were undertaken by Toyotomi Hideyoshi, whose exploits up to this time in the central provinces have been touched on in the preceding section; it is suffice to say here that he was by this time reaching the pinnacle of his power, and would shortly to seek the title of *shogun*.

Hideyoshi's first target was to be Shikoku, where the emerging power was the Chosogabe clan. Thus far we have heard little about the battles in southern Shikoku—the province of Tosa—separated from the more prosperous north by an imposing mountain range, and where power focused on the long but narrow Kochi Plain abutting the Pacific Ocean. In the mid-16th century Motochika Chosogabe had emerged to challenge the authority of the established Tosa clans, the Ichijo, Motoyama, and Aki. Under Chosogabe, the Motochika began to assert their independence from the Ichijo, to whom they were vassals. In 1562 he defeated the Motoyama at the Battle of Asakura (Motoyama) and thereafter built his power base on the Kochi Plain through alliances with other local families.

While remaining ostensibly loyal to the Ichijo over the next few years, Motochika's power grew. He defeated the Aki in 1569, and in 1573 finally turned on the Ichijo. Seizing on suggestions of dissonance among the retainers of Ichijo Kanesada, Motochika marched on the Ichijo's headquarters at Nakamura and in 1573 Kanesada fled to Bungo, defeated. Although the Otomo later supplied Kanesada with a fleet, with which he returned to Shikoku, this was quickly crushed by Chosokabe. With the conquest of Tosa complete, Chosogabe turned north, in 1580 leading some 30,000 men into Iyo and forcing encumbent *daimyo* Kono Michinao to flee to Bungo. Chosokabe pressed onwards; in 1582 he stepped up ongoing raids into Awa, and then defeated Sogo Masayasu decisively at Nakatomigawa. By 1583, Chosokabe troops had subdued all of Awa and neighboring Sanuki, and Motochika's ambitious plan to rule all of Shikoku was near fruition. However, in mid-1585 Hideyoshi brought a large host over to Shikoku and accomplished a quick victory over the Chosokabe army, and Motochika accepted his rule.

The Battle of Okitanawate

With the subjugation of Shikoku accomplished, Hideyoshi could now focus his efforts on Kyushu, where numerous enemies promised stiff resistance. Hizen, in northwestern Kyushu, was divided among many daimyo.

Two of the clans contesting land titles were the Arima, who controlled the Shimabara Peninsula, and the Ryuzoji, formerly retainers of the Shoni family until Ryuzoji Takanobu overthrew his masters in 1553. In the late 1570s Takanobu then began expanding into the Shimabara Peninsula. He enjoyed a strong advantage in numbers over the Arima, yet the Arima clan had connections with Jesuit missionaries and through them secured quantities of Portuguese weapons and ships, balancing the field a little more evenly. Even so, in 1582 Harunobu lost his important Shimabara

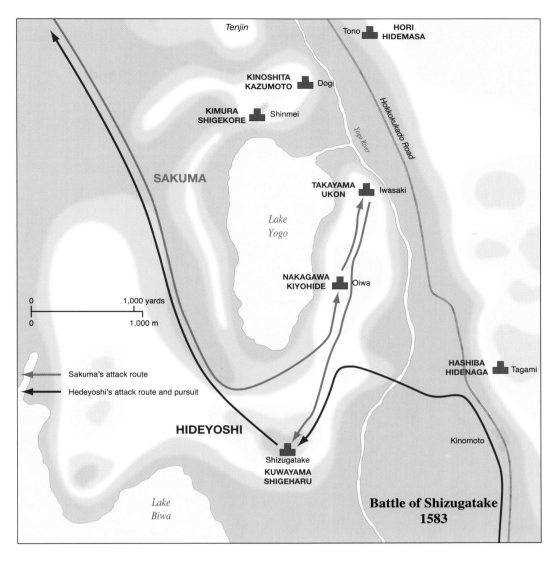

Castle and was soon reduced to holding a thin strip of the peninsula. In a much-weakened state, he turned for succor to the Shimazu clan, which was at the time at war with the Ryuzoji in Higo Province. The Shimazu responded to these entreaties by dispatching a force under Shimazu Iehisa to Shimabara.[154]

Eyeing the chance to neutralize both threats in one strike, in 1584 Ryuzoji Takanobu marched onto the Shimabara Peninsula at the head of a 25,000-strong army. Against him Arima and Shimazu could together field only 3,000 men. On May 5 the two antagonists met at Okitanawate. Advancing in two columns, the Ryuzoji were held fast in front of the allied positions. Exploiting a moment in the confused melee, a flying column of Shimazu suddenly pushed at Takanobu's position. Seeing this, Takanobu seems to have supposed, mistakenly, that his own men had turned on each other and, fatally, made no attempt to safeguard himself. By the time he had

realized his mistake, the enemy swordsmen were upon him. His guards were quickly overwhelmed and Takanobu himself was killed. As news of the loss of their leader spread through the Ryuzoji ranks, panic broke out and, although the Ryuzoji commanders struggled in vain to restore some discipline, their troops fled the field. For the Ryuzoji, the defeat at Okitanawate marked the eclipse of their once powerful position in northern Kyushu.

The Siege of Iwaya

By the mid-1580s, the subjugation of the Ryuzoji had been successfully accomplished, and the Shimazu clan could claim to hold sway over most of Kyushu.[155] However, they had as yet not made significant inroads in Bungo, Buzen, and Chikuzen, where the Otomo clan was all-powerful. Soon they began deep probes into Otomo territory, one of which, a drive into Chikuzen Province in 1586, culminated in the Siege of Iwaya.

Iwaya castle, in the former political and administrative center of Dazaifu (in present-day Fukuoka Prefecture), was the stronghold of an important Otomo ally, Takahashi Shigetane, whose family had received it as a reward from the Otomo in 1555. Shimazu Yoshihisa, the *daimyo* of Satsuma, attacked Iwaya with a force of 15,000, holding a massive numerical advantage over Shigetane's 760 defenders. Unsurprisingly, the castle fell after two weeks, during which time it was witness to much bravery on the part of the outnumbered defenders. Much of this, it appears, was inspired by the personal heroics of Shigetane himself, who took his own life rather than suffer the humiliation of capture.

The Battle of Hetsugigawa

In November 1586 Shimazu Yoshihisa renewed efforts to bring all of Kyushu under his control, marching a powerful army of 82,000 men far into Otomo-controlled Bungo. There were three columns, one led by Yoshihisa, and the others by Iehisa and Yoshihiro. This force began to threaten Funai, which prompted the intervention of Toyotomi Hideyoshi, who dispatched a large body of reinforcements across the *Hoya-kaikyo*[156] under Chosokabe Motochika[157] and Sengoku Hisahide, bringing the allied strength up to 7,000. Despite Hideyoshi's orders to maintain a defensive posture,[158] and Chosokabe's appeal to exercise caution, Hisahide and Otomo Yoshimune resolved to strike out and attempt the relief of Toshimitsu, an Otomo castle that was under seige by the Shimazu general, Niiro Tadamoto. But when the allied force arrived at Toshimitsu they discovered it had already fallen. A battle with the Shimazu army under Shimazu Yoshihiro and Iehisa ensued at Hetsugigawa, and during this the hapless pair were fooled again, this time into launching an attack in the immediate aftermath of a feigned retreat. The allies were soundly defeated and put to flight, leaving many casualties on the battlefield. For the Chosokabe it was a disaster, presaging their decline and eventual fall. Among the many dead were Chosogabe Nobuchika, Motochika's eldest son, and many of the Chosogabe retainers. For the Shimazu it was an unqualified success. The Chosogabe and Sengoku

armies abandoned their campaign in Bungo.

With this victory, Shimazu Yoshihisa was, albeit briefly, peerless in all of Kyushu. His reign was nevertheless a short-lived one. Events elsewhere, which are subsequently explained, had conspired to bring Toyotomi Hideyoshi to a position of almost unassailable power. His mission to dominate and unify Japan at the end of the Sengoku jidai had already led to the subjugation of much of Honshu and Shikoku, and with his eye on the ultimate goal of invading the continent, Hideyoshi turned his attention to Kyushu, southernmost of the main Japanese islands and a key staging point for this endeavor.

On January 20, 1587, the first element of a huge Toyotomi army[159] arrived in Kyushu for a decisive campaign of conquest. Led by Toyotomi's half-brother Hashiba Hidenaga, these 60,000 men were followed by Kobayakawa Takakage and the Môri, who had with them a further 90,000. Thus together they commanded about 150,000 men, the mightiest army ever seen in Japan. Faced with this, the Shimazu quit Funai on January 24 and rapidly withdrew south, allowing Hidenaga to proceed with an advance along the eastern coast of the island toward Kagoshima, the center of the Shimazu clan's domains. Hideyoshi himself arrived with yet another 30,000 men in February and secured the submission of most of the warlords of the provinces conquered by the Shimazu in the

Shimazu Yoshihisa (1533–1611)

Shimazu Yoshihisa became chief of the Shimazu in 1566, whereupon he embarked on an ambitious program to unify Kyushu under his control. Satsuma had been secured by 1572, but Yoshihisha was then faced by the man who would become his greatest rival, Ito Yoshisuke, although Yoshihisa was victorious at Kigasakihara, Takabaru (1576), and Kamiya (1578), after which the Ito ceased to be a threat.

Yoshihisa's successes continued until victory over the Ryuzoji clan (1584) left him on the verge of realizing his dream of unification. But Toyotomi Hideyoshi then sent a 200,000-strong army against him and the Shimazu were driven back to Satsuma province, Yoshihisa surrendering in June 1587. He became a Buddhist monk and died in 1611.

past decade, including the Akizuki, Arima, Goto, Nabeshima, Omura, and Ryuzoj, while his forces marched towards Kagoshima on the opposite side of the island.

The Battle of Sendaigawa

The Sendai River north of Kagoshima is the last natural obstacle in front of Kagoshima. Here, in June 1587, the final act of the war in the west was played out. Considering the vast numerical superiority that he enjoyed, Hideyoshi's advance to this point was protracted, but for even the most cautious observer the result must have seemed a foregone conclusion. The approaches to Kagoshima lay open, and Toyotomi troops were pouring into Satsuma. On June 6 Hideyoshi and Hidenaga[160] met a 5,000-strong Shimazu army, led by Niiro Tadamoto, near the river. Despite being vastly outnumbered Niiro led his men in a brave charge against the Toyotomi force, and even engaged the famous warrior Kato Kiyomasa in personal combat before retreating under cover of night. Outnumbered and facing imminent defeat, on June 14 Shimazu Yoshihisa surrendered. Fortunately for them, although Yoshihisa was obliged to retire, his family retained the provinces of Satsuma and Osumi, and part of Hyuga. Most of the other defeated clans were not so fortunate, as Toyotomi carved up Kyushu between his generals.

The Northern Provinces

With the surrender of the Shimazu of Satsuma in 1587, Toyotomi Hideyoshi completed his campaign of conquest in Kyushu. So far we have heard nothing of the northern provinces of Japan—Dewa and Mutsu, in the Tokoku region. During the Sengoku Period various clans ruled different parts of the region. In Mutsu, the two most powerful were the Date and the Hatekayama. After ascending to headship in the 1560s, Hatekayama Yoshitsugu consistently clashed with the Date and another of the Mutsu clans, the Ashina. In November 1585, Yoshitsugu attempted to mediate with Terumune, but then followed this by attempting to spirit him away to his Nihonmatsu Castle. Date Masamune, Terumune's son, immediately took pursuit, and caught up with the

Above: Shimazu Yoshihisa was probably the greatest 16th century Kyushu general, although he was lucky to have the martial skills of the Satsuma warriors at his command, and the outstanding military abilities of his brothers to help him. *(British Museum/Jo St Mart)*

hostage party by the Abukuma River. In the ensuing fight, Terumune and the most of his kidnappers were killed, while Yoshitsugu managed to return to Nihonmatsu castle with a few survivors.

Open war now broke out between the Date and Hatakeyama, with the Hatakeyama drawing on support from the Satake, Ashina, Soma, and other local clans. These allies, who together mustered some 30,000 troops, marched to within half a mile of Masamune's Motomiya Castle (which was in modern-day Fukushima), and prepared for an assault. Masamune, having only 7,000 warriors of his own, opted for a defensive strategy based on the series of forts that guarded the approaches to Motomiya. The fighting began on November 17, and from the outset things began to go badly for Masamune. Three of the vital outer forts were taken, and one of his chief retainers, Moniwa Yoshinao, was killed in a duel with an opposing commander. The attackers then started a drive towards the Seto River, the last obstacle between them and Motomiya. Masamune attempted to rebuff them at the Hitadori Bridge, but was driven back, and so pulled his remaining forces back within Motomiya's walls, and prepared for a last stand.

Night passed quietly and, seemingly by some act of providence, when the defenders looked out the next morning, the bulk of the enemy contingent had vanished. As it transpires, sometime during the previous few days, Satake Yoshishige had received word that his lands in Hitachi were under attack by the Satomi, and during the previous night, marched his sizeable army hurriedly away. This so weakened the allies that they felt unable to bring down Motomiya Castle, and the remainder of the allied army had quit the locale by the end of the day.

A few years later, in 1589, Masamune defeated the Soma, and next sought a conclusion to the decades-old rivalry between his clan and the Ashina. To this end, he bribed an important Ashina retainer, Inawashiro Morikuni, over to his side. Taking advantage of the confusion this defection caused, he assembled a powerful force of 23,000 men and marched straight for the Ashina's headquarters at Kurokawa.

They ran into the 16,000-strong Ashina forces at Suriagehara on June 5. The Ashina began well, but were compelled to retreat when Masamune himself led a charge against faltering Ashina ranks, breaking them. Unfortunately for the Ashina, the Date forces had destroyed their avenue of escape, a bridge over the Nitsubashi River; those who did not drown attempting to swim to safety were mercilessly slaughtered. It is estimated that during this bloody, decisive battle something like 2,300 enemy heads were taken.

Masamune now pressed on to Kurokawa itself, which fell easily. Morishige escaped to the lands of the Satake, and Masamune, for a short period, was the greatest northern warlord. This would be his last expansionist adventure, however, for the following year Hideyoshi besieged the Hojo's Odawara Castle, and for this adventure demanded the participation of his allies.

Battle of Odawara

Now only the recalcitrant Hojo clan remained for Hideyoshi to subjugate. Impelled by their stubborn refusal to accept his authority, Hideyoshi invaded the Kanto in 1590 with an enormous army of an estimated 200,000 men, fronted by a reinstated Tokugawa Ieyasu. Clinging to the slender hope that Hideyoshi would be hamstrung by difficulties in provisioning such a large army, Hojo Ujimasa withdrew the bulk of his forces to within the walls of the Hojo capital, Odawara, to sit out the expected siege. Odawara, located in the modern city of Odawara in Kanagawa Prefecture, was at that time one of the most heavily fortified castles in Japan, and a formidable challenge for any attacker.

Situated on a hill, surrounded by moats with water on the low side, and dry ditches on the hillside, with banks, walls and cliffs located all around, the Odawara defenses had frustrated previous attempts by no less than Uesugi Kenshin and Takeda Shingen to take the castle. Hideyoshi seems to have paid heed to this, for he brought with him twenty cannon to reduce the defenses. The Hojo too seem to have used artillery. Delmer Brown cites an account of the battle that states Hojo Ujinao, keeper of the castle, "placed three muskets and one cannon at each loophole in his castle."[161]

In the event, there was little actual fighting to speak of, for Hideyoshi paid good heed to his logistical needs, and was content to carry on a leisurely siege.[162] That siege was apparently highly unusual, resembling more of a huge fair, with a vast entourage of camp followers in attendance. Inside the castle, conditions were quite different, and after three months, facing starvation, the defenders of Odawara surrendered.[163] Ujimasa and his younger brother Ujiteru committed suicide; Ujimasa's heir, Ujinao, was exiled. After the battle other Hojo forts at Hachioji, Yorii, and Shizuoka were quickly taken, and the Hojo relinquished the Kanto forever.[164]

Battle of Sekigahara

To all intents and purposes, elimination of this last pocket of resistance to Hideyoshi's authority signified the end of the Sengoku Period. Although denied the title of *shogun* by

Above: Date Masamune's equestrian statue is located in Sendai, the city he founded. *(Michael S. Yamashita/Corbis)*

the emperor, Hideyoshi was by now indubitably ruler of Japan. Already he had instituted several programs to consolidate the peace,[165] including the establishment of a council of regents to rule until his son, Hideyori, came of age. Hideyoshi hoped that these five elder statesmen, or *go-tairo*—Ukita Hidiei, Maeda Toshiie, Uesugi Kagekatsu, Môri Terumoto, and Tokugawa Ieyasu—would each moderate the power of the others, thereby dissuading any one individual from moving to overthrow the council.

Although ultimately the council imploded, Hideyoshi's attempt to bring about some kind of accord between the *daimyo* may in fact have been driven by a desire to have domestic peace while he embarked on a wider quest. From 1592 until he died in 1598, Hideyoshi's restless ambition drove him to persevere with an ill-starred campaign on the Korean peninsula. The collapse of this venture, which achieved little at great cost in lives and money, badly compromised the authority of his successor, Toyotomi Hideyori, and considerably weakened the Toyotomi's power and prestige.

Hideyoshi's death, after a long period of illness that had seen him grow weaker in body and mind, was the catalyst for the political intrigues that ultimately led to the military campaign that culminated in the battle at Sekigahara. After the event the *go-tairo* soon split into two factions, one driven by the resurgent ambitions of Tokugawa Ieyasu, and the other by those who opposed him, led by the Toyotomi clan bureaucrat Ishida Mitsunari. The rival factions continued their feuding for two years, with each independently ambitious of creating an all-powerful new *shogunate*, until the fragile peace was finally broken and Ieyasu and Mitsunari faced up to each other on the battlefield, at what is now Sekigahara, in Gifu.

Ishida Mitsunari's claim to support the interests of Hideyoshi's son and elected heir, Hideyori, attracted many former Toyotomi allies to his side, and this despite his relative lack of experience on the battlefield. He was thus able to call on the support of many clans of the recent past, such as the Môri, the Kobayakawa, the Kikkawa, the Ukita, and the Shimazu, and bring an army of some 80,000 to Sekigahara. As most of these families had their power-base in western Japan, Ishida's forces are generally referred to as the "Army of the West."

Ieyasu, by then the most powerful individual on the council and with a distinguished military career behind him, was considerably better versed in matters of war than his rival. Supported by his family, the Matsudaira, and capable generals such as Ii Naomasa, Ieyasu had also been successful in gaining the alliance of several notable *daimyo* families, including the Kato, the Hosokawa, and the Kuroda.[166] Collectively referred to as the "Army of the East," (as they were mostly based in the eastern provinces), together they numbered some 74,000.

The size of these two forces means that, in sheer numbers, Sekigahara was by some measure the biggest military action of the age, and perhaps also the most important.[167] Maeda Toshiie was the only member of the council with the power to keep a rein on Ieyasu; when he died in 1599 Ieyasu took over Osaka Castle, the former residence of Hideyoshi and then occupied by his heir, Hideyori. By this act he ostracized the remaining regents. Ishida Mitsunari accused Ieyasu of disloyalty to the Toyotomi name, and with others began to plot against

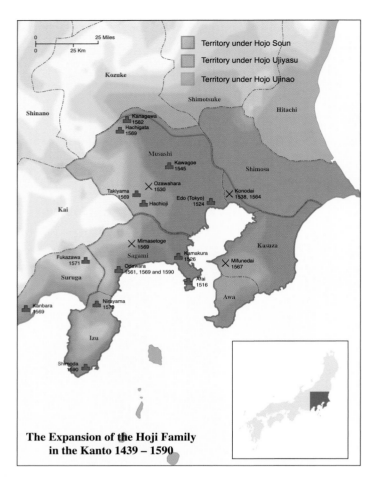

The Expansion of the Hoji Family in the Kanto 1439 – 1590

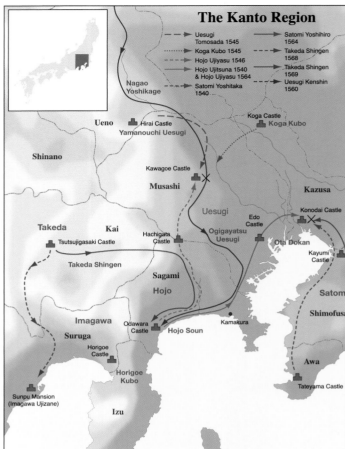

The Kanto Region

him. But Ieyasu soon got wind of the plot and demanded that the man he believed was behind it, Uesugi Kagekatsu, come to Kyoto to explain himself before the emperor. Kagekatsu responded by questioning the legality of Ieyasu's own actions.

Ishida Mitsunari (1560–1600)

Ishida Mitsunari entered the service of Toyotomi Hideyoshi in 1578, primarily as a financier. In 1585, he and his brother Masazumi were appointed administrators of Sakai Province and later Mitsunari became *daimyo* of Sawayama.

Mitsunari was disliked by the generals for his unmilitary appearance and scheming, but when Hideyoshi died he was appointed one of five regents responsible for governing until Hideyoshi's son came of age. Mitsunari's relationship with Tokugawa Ieyasu deteriorated, leading to the Battle of Sekigahara (1600), fought between Mitsunari's Western Army and the Eastern forces of Tokugawa Ieyasu and Maeda Toshinaga. The Easterners won the day, and Mitsunari was caught, taken to Kyoto, and beheaded.

The path to war had been laid. Knowing that a major confrontation was imminent, Ieyasu left a castellan in control of Osaka Castle, and another garrison at Fushimi Castle under the command of Torii Mototada. Beginning on July 8, the Army of the East began moving slowly northward from Edo for an attack on the Uesugi's mountain fortress, Aizu Castle. An advance force led by Sakakibara Yasumasa was followed two weeks later by Ieyasu's son and heir, Tokugawa Hidetada, with the main host of 37,000. At the same time thousands more troops from the Date, Maeda, Mogami, and other clans began advancing on the Uesugi's territories from the north, east and west. On the 21st, Tokugawa Ieyasu himself set out with an additional 32,000 troops.

With Ieyasu away from Edo, Ishida Mitsunari seized the opportunity to strike, calling on his western allies to mount an attack on Ieyasu from the rear. He planned to first eliminate the threat posed by Fushimi, then advance east.

After quickly ousting the castellan guard at Osaka Castle, in August troops coordinated by Môri and Ishida moved to attack Fushimi, just south of Kyoto, which was

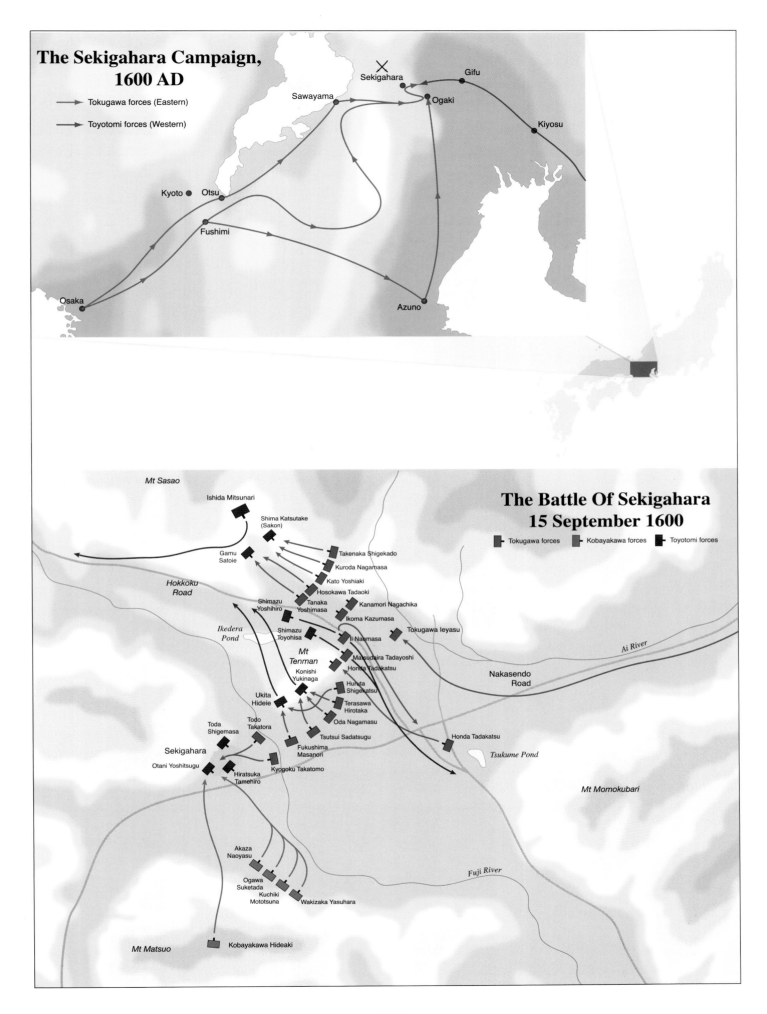

The Sekigahara Campaign, 1600 AD

→ Tokugawa forces (Eastern)

→ Toyotomi forces (Western)

Sekigahara

Gifu

Ogaki

Sawayama

Kiyosu

Kyoto • Otsu

Fushimi

Azuno

Osaka

The Battle Of Sekigahara
15 September 1600

■ Tokugawa forces   ■ Kobayakawa forces   ■ Toyotomi forces

Mt Sasao

Ishida Mitsunari

Shima Katsutake
(Sakon)

Gamu
Satoie

Takenaka Shigekado

Kuroda Nagamasa

Kato Yoshiaki

*Hokkoku
Road*

Hosokawa Tadaoki

Shimazu
Yoshihiro

Tanaka
Yoshimasa

Kanamori Nagachika

Ikoma Kazumasa

*Ikedera
Pond*

Shimazu
Toyohisa

Ii Naomasa

Tokugawa Ieyasu

Ai River

*Mt
Tenman*

Matsudaira Tadayoshi

Konishi
Yukinaga

Honda Tadakatsu

*Nakasendo
Road*

Huruta
Shigekatsu

Ukita
Hideie

Terasawa
Hirotaka

Toda
Shigemasa

Todo
Takatora

Oda Nagamasu

Honda Tadakatsu

Tsukume Pond

Tsutsui Sadatsugu

Sekigahara

Fukushima
Masanori

Otani Yoshitsugu

Kyogoku Takatomo

Hiratsuka
Tamehiro

Mt Momokubari

Akaza
Naoyasu

Fuji River

Ogawa
Suketada

Kuchiki
Mototsuna

Wakizaka Yasuhara

Mt Matsuo   Kobayakawa Hideaki

defended by Ieyasu loyalist Torii Mototada, a close compatriot of Tokugawa Ieyasu.

Here unfolded one of the most celebrated acts of heroism recorded in Japanese history, and a crucial development in the run up to the battle at Sekigahara. Mitsunari's army began their assault on August 27, but after ten days he had made little progress against the bastion. A message was then sent into the castle tied to an arrow, revealing that the besieging army had taken the wife and children of one of the defenders hostage, and that they would suffer crucifixion unless the man betrayed his fellow defenders. With little choice but to comply, on September 8 one of the towers was set aflame from within the castle, and a number of Ishida's men were able to penetrate the castle defenses. The central keep was then burnt, but Torii and his garrison battled on, despite knowing of their inevitable defeat, until all but ten of them were still standing. Mototada then killed himself and his family, and the castle fell into Mitsunari's hands. Nevertheless, by this supreme act of self-sacrifice Ishida Mitsunari's attention was diverted away from his Nakasendo fortresses, which were then attacked by Ieyasu. It thus served a crucial role in allowing for more important strategic gains for Tokugawa, and has ever since been hailed as a shining example of the *samurai* spirit.

Ieyasu's elaborate network of *shinobi* (spies)[168] had alerted him to Ishida's movements. He countered by diverting the bulk of his army west towards Kyoto, while forces led by Date Masamune continued north to feign an attack and keep the Uesugi in check. Ieyasu's forces marched out along the Tokaido, while his son Hidetada moved his 37,000 men along the route of the Nakasendo.[169] As it transpired, a battle against former Ieyasu ally Sanada Masayuki in Shinano Province would delay Hidetada, and prevent him from joining the main action.[170]

Moving swiftly and stealthily, Ieyasu succeeded in blocking the highways to Edo by taking the Nakasendo fortresses at Gifu and nearby Konosu.

Meanwhile, Ishida was at Ogaki, his advance much delayed by the protracted siege of Fushimi Castle.

Right: Torii Mototada on horseback with his retinue. *(British Museum/ Jo St Mart)*

Tokugawa Ieyasu (1543–1616)

Born in Mikawa province, for most of his childhood Tokugawa Ieyasu was a hostage of the Imegawa clan and he fought for them in their war against Nobunaga. Later, however, he transferred allegiance to Nobunaga and became a *samurai*. When Nobunaga died Hideyoshi and Ieyasu were initially in conflict but, having fought each other to a draw, they became good friends. Ieyasu did not take part in the Korean campaigns and by 1600 had consolidated his position as the most powerful feudal lord in the country.

Ieyasu's only rival was an alliance headed by Ishida Mitsunari and, after a campaign revolving around control of the two great highways, the *Tokaido* and the *Nakasendo*,

Mitsunari was defeated at the Battle of Sekigahara (1600), the largest single military engagement in Japanese history. Ieyasu was granted the title *shogun* in 1603 by Emperor Go-Yozei, enabling him to proceed to establish a system of feudal government that was so stable and effective that it lasted for 250 years. As *shogun*, Ieyasu laid down rules and regulations for the *daimyos*, severely limiting their power, and for their *samurai*, whom he encouraged to pursue scholarly learning in addition to their military skills.

Now aged sixty, Ieyasu was at last able to create and solidify the Tokugawa *shogunate*, as well as undertaking civil works such as building Edo Castle, and remodeling of

the imperial court and buildings in Kyoto. He handed the title of *shogun* to his third son, Hidetada, in 1605, but Ieyasu did not retire from public affairs. Starting in 1609, he began to isolate Japan from European influence, culminating in 1614 with the Christian Expulsion Edict, banning the Christian religion and practices, as well as expelling all foreigners. Then in 1615 the authority of the *shogunate* was challenged by Toyotomi Hideyori, but Ieyasu took to the field once more and held his own, defeating his opponent at the Siege of Osaka Castle. The following year Ieyasu, now aged seventy-five, died. The Tokugawa *shogunate* he established survived for two-and-a-half centuries, a remarkable testimony to a remarkable man.

Above: Most unusually Konishi Yukinaga was a devout Christian (in which capacity he was known as Dom Agostinho) and consequently would not commit *seppuku* after being defeated at the Battle of Sekigahara (1600). He was executed by his enemies instead. *(British Museum/Jo St Mart)*

Reports of Ieyasu's brisk approach were greeted with some alarm at the Ishida camp, and further confusion was spread by the *shinobi*, who intimated falsely that Ieyasu planned to by-pass Ogaki Castle and attack Ishida's own stronghold at Sawayama. Such a move, as Ishida was aware, would leave the path open for a march by the Tokugawa forces to Kyoto and Osaka.

On October 20, Ieyasu arrived at Akasaka, less than three miles away from Ogaki, where the rest of his allies were encamped. Ishida therefore decided to retreat from Ogaki Castle and defend the pass on the Nakasendo at Sekigahara, to block any further westward movement by his enemy. Thus, unwittingly, he played into the enemy's hands, for, despite inferior numbers, Ieyasu was a great deal more experienced in open battle.

Heavy rain fell that night, and when dawn broke a thick mist hung over the battlefield, limiting visibility to

just a few feet. Under this dense blanket, the two commanders arrayed their forces for the battle. Ishida positioned himself and 4,000 of his 6,000 men on the lower level of Sasaoyama, overlooking the Hokkoku Kado Road. To the front of his position, behind a specially constructed palisade, he placed his remaining 2,000 men under Gamo Bitchu and Shima Sakon. Behind the main body were 2,000 men under Oda Nobutaka, Kishida Tadauji, and Ito Morimasa. The Shimazu took up position with their 3,000 troops on a small hill to the right of Ishida. Konishi Yukinaga placed his 4,000 to the right of the Shimazu. To his right were Ukita Hidiie and his huge contingent of 17,000. Further on were Toda's and Hiratsuka's 1,500. Slightly to the rear of Toda were 600 more under Otani Yoshitsugu, while Otani Yoshimatsu placed his 3,500 in the woods on the opposite side of the Fuji River. On a small hill overlooking the village of Matsuo, Wakizaka Yasaharu had more men, and there were others too on the other side of Mount Nangu, under Môri, Kikkawa, Ankokuji, Natsuka, and Chosokabe. Kobayakawa Hideaki, with his powerful 15,600-strong host, maintained a position on a hill above the southern end of the line.

Ieyasu had arrayed just over 19,000 men, under Kuroda Nagamasa, Hosokawa Tadaoki, Kato Yoshiaki, Tsutsui Sadatsugu, and Tanaka Yoshimune, in a long line extending from Mount Sasao to the village of Sekigahara. A further 6,000 under Fukushima were between the Nakasendo Road and Fuji River. Behind the first line stood 3,600 of Ii Naomasa's cavalry and Matsudaira Tadayoshi's 3,000. In the third line were 4,600 men under Furuta Shigekatsu, Oda Yuraku, Kanamori Nagachika, and Ikoma Kazumasa. More still under Honda Tadakatsu and Tagawa Michiyasu were down on the Ise Road. Ieyasu's personal command of 30,000 took up a position behind the third line, straddling the Nakasendo, while various commanders positioned themselves to counter Môri's forces.

At eight in the morning the mist cleared, revealing these two vast armies. Suddenly out of the haze appeared the distinctive figure of Ii Naomasa, immediately recognizable by his golden-horned helmet. Riding at the head of his cavalry he raced through the Tokugawa front lines and charged towards the massed ranks of the Ukita.

The other Tokugawa commanders immediately joined battle. Fukushima Masanori charged headlong into the Ukita, and others at Otani's and Ishida's men. The troops in the Ishida's front line quickly took cover behind the palisade and unleashed a heavy fire on the attackers, but were overrun. Kuroda Nagamasa now began to move up the hill towards Ishida's command post, but concentrated *arquebus* fire stopped him short. Ishida then brought up five cannon and used them to pummel back the Tokugawa forces.

As the morning wore on a battle of attrition developed as commanders ordered their men into the fray along the wavering battlefront. The Tokugawa army made some ground on the northern flanks of the valley, where Ishida had his command post, but at the southern end of the line, stalwartly defended by the troops of the Otani, they were held in check.

The turning point in the battle came shortly after noon. Thus far the Kobayakawa Hideaki, a notional Ishida ally, had not committed forces to the fighting, and

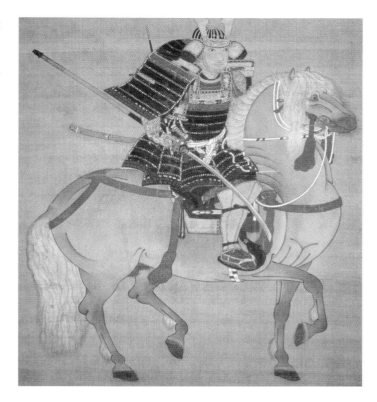

Above: Hosokawa Sumimoto was declared *kanrei* and inherited all of the Hosokawa's holdings on Shikoku. *(Sakamoto Photo Research Laboratory/Corbis)*

Below: Kuroda Nagamasa beating Watanabe Shinnojio during the Battle of Sekigahara on October 21, 1600. The result of victory was to allow Tokugawa Ieyasu to become *shogun*. *(via Clive Sinclaire)*

Above: Fukushima Masanori was rewarded for his support of Toyotomi Hideyoshi throughout the Shizugatake Campaign with a gift of land worth 5,000 *koku*. *(via Clive Sinclaire)*

held firm on his hilltop overlooking the field. Ishida had already sent frantic signals to his ally to relieve the pressure on the Otani by attacking the Ieyasu from the rear, but thus far Hideaki had not acted. Ieyasu, meanwhile, kept a wary eye on events, for in the event that the Kobayakawa forces did make such a move his position would become untenable. This apparently precarious situation was made worse by the fact that Hidetada had failed to arrive with his 38,000 troops.

But Ieyasu was a wily adversary, and not easily outdone. Already, before the battle, his agents had been in action and swayed Kobayakawa to his side. And so,

when Kobayakawa's men finally made their charge down the hill, it was against Otani Yoshitsugu's troops that they directed their fury. The Otani fought bravely, despite being heavily outnumbered, but other defections to the Eastern army eventually overwhelmed them. Yoshitsugu, faced with defeat, killed himself.

With the southern flank lost, Ishida's army now realized victory was with the enemy. Dropping their weapons, most—including Ishida himself—fled to the northern hill slopes and the shelter of Mount Ibuki. Only Shimazu remained on the field, fighting Ii Naomasa and his cavalry. Eventually Shimazu too was persuaded to quit the field, but with retreat to the north now cut off, his only option was to charge straight through the Tokugawa center and head for the Ise road. This he did, with Naomasa in close pursuit, eventually making it back to

Kyushu with just eighty of his men. Ishida was caught three days after a battle on Mount Ibuki, and executed with other captured leaders of the Western army on the riverbed at Kyoto a few days later.

Generally regarded as the last major conflict of the Sengoku jidai, Ieyasu's victory at Sekigahara, which had swung "on the defection of Kobayakawa Hideaki,"[171] marked the end of the Toyotomi reign. The way was now open for Tokugawa Ieyasu to become *shogun*. Three years later, Ieyasu received the title *Seii Taishogun*, and established Japan's final *shogunate*, which endured until the Meiji Restoration in 1868.

NOTES

1 Sengoku Jidai—this term was appropriated from Chinese terminology. It is usually translated as warring states era, although some authors think it more appropriate to use "Warring Warlords Period." For more on the debate over this issue see Mark Ravina, Mary Elizabeth Berry, and Conrad Totman, who argue that the han (feudal domains) were not unlike quasi-independent states, and that the term is thus more or less appropriate.

2 Stephen Turnbull points out that, although historians have traditionally written about a decline in horseback fighting, it is more accurate to see it as a "radical change." *War in Japan 1467-1615* p.16. See also Delmer M. Brown *The Impact of Firearms on Japanese Warfare 1543-98* The Far Eastern Quarterly 7: 3; p.244.

3 Fernao Mendes Pinto, a Portuguese trader shipwrecked on the Shimazu island of Tanegashima, first introduced the European *arquebus* to Japan in 1543. In 1549 Shimazu Takahisa used European–styled *teppo* against the fortress of Kajiki in Osumi Province and within two or three years the Japanese were producing quantities of these simple firearms for themselves. By the 1550s the *teppo* was commonly deployed on the field of battle.

4 Quoted in Delmer M. Brown *The Impact of Firearms on Japanese Warfare 1543-98* The Far Eastern Quarterly 7: 3; p.237.

5 Delmer M. Brown *The Impact of Firearms on Japanese Warfare 1543-98* The Far Eastern Quarterly 7: 3; p.237.

6 Delmer M. Brown *The Impact of Firearms on Japanese Warfare 1543-98* The Far Eastern Quarterly 7: 3; p.239.

7 Stephen Turnbull *War in Japan 1467-1615* p.16.

8 In some cases the breastplate was modeled on European patterns, and known as the okegawa-do.

9 That necessity being the need for protection against increasing numbers of cannon being fielded. See Delmer M. Brown *The Impact of Firearms on Japanese Warfare 1543-98* The Far Eastern Quarterly 7: 3; p.247.

10 John Whitney Hall *Foundations of the Modern Japanese Daimyo* The Journal of Asian Studies 20: 3; p.320-21.

11 John Whitney Hall *Foundations of the Modern Japanese Daimyo* The Journal of Asian Studies 20: 3; p.320-21.

12 John Whitney Hall *Foundations of the Modern Japanese Daimyo* The Journal for Asian Studies 20: 3; p.318.

13 Carl Steenstrup's *Hojo Soun's Twenty-Four Articles. The Code of Conduct of the Odawara Hojo* Monumenta Nipponica 29: 3; pp.284.

14 One of the best sources of information on Hojo Soun's early life is Carl Steenstrup's *Hojo Soun's Twenty-Four Articles. The Code of Conduct of the Odawara Hojo* Monumenta Nipponica 29: 3; pp.283-303.

15 Stephen Turnbull says that his family was in fact quite established *War in Japan 1467-1615* p.30.

16 Carl Steenstrup's *Hojo Soun's Twenty-Four Articles. The Code of Conduct of the Odawara Hojo* Monumenta Nipponica 29: 3; pp.284.

17 For a biography of Ujichika, the leader of the clan 15th and early 16th Century, see Terje Solum and Anders K. Rue *Saga of the Samurai: Shingen in Command*. Anaheim. Brookhurst Press, 2006. p.64.

18 Terje Solum and Anders K. Rue *Saga of the Samurai: Shingen in Command*. Anaheim. Brookhurst Press, 2006. p.13.

19 The strategic location of this fortress on the Tokaido, between mountainous Hakone and Sagami Bay, gave it a key role in the wars of the Sengoku jidai, and in much subsequent Japanese history.

20 Carl Steenstrup's *Hojo Soun's Twenty-Four Articles. The Code of Conduct of the Odawara Hojo* Monumenta Nipponica 29: 3; pp.285.

21 Carl Steenstrup Hojo Soun's Twenty-One Articles: The Code of Conduct of the Odawara Hojo Monumenta Nipponica 29: 3; 285.

22 As an aside, it appears also that Hojo Soun's successor, Ujitsuna, was the first Japanese to embrace firearms, when in 1510 he received a Chinese matchlock.

23 John Whitney Hall *Foundations of the Modern Japanese Daimyo The Journal for Asian Studies* 20: 3; p.318.

24 Terje Solum and Anders. K. Rue *Saga of the Samurai: Takeda Rises to Power*. Anaheim. Brookhurst Press, 2003.

25 Michael Solomon provides a more detailed look at the role of the Honganji in *The Dilemma of Religious Power. Honganji and Hosokawa Masamoto* Monumenta Nipponica, 33:1: pp. 51-65.

26 It was at this time that the 8th abbot of Jodo Shinshu, Rennyo, was appointed to the position of abbot of Hongan-ji, and it is said that the *ikki* began then.

27 For a more detailed look at this rebellion, and the history of the ikko-ikki see Michael Solomon *The Dilemma of Religious Power: Honganji and Hosokawa Masamoto* Monumenta Nipponica 33: 1; p.51-65.

28 Ashikaga Yoshihisa died on campaign, and was succeded by Yoshitane.

29 Michael Solomon *The Dilemma of Religious Power: Honganji and Hosokawa Masamoto* Monumenta Nipponica 33: 1; p.64.

30 Although there is considerable debate over whether the *ikko-ikki* and the Yamashiro-ikki were truly revolutionary, they certainly represent another expression of the *gekokujo* process.

31 The area commonly known and referred to in this text as Chugoku, and which comprises the northern San'yo region and southern San'in region.

32 All Japanese school textbooks contain the Mitsuya no kyokun, Môri's famous lesson to his three sons that teaches that while one arrow is easily bro-ken, three arrows together cannot be broken.

33 For details on Harukata's revolt against Ouchi Yoshitaka see Stephen Turnbull *War in Japan 1467-1615* p.35.

34 Sanehisa also suffered the loss of a number of his forts, among them Ichiku.

35 Stephen Turnbull *War in Japan 1467-1615* p.35.

36 Motonari's victory here had been much aided by the assistance of the Murakami, a family of pirates whose friendship Motonari had been courting for some time. For more on the Murakami see Peter D. Shapinsky, *Japanese Pirates and Sea Tenure in the Sixteenth Century Seto Inland Sea: A Case Study of the Murakami kaizoku."* Paper presented at Seascapes, Littoral Cultures, and Trans-Oceanic Exchanges, Library of Congress, Washington D.C., February 12-15, 2003. <http://www.historycooperative.org/proceedings/seascapes/shapinsky.html>.

37 Stephen Turnbull notes that this siege saw the employment of two Portuguese cannon, "although the effect of (the cannon) were probably more psychological than material." Stephen Turnbull *Samurai Commanders 1577-1638* p.20.

38 Stephen Turnbull *War in Japan 1467-1615* p.37.

39 The Chubu, Kanto and Kansai regions.

40 Numerous sayings attributed to Norikage survive. The most famous, also quoted previously in this book, is "The warrior may be called a beast or a dog; the main thing is winning."

41 The ji-zamurai, also known as kokujin, were lords of smaller rural domains in feudal Japan.

42 In succession, he changed his name to Uesugi Masatora, when he inherited the Uesugi family name in order to accept the official title of Kanto Kanrei; then he changed it again to Uesugi Terutora to honor the Shogun Ashikaga Yoshiteru, and finally to Kenshin after he became a Buddhist monk.

43 Carl Steenstrup *Hojo Soun's Twenty-One Articles: The Code of Conduct of the Odawara Hojo* Monumenta Nipponica 29: 3; 286. For a brief biography of Ujitsuna see Terje Solum and Anders K. Rue *Saga of the Samurai: Shingen in Command*. Anaheim. Brookhurst Press, 2006. p.64.

44 Carl Steenstrup *Hojo Soun's Twenty-One Articles: The Code of Conduct of the Odawara Hojo* Monumenta Nipponica 29: 3; 286.

45 Official recognition for the Hojo's possession of Sagami and Izu had come from the Imperial Court in 1533.

46 Terje Solum and Anders K. Rue *Saga of the Samurai: Takeda Nobutora*. Anaheim. Brookhurst Press, 2004. p.49.

47 Stephen Turnbull *War in Japan 1467-1615* Osprey (2002) p.32.

48 Carl Steenstrup *Hojo Soun's Twenty-One Articles: The Code of Conduct of the Odawara Hojo* Monumenta Nipponica 29: 3; 286.

49 Stephen Turnbull *War in Japan 1467-1615* Osprey (2002) p.32.

NOTES CONTINUED

50 For a brief biography of Ujiyasu see Terje Solum and Anders K. Rue *Saga of the Samurai: Shingen in Command*. Anaheim. Brookhurst Press, 2006. p.64.

51 Stephen Turnbull *War in Japan 1467-1615* Osprey (2002) p.32.

52 A figure of 80,000 to 85,000 has been suggested but few scholars give this much credence.

53 Stephen Turnbull *War in Japan 1467-1615* Osprey (2002) p.33.

54 The clan, through its close relationship with the Ashikaga *shoguns*, had been gifted lands in Totomi, Suruga and Mikawa.

55 In time, however, they were to prove a obstacle to Hojo aspirations.

56 For a biography of Yoshimoto, the leader of the clan 15th and early 16th Century, see Terje Solum and Anders K. Rue *Saga of the Samurai: Shingen in Command*. Anaheim. Brookhurst Press, 2006. p.65.

57 Much about Nobutora's early life is described in Terje Solum and Anders K. Rue *Saga of the Samurai: Takeda Nobutora*. Anaheim. Brookhurst Press, 2004. p.17.

58 Terje Solum and Anders K. Rue *Saga of the Samurai: Takeda Nobutora*. Anaheim. Brookhurst Press, 2004. p.18.

59 Terje Solum and Anders K. Rue *Saga of the Samurai: Takeda Nobutora*. Anaheim. Brookhurst Press, 2004. p.37.

60 Terje Solum and Anders K. Rue *Saga of the Samurai: Takeda Nobutora*. Anaheim. Brookhurst Press, 2004. p.38-39.

61 Terje Solum and Anders K. Rue *Saga of the Samurai: Takeda Nobutora*. Anaheim. Brookhurst Press, 2004. p.55.

62 Terje Solum and Anders K. Rue *Saga of the Samurai: Takeda Nobutora*. Anaheim. Brookhurst Press, 2004. p.55.

63 Terje Solum and Anders K. Rue Saga of the Samurai: Takeda Nobutora. Anaheim. Brookhurst Press, 2004. p.58.

64 Although the Takeda and Hojo made peace, Nobutora's alliance with Yoshimoto split the Hojo-Imagawa union and the two clans began fighting.

65 It should be noted here that, given the lack of reliable sources, several Japanese historians consider this story to be fictional.

66 Terje Solum and Anders. K. Rue *Saga of the Samurai: Takeda Shingen*. Anaheim. Brookhurst Press, 2005. p.9.

67 Nonetheless, Nobushige was to lend vital support to his brother during the following two decades.

68 For a biography of Ogasawara Nagatoki see Terje Solum and Anders K. Rue *Saga of the Samurai: Shingen in Command*. Anaheim. Brookhurst Press, 2006. p.65.

69 For a biography of Yoshitomo see Terje Solum and Anders K. Rue *Saga of the Samurai: Shingen in Command*. Anaheim. Brookhurst Press, 2006. p.65.

70 At Sezawa "In the course of a six hour period, as many as nine battles were fought between the two armies." Terje Solum and Anders K. Rue *Saga of the Samurai: Takeda Shingen*. Anaheim. Brookhurst Press, 2005. p.16-17.

71 For a biography of this man see Terje Solum and Anders K. Rue *Saga of the Samurai: Shingen in Command*. Anaheim. Brookhurst Press, 2006. p.64.

72 Terje Solum and Anders K. Rue *Saga of the Samurai: Takeda Shingen*. Anaheim. Brookhurst Press, 2005. p.43.

73 Terje Solum and Anders K. Rue *Saga of the Samurai: Takeda Shingen*. Anaheim. Brookhurst Press, 2005. p.45.

74 The exact number is much disputed, ranging from over 4,000 to the figure quoted here.

75 Terje Solum and Anders K. Rue *Saga of the Samurai: Takeda Shingen*. Anaheim. Brookhurst Press, 2005. p.57-58.

76 Terje Solum casts doubt on the evidence for the contention that Murakami used *teppo* on the battlefield, given that it was only five years since firearms had been introduced to Japan. *Saga of the Samurai: Takeda Shingen*. Anaheim. Brookhurst Press, 2005. p.61.

77 Terje Solum and Anders K. Rue *Saga of the Samurai: Takeda Shingen*. Anaheim. Brookhurst Press, 2005. p.63, *Saga of the Samurai: - Shingen in Command*. Anaheim. Brookhurst Press, 2006 p.37.

78 Terje Solum and Anders K. Rue *Saga of the Samurai: Saga of the Samurai: - Shingen in Command*. Anaheim. Brookhurst Press, 2005. p.9.

79 Terje Solum and Anders K. Rue *Saga of the Samurai: Saga of the Samurai: - Shingen in Command*. Anaheim. Brookhurst Press, 2005. p.37.

80 Terje Solum and Anders K. Rue *Saga of the Samurai: Saga of the Samurai: - Shingen in Command*. Anaheim. Brookhurst Press, 2005. p.15.

81 Harunobu changed his name to the more familiar Shingen in 1551.

82 For a biography of Uesugi Kenshin see Terje Solum and Anders K. Rue *Saga of the Samurai: Shingen in Command*. Anaheim. Brookhurst Press, 2006. p.67.

83 Terje Solum points out that there is some controversy over the exact number and dates of the confrontations that place on the Kawanakajima Plain. See Terje Solum and Anders K. Rue *Saga of the Samurai: Shingen in Command*. Anaheim. Brookhurst Press, 2006. Appendix 3.

84 See Terje Solum and Anders K. Rue *Saga of the Samurai: Shingen in Command*. Anaheim. Brookhurst Press, 2006. p.42.

85 The army was made up of troops from the Murakami, Takanashi, Inoue, Shimazu, Suda and Karita families.

86 Stephen Turnbull *War in Japan 1467-1615* p.35.

87 Military historians find much of interest in the tactics employed by the opposing commanders. It is also worth noting that this resulted in greater casualties for both sides, as a percentage of total forces, than any other battle in the Sengoku Period.

88 The Takeda clan established an extensive network of signal-fires that could be used to warn of an enemy's movements. The equipment consisted of an iron bucket at the end of a long wooden pole, which pivoted on a wooden watchtower. Once the enemy was spotted, the flammable contents of the bucket were set alight and the bucket raised.

89 Apparently, cloth was wrapped on the horses' hooves to deaden the noise they make *en marche*.

90 This tactic was known as the *kuruma gakari* formation, in which every unit is replaced by another as it becomes weary or destroyed.

91 This was generally just a four-walled screened enclosure.

92 In 1551, at Harai, Ujiyasu defeated Uesugi Norimasa and drove him to seek exile in Echigo under protective custody of one Nagao Kagatora. Nagao henceforth assumed control of the Uesugi, and later took the name Uesugi Kenshin.

93 Events prompted by a succession dispute after the death of Yoshitaka.

94 Stephen Turnbull *War in Japan 1467-1615* p.34.

95 Stephen Turnbull *War in Japan 1467-1615* p.34-35.

96 Literally, Wind, Forest, Fire, Mountain. This was written on Takeda's battle standard and referred to the following passage in Sung Tsu's *The Art of War*.

"Move as swift as a wind, stay as silent as forest, attack as fierce as fire, unmovable defence like a mountain."

97 Stephen Turnbull *War in Japan 1467-1615* p.41.

98 The only really *extensive* biography of Oda Nobunaga in English is *Japonius Tyrannus: The Japanese Warlord Oda Nobunaga Reconsidered* by Jeroen Lamers Hotei Publishing (2001).

99 In return he offered to send his only son Matsudaira Takechiyo as a hostage. The child (Tokugawa Ieyasu) was duly dispatched eastward but was intercepted and spirited away by Toda Yasumitsu, to become a hostage of the Oda. Nonplussed, Hirotada stubbornly refused to change his allegiances, and in the end no harm came to the boy.

100 His main rival was his uncle Nobutomo, and his brother Nobuyuki, the latter favored by many of the clan retainers to assume leadership of the clan. Nobunaga had Nobutomo assassinated in 1555, and Nobuyuki in 1557.

101 The best biography in English is Conrad Totman *Tokugawa Ieyasu: Shogun* Heian International (1983).

102 This was the first time since 1508 that an expedition against the capital had been undertaken.

103 The latter was invested by forces led by Tokugawa Ieyasu, who used ranks of *teppo* to lay down concentrated fire on the defenders.

104 Stephen Turnbull *War in Japan 1467-1615* Osprey (2002) p.42

105 Stephen Turnbull *War in Japan 1467-1615* Osprey (2002) p.42

106 Toyotomi Hideyoshi played an active part in these negotiations. In 1564 he managed to convince, mostly with liberal bribes, a number of Mino warlords to desert the Saito clan.

107 In 1570, the Rokkaku tried to take back Chokuji castle, by cutting off the water supply and placing the castle under siege. Shibata Katsuie, the commander entrusted with defending the castle, led his forces in sallying out of the castle to face the besiegers, succeeding in the end. See Stephen Turnbull *Samurai Commanders* Osprey (2005) p.32.

108 Stephen Turnbull *War in Japan 1467-1615* Osprey (2002) p.42.

109 Stephen Turnbull *Samurai Commanders 1577-1638* p.6.

110 The best biography in English on Hideyosh is Mary Elizabeth Berry *Hideyoshi* Harvard University Press (1982).

111 Tokugawa Ieyasu attacked the *ikko-ikki* of Mikawa in 1564, in the Battle of Azukizaka, and failed to defeat them. Shortly afterwards, with a contingent of *sohei* from his own religious sect, Jodo shu, he defeated the *ikki* adherents in battle, burned all their temples to the ground.

112 During Oda Nobunaga's rise to power, the monks of Enryakuji had regained their military might, and fought a number of skirmishes, in the streets of Kyoto, against Nichiren followers. They eventually burned all of Kyoto's Nichiren temples to the ground, and then proceeded to seek allies among the local lords, or *daimyo*. In the late 16th century, it was common for temples in the Kyoto area to form such alliances to bolster their already considerable strength and influence. See Mary Elizabeth Berry *The Culture of Civil War in Kyoto* University of California Press (1994) Chapter 4.

113 Stephen Turnbull *War in Japan 1467-1615* Osprey (2002) p.45.

114 Stephen Turnbull *Samurai Commanders 1577-1638* p.7.

115 Stephen Turnbull *War in Japan 1467-1615* Osprey (2002) p.44.

116 Stephen Turnbull *War in Japan 1467-1615* Osprey (2002) p.44.

117 Nobunaga was a noted proponent of firearms on the battlefield. Delmer M. Brown notes that as early as 1549, Nobunaga "placed an order for five hundred matchlocks with the gunsmiths of Kunitomo."

118 Kuki Yoshitaka (1542-1600), head of Toba castle and admiral of the *Kumano Suigun* Navy, is regarded as founder of the Japanese Navy.

119 Both of these weapons had been adopted from the Chinese, and were by this time in widespread use as naval weapons in Japan. Delmer M. Brown discusses the adoption and uses of artillery, both field and naval, in *The Impact of Firearms on Japanese Warfare 1543-98* The Far Eastern Quarterly 7: 3; p.239-243.

120 According to the *Nobunagakoki* (Chronicle of Nobunaga), Yoshitaka brought his ship *Nihon Maru*, up close to Ganshoji temple, where the waters were shallow, and blasted off the main gate to the castle, leading his side to victory.

121 Stephen Turnbull *War in Japan 1467-1615* Osprey (2002) p.45.

122 In October 1580, with the Takeda in a condition of terminal decline, the Tokugawa moved to take back the Taketenjin fortress. A siege lasting some six months culminated in surrender of the defenders on March 22, 1581, and custody of Taketenjin was returned to the Tokugawa.

123 Stephen Turnbull *War in Japan 1467-1615* Osprey (2002) p.47.

124 Stephen Turnbull, speaking of Ieyasu's uncanny good fortune in battle, says about Mikatagahara that it was "a defeat that the onset of winter saved from being a rout." Stephen Turnbull *Samurai Commanders 1577-1638* Osprey (2005) p.16.

125 Stephen Turnbull *War in Japan 1467-1615* Osprey (2002) p.48

126 The *Koyo Gunkan* is a contemporary record of the military exploits of the Takeda family, describing their major battles and tactics, and detailed breakdowns of their military formations

127 Delmer M. Brown put the figure much higher, at 70,000.

128 Delmer M. Brown *The Impact of Firearms on Japanese Warfare 1543-98* The Far Eastern Quarterly 7: 3; p.239.

129 Delmer M. Brown *The Impact of Firearms on Japanese Warfare* 1543-98 The Far Eastern Quarterly 7: 3; p.245.

130 The events at Mikatagahara may have influenced this tactic.

131 Delmer M. Brown *The Impact of Firearms on Japanese Warfare* 1543-98 The Far Eastern Quarterly 7: 3; p.245.

132 This is the first documented use of large-scale volley fire worldwide, 25 years before it is seen in Europe.

133 It took on average 15-20 seconds to reload the *teppo*.

134 The exact number of casualties on the Takeda side is disputed, with some sources placing it much lower. Among them were: Takeda Nobuzane, Baba Nobufusa, Yamagata Masakage, Naito Masatoyo, Hara Masatane, Sanada Nobutsuna, Sanda Masateru, Kasai Mitsuhide, Wada Narishige, Yonekura Shigetsugu, Atobe Shigemasa. Most had died leading their cavalry units in the charge.

135 See Delmer M. Brown *The Impact of Firearms on Japanese Warfare 1543-98* The Far Eastern Quarterly 7: 3; p.241-244 for a full discussion of the adoption of cannon by the Japanese. Brown reports that the first were introduced in 1551 as a gift to

Otomo Yoshiuzume, quickly copied (with varying success) and championed by Oda Nobunaga. By 1582 they were apparently in widespread use.

136 Mitsuhide was charged with the San'in region of southern Honshu, including the provinces of Tamba, Tango, Tajima, Inaba, Hoki, Izumo, Iwami and Oki while Hideyoshi was sent against neighboring San'yo — (Harima, Mimasaka, Bizen, Bitchu, Bingo, Aki, Suo and Nagato).

137 To put this into persepective, Arthur Marder points out that during the Sengoku Period "Sea battles were uncommon. The fleets which participated in the battle at the entrance to Osaka Bay in Nobunaga's Ishiyama offensive...existed primarily for the purpose of attacking a fortress from the sea in conjunction with a land offensive." Arthur J. Marder *From Jimmu Tenno to Perry: Sea Power in Early Japanese History* The American Historical Review 51: 1; p.21. Besides Kawanakajima, the only other naval battles of note were off Omosu in 1580, and Shimoda in 1590.

138 One of the key reasons that the Oda army could not break the siege laid by the Mōri army at Kozuki was that they were currently engaged in the reduction of Miki Castle.

139 Stephen Turnbull *Samurai Commanders 1577-1638* p.9.

140 Although it is sometimes suggested that these *o-adakebune* were the first ironclad battleships, it is more likely that they had iron plating in strategic locations. They were apparently 72 feet long and 42 feet wide.

141 During this battle a major flaw in the design of these giant floating gun platforms was revealed. In one catastrophe, as Mōri *samurai* boarded one of the great ships, all the defending warriors ran to that side of the deck *en masse*, shifting the center of gravity to such an extent that it capsized. See Delmer M. Brown *The Impact of Firearms on Japanese Warfare* The Far Eastern Quarterly 7: 3; p.250.

142 Katsuiie had recovered from the injuries he sustained at Nagashima against the *ikko-ikki* and subsequently conducted a successful camapign against the *ikko-ikki* in Echizen, for which he was assigned territories.

143 Stephen Turnbull *Samurai Commanders 1577-1638* p.42.

144 Stephen Turnbull *Samurai Commanders 1577-1638* p.8.

145 In light of subsequent events much has been been made of this by contemporary analysts. Some say Hideyoshi had no need for reinforcements, and asked for them because he desired to appear humble in the face of envious generals in Nobunaga's retinue, wherein there were many who resented his swift promotion from footman to general. Others have intimated that Hideyoshi and his confidantes, by way of a plot to assassinate Nobunaga, drew him into a trap.

146 Stephen Turnbull *War in Japan 1467-1615* Osprey (2002) p.52, 53.

147 Stephen Turnbull *War in Japan 1467-1615* Osprey (2002) p.54.

148 On June 25, surrender terms were agreed with Shimizu Muneharu, one of which was a requirement that he commit *seppuku* (ritual suicide) in a boat on the artificial lake created by the flooding, in full view of onlookers.

149 Stephen Turnbull *Samurai Commanders 1577-1638* p.9.

150 A. L. Sadler, *The Maker of Modern Japan: The Life of Tokugawa Ieyasu* (London: George Allen & Unwin, 1937) 120.

151 The son of Nobutada, who had been killed at Honno-ji alongside Nobunaga. After Nobutada's

death Hideyoshi, Nobukatsu and Nobutaka were assigned to be guardians of the new lord.

152 Stephen Turnbull *Samurai Commanders 1577-1638* p.10.

153 154 See Delmer M. Brown *The Impact of Firearms on Japanese Warfare* The Far Eastern Quarterly 7: 3; p.246.

155 Stephen Turnbull *War in Japan 1467-1615* p.37.

156 Stephen Turnbull *War in Japan 1467-1615* p.64.

157 The body of water separating Shikoku from Kyushu.

158 In mid-1585 Chosokabe Motochika had been defeated by Toyotomi Hideyoshi and his holdings reduced to Tosa Province.

159 Stephen Turnbull *Samurai Commanders 1577-1638* p.21.

160 Stephen Turnbull says this operation was the 'biggest military operation ever seen in Japan" Stephen Turnbull *War in Japan 1467-1615* p.64.

161 See Delmer M. Brown *The Impact of Firearms on Japanese Warfare 1543-98* The Far Eastern Quarterly 7: 3; p.246.

162 Delmer M. Brown The impact of firearms on Japanese Warfare *1543-98* The Far Eastern Quarterly 7: 3; p.240. Brown also says that by the time of the campaign against the Hojo "'t is clear that the employment of heavy artillery had become a basic element in Japanese warfare" p.243.

163 One way that Hideyoshi tried to enter Odawara was through tunneling, as he apparently employed miners to dig shafts under the outer defenses of the stronghold.

164 Stephen Turnbull notes that, unusually, Odawara was not sacked after the surrender, as was generally the case after the successful conclusion of a siege. *War in Japan 1467-1615* p.74.

165 The Hojo's lands were gifted to Tokugawa Ieyasu. Carl Steenstrup *Hojo Soun's Twenty-One Articles: The Code of Conduct of the Odawara Hojo* Monumenta Nipponica 29: 3; 286.

166 In 1588, Hideyoshi forbade ordinary peasants from owning weapons and started a sword hunt to confiscate arms. The swords were melted down to create a statue of the Buddha. This measure effectively stopped peasant revolts and ensured greater stability at the expense of freedom of the individual *daimyo*.

167 The Kato and Kuroda clans were of course led by two highly experienced and respected veterans of the Korean campaigns, respectively Kiyomasa and Nagamasa.

168 For those reasons, it is also the most widely documented of all the *samurai* battles, the inspiration for film directors, game makers and authors alike.

169 *Shinobi* were used extensively throughout the Sengoku jidai to gather information on enemy troop concentrations, castle defenses, logistics and so forth.

170 Under the Tokugawa *shogunate*, five roads of Japan's thousand-year-old highway system were formally nominated as official routes. Two of these Five Routes of Japan connected Edo (modern-day Tokyo) to Kyoto in Japan. The first, the Tokaido (Eastern Ocean Road) was the most important of the Five Routes. Another, the Nakasendo (road through the central mountains, was inland and less heavily traveled.

171 Stephen Turnbull *War in Japan 1467-1615* p.81.

THE FAILED QUEST—
JAPANESE INVASIONS OF KOREA

In the last years of his reign Toyotomi Hideyoshi undertook two invasions of Korea, the first in 1592 and another in 1597, planning to use that country as a stepping-stone for the wider conquest of Ming Dynasty China—an accomplishment that had also been the dream of Oda Nobunaga. Ultimately, both campaigns ended with the withdrawal of Japanese forces, perhaps not in abject defeat but certainly without the accomplishment of those great ambitions to trumpet. Viewed in hindsight, the Korean invasions are particularly significant,[1] marking "the first time in Asian history that massive armies equipped with modern weaponry clashed on the field of battle."[2] The social and political legacy of the wars can be seen in many areas, including the influence on subsequent relations between Japan and her continental neighbors, and also Japan's decision to isolate itself from the world for two-and-a-half centuries.

Hideyoshi did not outlive his grand scheme, dying in the final months of the second invasion. But whereas in the past it was the habit of historians to attribute the failure of the invasions to the sudden loss of its motive force, more recent scholarship points to inherent weaknesses in the planning of the campaigns, and the forces employed to execute them, as the true cause.

Hideyoshi's motives for launching the campaigns are not clear. The traditional view is that in his later years, Hideyoshi was driven by a yearning for some great achievement to solidify his legacy, and thus began to contemplate the scheme that his mentor, Oda Nobunaga, had envisioned as his great destiny. However, Hideyoshi's need to fulfill personal ambitions has historically been seen as *cassus belli*; potentially there were other more concrete incentives for the invasions.[3] One was a requirement to allay the threat of domestic unrest posed by the glut of (now redundant) *samurai* and soldiers. The coalition through which he ruled Japan was based on the sharing of spoils, especially land, among the powerful *samurai* lords that comprised Hideyoshi's power base. By 1592, land was a scarce commodity in Japan, and Hideyoshi needed to find land in order to appease his rapacious supporters. The only real way to achieve this was by attacking foreign soil. A further incentive was a requirement to justify his rule—which lacked royal authority—by establishing military supremacy over his neighbors.

Hideyoshi had "good reason to be confident"[4] of success. After a century and a half of warfare the Japanese military had been honed into a formidable force. Forged together, as an army, it was by most measures the most professional army in Asia; Kenneth M. Swope contends that it was "arguably the most skilled in the world at the time."[5] This army could draw on a pool of half a million battle-hardened soldiers, was led by experienced and resourceful officers, was equipped with the latest in personal weapons, and skilled in their use. As its supreme commander, Hideyoshi seemed to have in his hands the means by which to fulfill long-nurtured ambitions.

Long before completing the unification of Japan, Hideyoshi began planning for a possible war on the mainland. Efforts to prepare the military for the grand venture began as early as 1586, when the keels for the first of what would be a great fleet of two thousand ships were laid. The following year, to gather intelligence on Korean military strength and suitable landing points, a reconnaissance force of twenty-six ships was dispatched to the southern coast of Korea on a limited incursion.[6] The Japanese party met with only desultory resistance, and from that Hideyoshi concluded that the Koreans were ill-prepared to face an invasion of their shores. Nonetheless, perhaps mindful that the true prize was not Korea but her Chinese neighbor, Hideyoshi began communicating with the Koreans in 1587,[7] inviting the Korean King Seonjo to submit to Japanese rule and embark on a joint quest with him against China. At first talks were refused entirely, and so too were requests in April and July 1591 for unmolested passage across Korean territory and into China. Having failed to secure an accord with the Koreans, in August Hideyoshi ordered final preparations for invasion to begin. Construction was already underway of a purpose-built castle at Nagoya on Kyushu (in modern-day Karatsu), from which he planned to oversee the operation, and which would serve as an enormous staging area for the invasion forces.

At Nagoya, the point in Japan closest to Korea, Hideyoshi gathered a massive host, composed largely of the armies of western *daimyo* families, notably the Mori, Chosokabe, Shimazu, Nabeshima, Kato, and Konishi. Hideyoshi opted to remain at Nagoya. The army consisted of nine divisions totaling 158,800 men; the last two divisions, 21,500 men, were stationed as reserves in Tsushima and Iki, respectively. In total, during the war,

Japan used a total of 500,000 troops. Most of these were *ashigaru*. While Japanese divisions included cavalry as well, in light of their experiences with the use of guns during the Sengoku jidai, cavalry was used less. The *teppo* had come to be widely used by *ashigaru*.[8] They also used a good compound bow, and the *samurai* also had his long *katana* and short *tanto* swords. However, the swords saw only very infrequent use, as most engagements were fought at ranges where the Japanese soldiers relied mostly on the musket and bow.

Cavalrymen were equipped variously with spears or glaives, or sometimes with smaller guns designed specifically for use on horseback. All men regardless of rank wore some form of armor, ranging from the simple chainmail and bamboo armor of the *ashigaru* through to the complex and weighty *o-yoroi*.

Tactically, at least in the first phase of the war, the Japanese were able to gain a significant advantage over the Koreans by fielding a large concentration of *teppo*, which had a greater effective range (600 yards compared

---

Below: From humble beginnings, Toyotomi Hideyoshi (shown here enjoying his first battle) was a heroic warrior who brought peace to Japan after more than a century of civil war, while also harboring plans for expansion beyond the nation's shores. *(via Clive Sinclair)*

with 500 yards for the Koreans' bow—and 350 yards for the Japanese bow, come to that). The *teppo* bullets also had greater penetrating power than arrows, and they could be fired in concentrated volleys to make up for the lack of accuracy.

But the undoubted strength of the Japanese land forces masked a crucial weakness within its forces at sea. The comparative rarity of naval actions during the Sengoku jidai had perhaps led to neglect in this branch of the military, for in terms of experience and equipment Japan was ill-prepared to launch an invasion that would depend so heavily on maritime support.

One problem was in the design of its warships. Despite the fact that Japan had close commercial ties with seafaring nations such as Spain and Portugal, and thus exposure to modern techniques of shipbuilding,[9] the evolution of the Japanese fighting ships had lagged behind. In fact, during the invasions, the fleet was primarily composed not of ships purpose built for fighting but rather merchant ships modified for the transportation of troops. Propulsion was provided by but a single, square sail, and though by merit of hull-design the ships were reasonably fleet, they were also quite difficult to maneuver. Another problem was in the construction techniques employed by the Japanese shipwrights, namely their use of iron nails, which rusted and loosened in water. Furthermore, the great majority of Japanese warships at this time were not armed with cannon (and lacked provision for such), and were generally used instead as firing platforms for archers and musketeers. This meant that the Japanese expected to engage at relatively close range, and overcome enemy ships after boarding them in *melee* fighting.

Another interesting factor that Arthur Marder points to is the lingering influence of the so-called *wako* pirates, whose heyday was from the end of the Mongol invasions to the time of the Japanese invasions of Korea. During this time "The warlike spirit stimulated by the Mongol campaigns and the incessant domestic turmoil made many Japanese bellicose and restless. Many feudal lords and their retainers along the western coast took up piracy as a livelihood from the middle of the fourteenth century

Right: Until the 16th century, bows and arrows (*yamiya*) were the most potent weapon of warriors on land and at sea. Arrows could be fired by dismounted men or from a horse, usually at the gallop, when the archer shot at right-angles to the direction of travel. Bows designed for use on horseback could neither be too long or too heavy. Many bows had a handgrip about one-third of the distance from the top of the bow, thus making them easier to use on horseback. There were many different types of bows in use by Japan's military, including several crossbows. However, from 1543, the introduction of firearms led to a decline in the art of archery in favor of the arquebus. *(via Clive Sinclaire)*

on.... In one way the period of piracy may have retarded Japan's naval development. Since the pirates did their fighting on land, their ships were not effective as warships. This may have been a contributing factor toward the ineffectiveness of the warships of Hideyoshi's Korean campaigns."[10]

In fairness, Hideyoshi does seem to have made efforts to address some of the problems, attempting unsuccessfully to purchase on separate occasions both Spanish and Portuguese vessels,[11] but he failed to grasp that simply building great numbers of (inadequate) ships and crewing them with inexperienced men would not suffice. Furthermore, by enacting ordinance in 1587 to curb the activities of pirates he inadvertently propagated the rapid downfall of the only body of men with seafaring experience. Simply, "He did not foresee how important control of the seas would be during the campaign."[12]

The Koreans, whose fighting strength Hideyoshi had already desultorily dismissed, was at that time under the two-hundred-years-old Joseon Dynasty. The current incumbent, Seonjo,was the fourteenth king of the dynastic line. Unlike previous Korean polities, which had hostile relations with their neighbors, the Joseon Dynasty had established close trading and diplomatic relations with Ming China, and also continuous trade relations with Japan.

As for the military situation, the Koreans had adopted a largely defensive posture in response to the two major security threats. Like their Chinese neighbors, the Koreans were at this time harassed by Jurchen[13] raiders, and to counter the threat the Koreans constructed an extensive line of fortresses along their northern borders on the Tumen River. The other external threat was the marauding fleets of *wako*, who pillaged the coastal villages and trade ships.[14] These *wako* ranged out of Tsushima and Iki in the Sea of Japan, and the Goto Islands near to Nagasaki and other islands off Kagoshima. The pirate fleets were as many as two hundred strong, and operated with impunity and without interference from the government. For many years[15] the entreaties of Korean and Chinese officials to the Japanese were ignored, and the *wako* "caused all the countries of the Asiatic continental shore to tremble with fear."[16]

In response to the *wako*, the Koreans developed a powerful navy, without doubt the strongest branch of their military. This had been continuously developed since the 10th century, with knowledge from China, and was highly advanced by the beginning of the Joseon Period in 1392. At the time of the Japanese invasions the Koreans had large numbers of heavy warships, known as *panokseons*, that completely outclassed anything that the Japanese could field. These mounted a variety of weapons, but most importantly, cannon. The Ming Dynasty in China "had been developing cannon and other firearms based on Portuguese models since early in the reign of the Jiang Emperor"[17] and at that time led Asia in their development and manufacture. The technology had traveled to Korea, also, and their successful adoption of it would contribute to the in-war Sino-Korean dominance at sea.

In the first phase of the war the Korean fleets could bombard the cannon-less Japanese ships from outside of the range of the Japanese muskets, arrows, and catapults. Even when the Japanese attempted to arm their fleet with cannons, their lightweight ship design proved a serious limitation to the number that could be borne.

Korean ships had both sails and oars, and were flat-bottomed. Although less capable of blue-water operations, they were well suited to the type of inshore fighting that characterized the naval war. Furthermore, the Koreans used wooden dowels to fasten together the structure of their ships, and these tended to expand and add strength to the joints.

Despite the apparent strength of Korean naval forces, their land-based forces were in a parlous state from top to toe. First and foremost the navy was handicapped by a weak officer corps that was itself hamstrung by internal bureaucracy; to rise in ranks depended far more on social connections than military knowledge. Second, there were only a few regular military units and no field army, and national defense depended heavily on the mobilization of the citizen soldiers in the event of an emergency. With no standing army to speak of, new and ill-trained conscripts were expected to make up a significant portion of the army's ranks. Korean soldiers were on the whole disorganized, poorly trained and ill-equipped.

Above: In 1592, the Koreans were poorly equipped to counter a massed assault by experienced troops fielded by the Japanese. Their defenses mostly consisted of little more than a low stone wall around the base of a mountain, poorly provisioned with towers and fire positions.
(via Jo St Mart)

Furthermore, the Koreans based their defense plans on mountain fortresses, which they set the conscript soldiers to building. However, these mostly consisted of little more than a stone wall around the base of a mountain, poorly provisioned with towers and fire positions, and mostly low in height.

Both Korea and China had already been using firearms similar to the Portuguese *arquebus*, but focus in Korea rested primarily on artillery and archery. The Korean infantry—alongside swords, spears, and tridents—used one of the most advanced bows. Its maximum range was 500 yards, compared to the 350 yards for the Japanese bows. However, as the Japanese military had found, training a soldier to effectively use the bow was long, arduous and costly, unlike for the musket. Korea had cavalry divisions, but in the majority of engagements in

which they were used these proved ineffective. The mountainous terrain in Korea, and lack of fodder to provision the horses, hindered their operations, as did the Japanese use of muskets at long range.

In terms of pure numbers, during the first invasion the Koreans deployed a total of 84,500 regular troops throughout, bolstered by 22,000 irregular volunteers. Court adviser Lee Yul-gok had as early as 1582 recommended that the Yi court implement a nationwide expansion of troops up to 100,000, but his proposal was rejected. So too, was a 1588 proposal from a provincial governor to fortify the twenty islands along the southern coast of the peninsula, and another in 1590 to fortify the islands around the port city of Pusan. Thus, in 1592, the Koreans were poorly equipped to counter a massed assault by experienced troops.

In terms of armor, a great disparity existed between the Korean soldier and his Japanese counterpart: Korean soldiers had almost no armor at all. The Korean military seems to have believed that the soldiers had no need for armor as emphasis was placed on ranged weapons and agility/maneuverability, instead of hand-to-hand combat. Thus, what protection they did have consisted of a heavy leather black vest over their everyday white clothes, and a strictly ceremonial felt hat that offered some protection. Only the elite soldiers stationed at Seoul had armor. Korean captains and generals wore chainmail and scale armor, with shoulder, leg, and chest plates. Often, a padded piece of leather was worn around the waist.

The third belligerent was China, which beginning in early 1593 sent 80,000 troops to help the ailing Korean army when China's own southern borders were threatened. This in itself was not hugely significant,[18] but the fact that China at that time was the foremost manufacturer in Asia of medium and heavy artillery was. When the Chinese brought quantities of these weapons (which the Japanese had very few of) to the fight on the land, this may well have been a decisive factor.[19]

The Chinese used a great variety of infantry weapons, including crossbows and long bows, swords (also for its cavalry), and muskets. Their experiments with gunpowder had also led them to produce crude smoke bombs and hand grenades, all of which would be used during the course of the war.

The Chinese navy was also a major force, contributing many well-armed vessels to the allied cause.

First Invasion (1592–1593): Siege of Pusan and Battle of Tadaejin

By the spring of 1592 preparations for the invasion were complete. Hideyoshi summoned to Nagoya the two men he had charged with prosecuting the campaign to finalize

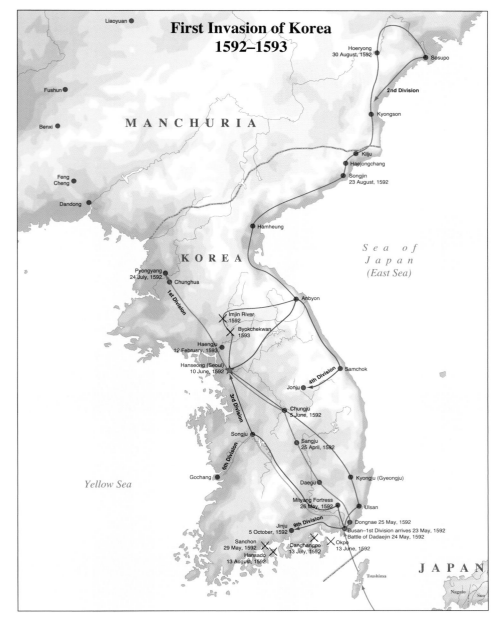

details of the planning. Both Kato Kiyomasa and Konishi Yukinaga had distinguished themselves in Hideyoshi's service during the Kyushu campaign, yet they were very different men, and also great rivals. Kato, a tough, uncompromising military man20 and a zealous supporter of the Buddhist Nichiren sect, despised Konishi's Christian beliefs. In Korea, their conflicting personalities would clash on several occasions.

The plan called for the invasion force to stage through Tsushima, the island that lies approximately halfway to Korea. The first wave of the invasion force, 150,000 men in 700 boats (including 9,200 seamen) under Konishi Yukinaga and So Yoshitoshi, sailed from Tsushima on May 23, 1592, heading for Pusan and various other landing points on Korea's southeastern coast. The Korean navy, having mistaken the fleet for trading vessels, took no action, and the ships made landfall at Pusan that evening unmolested. Even at this advanced stage there was a final Japanese plea to the Koreans for a safe passage to China, but this was refused.

At Pusan the invaders faced a 20,000-strong garrison under General Chong Pal, who tried to marshal his troops and deny the invaders a beachhead. But he had been caught by surprise and his outnumbered force was quickly overwhelmed. As Chong retreated back to the city in an attempt to reorganize, Japanese troops under So Yoshitoshi moved onto the mountain slopes overlooking the city to the west, from where they were able to pour fire down into the city. Under this cover the city walls were quickly scaled and Pusan fell within a few hours, providing the Japanese with a landing stage from which to support their armies.

Battle of Tongnae

Meanwhile, Konishi Yukinaga had invested the subsidiary harbor forts of Tadaejin and Seopyeongpo, and with these secured he wasted no time in striking out for the objective, Hanseong (the capital and present-day Seoul), some 205 miles to the northwest on the Yellow Sea coast. The road to Seoul was guarded by the mountain fortress of Tongnae, a few miles to the northeast of Pusan, where Yukinaga's force soon arrived. Before opening his assault the Japanese commander again demanded that the Koreans allow the Japanese to travel through the peninsula, but was met with rebuttal, and therefore proceeded to ring the fortress with his troops.

Although a Korean army under Yi Gak was approaching Tongnae from the north, he abruptly halted at Sonsan on hearing news of developments at Pusan. Without reinforcement, the 3,000 defenders of Tongnae were in a desperate position, and after twelve hours of battle Tongnae fell. The castle governor, Song San-hyeon, died in the battle but had shown such exemplary spirit in defense that he was accorded a proper burial ceremony by the victorious Japanese. Carrying the momentum Konishi shortly took the mountain fortress of Yangsan, apparently without a fight, as the defenders fled in fear upon being fired on by the Japanese scouts.

The advance through Gyeongsang

At the end of May, as Konishi's 1st Division started to roll north, Kato Kiyomasa's 2nd Division landed in Pusan, followed by Kuroda Nagamasa's 3rd Division, which came ashore west of the Nakdong River. Kuroda and Kato now embarked on separate lines of advance, the 2nd northeast toward Ulsan and the 3rd along the line of the Nakdong River toward Songu. By the end of the month Kiyomasa had captured Tongdo, and then Kyongju (Gyeongju). Meanwhile, after securing his beachhead, Nagamasa laid siege to nearby Gimhae castle, laying down gunfire on the defenders while his engineers constructed ramps up to the walls with plundered bundles of crops. By early June, Nagamasa had advanced nearly 100 miles through Gyeongsang, before finally taking Songju.

Below: A heavily stylized view of the melee fighting during the Battle of Tadaejin (also Dadaejin), one of the earliest battles of the first Japanese invasion of Korea. Japan's Konishi Yukinaga, commander of the First Division, met little resistance from the Korean commander, Yun Heung-sin. *(Wikipedia via Jo St Mart)*

To the west Yukinaga had captured the fortress at Miryang (Milyang, Gyeongsangnam-do), before moving on to secure Chongdo (Cheongdo) fortress. He then advanced to Daegu, the administrative, economic, and cultural center of the entire Gyeongsang region, and razed it. Less than three weeks after landing, Yukinaga was across the Nakdong River and at the Songsan mountain (near to present-day Gumi), a position from where he could threaten Sangju.

Battle of Sangju

The fortress of Sangju held a vital strategic position on the east-west transit route between the Gyeongju area and the Han River valley in the west, and was a natural focus for any invader. Already, as Japan's 1st Division had begun to press on Daegu, the man charged with holding the city, General Yi Il, had ordered the garrison to withdraw the fifty miles north up the road to Sangju. Recognizing that he could not withstand a protracted siege of the fortress, he opted to face the 1st Division head on. The few men that he had (fewer than 1,000) were deployed in front of the fortress on two small hills. On gaining the field, Yukinaga split his much larger force into three, and began laying musket fire down on the Korean positions. The hapless Koreans, armed only with bows, could not match the Japanese gunners for range and watched their arrows fall short. Yukinaga launched a three-pronged attack on the front and on the two flanks. Yi Il was ultimately forced to quit, for the loss of 700 men, and another key fortress fell into Japanese hands.

Battle of Chungju

With the fall of Sangju, the 1st and 2nd Divisions could now began to converge on the fortress of Ch'ungju, guarding the entrance to the Han River, and the last obstacle in front of Seoul. Hoping to break down the relentless Japanese advance, the Korean command resolved to make a stand at the Ch'ungju fortress. Located above the Choryong Pass, this was an "eminently defensible position along the route to Seoul,"[21] and the only path through the western end of the Sobaek mountain range. The position was held 8,000 troops,

under the command of the distinguished General Sin Ip. However, rather than try to hold the fortress, Sin Ip elected to attempt to confront the enemy in the open field, where he believed that his cavalry would be more effective. He also seems to have underestimated the Japanese *teppo* somewhat, stating. "The enemy are foot soldiers and we are cavalry. If we go forth and meet them on the open plain and use our iron clad cavalry, how can we not be victorious?"[22] With that he placed his units in a broad, flat valley at Tangeumdae to confront the enemy. Although open, this area was covered with flooded rice paddies and their associated dykes, which would clearly be a hindrance for the Korean cavalry, most of whom were new recruits. To exacerbate what was already a poor choice, he stood his men with their backs to a river.

Yukinaga had by now quit Sangju with his army of 18,000 men, and occupied an abandoned fortress at Mungyong. Marching out the next morning, Yukinaga arrived at Tangumdae in the early afternoon. Using the same approach as at Sangju, he split the division into three, which then swarmed into the valley on the front and flanks of Sin's position. As the exchanges began, the *teppo* again proved their worth, for the Korean archers could make no worthwhile response to the volleys of musket fire that tore into their ranks. Sin then tried to steady his withered ranks, personally leading two desperate cavalry charges at the Japanese, but neither could break their unyielding line. The battle now turned into a rout; fleeing the battlefield, many Koreans drowned in one of the two rivers that blocked their path of withdrawal. Sin himself died at his own hand, and in the *melee* that followed thousands of heads were taken by the pursuing Japanese—a practice that was continued by *samurai* with some fervor throughout the war on the continent.

The fall of Hanseong (Seoul)

By June 7 Yukinaga's army had pushed past Choryong and taken Ch'ungju. Shortly thereafter he was joined by Kato and Kuroda, who took him to task for not checking his advance at Pusan, as had been the prior arrangement, seemingly seeking all of the glory for himself.[23] Petty clashes of ego aside, the Japanese generals could between them reflect with some satisfaction on progress thus far. In just over ten days they had advanced more than a hundred miles from Pusan, meeting very little resistance on the way, and were now less than a hundred miles from Hanseong. With confident predictions from all, Hideyoshi himself was poised to cross the sea and take personal command.

In the interim, his generals went to work on planning the next phase of the conquest. Between them they determined to group the Japanese troops into two spearheads that would follow different lines of march to Hanseong. In the first week of July, the two forces, one under Kiyomasa and the other led by Yukinaga, began a race north to capture this vital prize. Within days Kiyomasa, following a shorter route, was halted at the Han River for a lack of boats to effect a crossing. Konishi's 1st Division, however, was able to cross further upstream where the river was more easily forded. Once across the river, he advanced swiftly on Hanseong. Finding the city sealed but apparently undefended— King Seonjo having fled the day before—on June 11 his troops managed to gain entry through a small floodgate in the castle wall, and opened the city gates from within. Once again, Yukinaga had beaten his rival to the goal. It was only after an ill-planned assault against his forces that

Above: Kiyomasa was one of the *Shizugatake no shichi-hon-yari* or Seven Spears of Shizugatake. *(via Clive Sinclaire)*

Kiyomasa was gifted a number of boats to cross the Han. When he finally arrived, along with other commanders and their troops,[24] he apparently had some difficulty convincing Yukinaga's troops to let him enter.

The Koreans did try to reclaim Hanseong, through the efforts of the governor of the Jeolla Province, Yi Kwang. With his regular forces bolstered by the addition of volunteers, Kwang rallied a substantial army of 50,000 men, which he led north to Suwon, just twenty-six miles south of Hanseong. On May 4, a scouting force attempted to take a fortress at Yong-in, which was held by a 600-strong Japanese garrison under Wakizaka Yasuharu. Before any impression could be made, a relief force arrived and launched a counterattack. Kwang's troops were driven off and forced to retreat.

Advance across the Imjin River

At a council of war between the important commanders in Hanseong it was now decided that Yukinaga's battle-weary troops would take a deserved rest, while Kiyomasa pressed on north to the Imjin River, a natural obstacle behind which the Korean General Kim Myong-won had deployed 12,000 troops concentrated at five key points where he expected the Japanese to try and cross. During his retreat to the river, Kim Myong-won had ordered land on the southern approaches to the river burnt to deprive the Japanese troops of sustenance and of materials with which to effect a crossing. Upon gaining the river, Kiyomasa sent yet another message to the Koreans imploring them to open the way to China, but this too was flatly rejected.

Denied the means to carry the advance over the river, Kiyomasa was compelled to sit tight for a whole month, before making what appeared to be a tactical withdrawal to the safety of the Paju fortress.[25] This was in fact a calculated deception, for when the obliging Koreans, interpreting withdrawal as retreat, launched an attack at dawn against the remaining Japanese troops on the southern shore of the Imjin River, they were struck by a sudden counterattack.[26] Isolated on the wrong side of the river, a great many were killed. More important, the Japanese acquired the Korean boats. As the Japanese began to pour across the river, Kim Myong-won fell back with his remaining forces to the Kaesong fortress. This too shortly came under attack by the Japanese, and Kim Myong-won was obliged to retreat yet further, to Pyongyang.

Now that they held a bridgehead across the river, the Japanese commanders could begin to look toward the next objectives. They settled on separate but complementary objectives: Yukinaga would continue north, to Pyongan Province, in pursuit of the retreating King Seonjo;[27] Kiyomasa would embark on an epic drive to Hamgyong Province, in the far northeastern part of the peninsula. The Sixth Division under Kohayakawa was to advance on Jeolla Province in the southwestern corner; the Fourth Division under Mori would secure Gangwon Province in the midwestern region; Kuroda Nagamasa's 3rd Division would stabilize Hwanghae; and other Japanese forces would move against Chungchon, Gyeongsang, and Gyeonggi.

The fall of Pyongyang

In the ensuing days and weeks along his northward line of march, Yukinaga occupied and sacked Pyongsan, Sohung, Pungsan, Hwangju, and finally Chunghwa, at which juncture he linked up with Kuroda Nagamasa's 3rd Division for a drive on Pyongyang. Approached from the south, the city is shielded by Taedong River, and behind this Yi Il and Kim Myong-won set 10,000 of their troops to repulse the 30,000 of the 1st and 3rd Japanese Divisions. The Korean soldiers then set about confiscating or destroying any boat, raft, or other vessel that could bear men on water, and thus be of use to the enemy. But, with this done, it is somewhat perplexing that, once the Japanese had gained the river and were encamped on its southern side, the Koreans resorted to the same tactic employed on Imjin, using boats to assault across the river for a surprise night attack.

This attack, although initially successful, provoked a strong counterattack by other elements of the Japanese army, threatening to cut of the Korean line of retreat. With reinforcements unable to cross the river, the position began to deteriorate, and it was only with some good fortune that the Korean troops were able retreat in order back over the river, whence they had come. Good fortune had been

Above: Above: Kato Kiyomasa, a Japanese commander during the invasions of Korea. *(China Tourist Board)*

visited on them simply because the Japanese had given up their pursuit, desiring instead to study the manner in which the Koreans made their river crossings. From these patient observations the Japanese commanders were able to discern the practicable fording points. The following day, as the Koreans fell back towards Pyongyang, the Japanese began sending troops over.

Having ceded another vital bridgehead, and the last defensible position in front of Pyongyang, the Koreans were impelled to abandon the city under the cover of darkness. On June 16, Yukinaga and Nagamasa entered the city in triumph, only to find it empty. Thus, with Pyongyang securely under control, the Japanese were poised to cross the Yalu River into China, and realize Hideyoshi's grand scheme.

The Gangwon, Hamgyong and Manchurian Campaigns

Earlier in June, Mori Yoshinari had set out northeastward from Hanseong, crossed into Kangwondo, and captured a string of fortresses down the eastern coast from Anbyon to Samchok. While he continued down the coast, another force under Shimazu Yoshihiro turned inland and took Yanggu, Chunchon, and Wonju, before establishing himself at the provincial capital of Wonju.

Meanwhile, Kato Kiyomasa led the 20,000-strong 2nd Division on a ten-day march across the peninsula, towards "the wildest area of Korea." This began Kato's Northern

Below: Kuki Yoshitaka came from a family of warlord pirates and was associated with maritime warfare all his life, including two invasions of Korea. *(British Museum/Jo St Mart)*

Campaign, described by Stephen Turnbull as "the crowning glory of his military career."[28] Although the subsequent actions that Kato fought were mainly confined to Hamgyong, there was at least one battle with Jurchen in the southeastern part of Manchuria, making him the only one of Hideyoshi's generals to stand on Chinese territory.

After making his eastward transit, Kato staged through Anbyon (captured earlier by Mori's 4th Division), south of modern Wonsan on the Eastern Sea coast of North Korea. He then followed the coast to the provincial capital of Hamgyong Province, Hamheung, and quickly secured it. Allocating men to oversee the defense and civil administration of the city, he led the remainder northeast along the coast towards Haejongchang.

On July 23 Kiyomasa fought against the southern and northern Hamgyong armies under the commands of Yi Yong and Han Kuk-ham, respectively, at Songjin (the modern-day Kimchaek). The open battlefield was played to advantage by the Koreans, who used a division of their cavalry to bottle up the Japanese forces in a grain storehouse.[29] The Japanese barricaded themselves with bales of rice, and drove off Korean forces with musket fire. Planning to renew the attacks in the morning, the Koreans retired, only to be ambushed and surrounded near a swamp. Many of those who tried to flee were mired in the swamp and slaughtered.

Survivors of the Songjin debacle soon spread the alarm among other garrisons, allowing the Japanese troops to push with some ease further north into mountainous North Hamgyong, capturing Kilju, Myongchon, and Kyongsong. From here they left the coast and headed directly north towards the Chinese border, through Puryong and toward Hoeryong on the Tumen River, a place so remote that it served as a penal colony. On July 30 Kiyomasa entered Hoeryong,[30] and soon after he accepted in tribute from a Korean bandit pack General Han Kuk-ham, bound in ropes, along with the head of an unnamed Korean general.

Kato was now at the extreme north point of his epic march, 300 miles distant from Pyongyang and the nearest Japanese troops. Not bowed by any feelings of isolation, Kiyomasa launched a limited excursion into southern

Above: Replica of a Korean Navy "turtle ship," which scored many victories against the Japanese invaders. *(Jo St Mart)*

China, the closest that any Japanese general came to realizing Hideyoshi's dream. However, soon after crossing the border he encountered the hard-fighting Jurchen, and after a tough battle withdrew back over the border, never to return. Instead, Kiyomasa continued to push east, capturing the fortresses of Chongsong, Onsong, Kyongwon, and Kyonghung, and finally arriving at Sosupo on the estuary of the Tumen River.

Thus far, the war on land had been nothing short of a disaster for the Koreans. Within the first three months of the war, the Japanese invasion force had advanced up the Korean peninsula from Pusan in the south to Pyongyang in the north, capturing all of the major cities and routing the Koreans in every battle. In June Hideyoshi was already confidently predicting that he would be in Peking by October.[31]

The beleaguered Korean regular army, lacking leadership and morale, was scattered throughout the countryside in disorganized units. Seeking assistance from China, King Seonjo petitioned the Ming Emperor Wanli, but with the Chinese currently engaged in suppressing a revolt among their own troops in Ningxia in northwest China, the Koreans were offered only a token force of 3,000 soldiers under Zu Chengxun,[32] which was unlikely to have much impact on events.

The war at sea

But this version of events somewhat clouds the actuality, for the Japanese themselves were not without their own woes. Their points of landing were in the far south, many miles distant. Thus far the land army had failed to secure their sea lines of communication. It was therefore badly extended, and forced to live off land that could barely support such a military juggernaut.

The Japanese had planned all along to use the waters west of the Korean peninsula to supply the invasion. Initially, the Korean navy seemed powerless to stop them. Soon after the landings at Pusan, the Left Naval Commander of Gyeongsang Province, Bak Hong,

Japanese text in vertical columns appears at the top of the page.

Above: Ukita Hideii (the overall commander of the Japanese Army of the Left), whose 55,000 men drove the 6,000 Chinese/Korean garrison from the walled city of Namwon. *(British Museum/Jo St Mart)*

destroyed his entire fleet, his base, and all armaments and provisions, and fled. His counterpart, Right Naval Commander Won Gyun, also destroyed and abandoned his own base, and fled to Konyang. Korea now had only two (out of four) remaining previous navies, and these were on the other (east) side of the peninsula. But fortunately for the Koreans, they possessed excellent vessels and fine seamen, the best of whom was the Admiral Yi Sun-sin,[33] whose actions against Japanese shipping had a major effect on the outcome of the war. Of the many qualities that Yi possessed as a naval commander perhaps the most crucial was that, "Yi broke with the Oriental tradition of using warships as mere platforms on which soldiers might fight. He regarded warships in terms of firepower."[34]

Battle of Okpo

The Japanese navy had no sailors of this caliber. "Of the nine squadron commanders, Kurushima Yasuchika, Wakizaka Yasuhara, Kato Yoshiaki, Kuki Yoshitaka, and Todo Takatora had some sea experience…But of the lot perhaps only Kuki had any real naval knowledge."[35] Furthermore, they were all equal in power, Hideyoshi having declined to elect one of them as overall commander, leading to inevitable clashes of personality with each striving for laurels. During the first landings, the fleet was nowhere to be seen, having delayed at Nagoya, and arrived at Pusan some two weeks after the first units had landed. Fortunately for them, the admiral in charge of defending the southeast coast, Won Kyun, took no action at a time when the Japanese were critically vulnerable. In a brief encounter off Kadok Island he turned tail and fled, seeking the assistance of the admiral of neighboring Jeolla, Yi Sun-sin.

The Japanese commanders quickly established bases of operation at Pusan, and began patrolling the sea lines between Pusan and Nagoya. Meanwhile, preparations were made to sail north up the western coast, to rendezvous with Konishi Yukinaga's 1st Division. On June 16, the Japanese convoy set out from their anchorage. Yi Sun-sin and Admiral Yi Ok-gi were already in the vicinity with one or two of the curious, newly completed, so-called "turtle" boats,[38] plus *panokseons*, small warships, and other boats. After rendezvous with Admiral Won's fleet, the flotilla of eighty-five ships moved out for Kadok, seeking out the enemy. Scouting vessels soon detected a sizeable force of Japanese vessels southwest of Pusan at Okpo harbor, on the east coast of Koje Island, where their crews were occupied ashore in plundering.

Upon sighting the approaching Korean fleet, some of the raiders attempted to flee in their ships, but were caught, and encircled. In the ensuing two-hour battle the Japanese, armed only with muskets and bows, proved no match for the Korean sailors, who laid off at a safe distance and rained down a barrage of fire-arrows, cannon fire, and primitive "bombs," closing only when an enemy ship was crippled. That night, four more Japanese vessels were sunk, and during the next day eleven more were sent to the bottom at Chokjinpo. The

Koreans, having lost not a single ship, had won a crucial victory and exposed Japan's Achilles heel—its fleet.

Battle of Sachon

About three weeks after the defeat at Okpo, the Japanese fleet had recovered strength enough for another attempt to force a passage to the north. In the first week of July they moved west along the southern tip of the peninsula, before seeking temporary harbor at the Bay of Sachon. Yi Sun-sin and Won Gyun, following these movements carefully through spies, ordered their combined fleets to set sail for Sachon. On July 8, the twenty-six ships arrived at the entrance to the bay, but a strong outgoing tide prevented them from entering. Yi therefore ordered the fleet to make show of withdrawing, "a favorite strategem,"[39] to draw the Japanese out to sea. Compliantly, the Japanese hurriedly embarked their twelve ships and pursued the Korean fleet. Yi Sun-sin then turned and counterattacked, with the "turtle" ship in the front, and successfully destroyed all twelve ships. A few days latr he attacked and sank another Japanese squadron west of Hansan Island, which lies to the west of Koje.

Battle of Danghangpo

Flushed with victory, Yi Sun-sin and Won Gyun were then joined by Admiral Yi Ok-gi's Eastern Jeolla Fleet and, working in union, they began to comb the waters off Gyeonsang for Japanese vessels. Once again, the "eyes and ears" of Yi's intelligence network were at work watching for movements. On June 13, the admirals received intelligence that a group of Japanese ships had been found at anchor in the Bay of Danghangpo. A flotilla was duly dispatched to challenge it. Entering the bay through a narrow gulf, Yi was confronted with the sight of twenty-six enemy vessels lying at anchor in the bay. Holding the rest of the fleet in check, Yi ordered a "turtle" ship in to penetrate the enemy formation. Once the "turtle" was among the enemy ships, Yi ordered his ship captains to stage a retreat, tempting the Japanese to take up the chase. With their enemy brought to open water, the Korean fleet turned and enveloped them, sending the "turtle" ship to harry the enemy flagship, and pounding the others with

cannon. Of the twenty-six Japanese ships only one managed to escape destruction, and that too was caught and sunk by a Korean ship the next morning.

Battle of Hansando

Toyotomi Hideyoshi now began to grow concerned about the success of the Korean navy against his ships, not least because the need to provision the armies in the north had become urgent. He therefore recalled three experienced naval commanders from their duties on land. These men, Wakizaka Yasuharu, Kato Yoshiaki, and Kuki Yoshitaka, hastily assembled a powerful squadron with which to break out of their enforced confinement on the southern coast and establish a secure passage to the northwest coast. In the second week of August, with the combined Korean navy of seventy ships under the commands of Admirals Yi Sun-sin and Yi Ok-gi at that time engaged off Jeolla Province, the Japanese fleet of eighty-two vessels moved up through the Hansan Strait, en route to Pyongyang, anchoring halfway up at the harbor of Gyeonnaeryang. Sailing from the Miruk Island at Dangpo, the Korean fleet reached the entrance to the bay on August 14, but because of the narrowness of the strait and the additional hazard posed by underwater rocks, Yi chose to employ his usual tactic. A small squadron of ships was duly sent in to lure the enemy into open water, and sure enough Wakizaka's squadron took the bait. This was at once surrounded by the Korean fleet, arrayed in semicircular formation of Yi Sun-sin's devising, called the "crane wing," with at least three of the vaunted "turtle" ships leading the attack. The Korean vessels fired a hail of cannonballs into the Japanese formation, and by standing off at a safe distance avoided Japanese counterfire. The battle was another crisp victory for Korea, with Japanese losses amounting to fifty-nine ships—forty-seven destroyed and twelve captured.

Those that survived fled to Angolpo, west of Pusan, but within two days they had been hunted down and were under attack. This time, however, the Japanese captains did not fall for Yi's mock retreat, and sat tight at anchor. Yi arrayed his ships and began a bombardment, sending many more enemy ships to the bottom. Unable to sustain losses of this scale, Hideyoshi now ordered a halt to all naval operations, and the fleet withdrew to the secure confines of Pusan. But even at anchor there they were not safe from attack.

Early in October, Yi led his 200-strong fleet into Pusan harbor[40] in a bold attempt to smash the Japanese fleet and sever their sea lines of communication. Finding nearly 500 Japanese ships anchored in five closely packed lines parallel to the shore, and well-protected by shore batteries, "back and forth the Korean ships plied, pouring in broadside after broadside. Lashed together, the flames spread rapidly from one to another of the Japanese fleet." Although he was eventually forced to retire, the damage wrought had been severe. As Arthur Marder observes, this meant "Yi now had undisputed command of the sea and controlled Japan's lines of communication and supply." In short, "The reinforcement and supply situation for the Japanese armies became acute."[41]

Siege of Jinju

Despite the catastrophic reverses they were suffering at sea, Hideyoshi's generals continued apace with efforts to subjugate Korean territory. For a time at least, Korea had appeared virtually defenseless,[42] but beginning in the late fall there were signs that the momentum of the attack was beginning to slow. One such indication was in Jeolla Province, in the southwest of the country, where Kobayakawa Takakage's 6th Division had been sent on a campaign of conquest. Marching first to Chonju he then moved left to Kumsan in Chungchong (central western South Korea), and secured this as a base for operations against the province.

Kobayakawa realized that possession of the powerful fortress at Jinju, and another on the approaches at Changwon, was crucial to establishing control over Jeolla. He therefore sent a 20,000-strong army under Hosokawa Tadaoki to capture Changwon, and then moved to reduce Chinju. Jinju was garrisoned by 3,000 troops under a capable commander, Kim Si-min. Although clearly at a disadvantage in pure numbers, somewhat unusually Kim had armed some of them with 170 recently acquired muskets, which were equal in quality to the Japanese

teppo, and also had cannon to bolster the defenses. On October 4, under a withering rain of cannons, arrows, and bullets, Kobayakawa's men began attempts to scale the walls, first using ladders, and then with a siege tower. When all attempts had been repulsed Hosokawa tried using his *teppo* squads to provide cover for the soldiers scaling the wall. Again, they were driven off, as Koreans smashed up the scaling ladders with rocks and axes. After nearly a week of this, facing a mounting tally of casualties, Hosokawa abandoned the siege. Consequently, the Japanese were prevented from taking Jeolla Province.

Intervention of Ming China

Elsewhere, an event of much greater significance had already taken place: the intervention of Ming China. On August 22, Zu Chengxun, Vice Commander of the northeastern city of Liaoyang, had crossed the Yalu with the 3,000 troops offered by the Ming Emperor, heading for Pyongyang.[43] After a difficult march through unfamiliar territory, the Chinese entered the apparently deserted city on August 23, only to be set on and slaughtered by Japanese troops that had hidden in wait. But despite this apparent victory, it was an ominous portent of what was to come. The Japanese commanders "…were ill at ease. They knew the Chinese would be coming in greater numbers, and despite Hideyoshi's bombast (he had belittled the fighting abilities of the Chinese), Japan's generals had a healthy respect for the military prowess of Ming China from the start."[44]

In China, fearing an imminent Japanese invasion, coastal defenses were hastily strengthened and men were called to arms. Meanwhile, the Chinese prepared to take the offensive, with plans for a large-scale intervention. Large numbers of new weapons were ordered, along with supplies, and new warships[45] constructed in time for a projected expedition in the new year. To this were committed 40,000 men[46] under Generals Song Yingchang and Li Rusong, the latter proudly boasting on the eve of the attack, "Our army is like the wind and rain. In the morning they will come together at the Yalu River and by evening we certainly will have smashed the enemy." Li's confidence stemmed from his firm belief in superior firepower, for in addition to a 3,000-strong contingent of skilled riflemen he could also field a sizeable detachment of artillery.

The Ming army crossed the Yalu River into Korea in January 1593, where it linked up with a group of Korean militias. By February 6 it was drawn up to the walls of Pyongyang, which it now besieged. Ringing the walls with his cannon, Li laid down a mighty barrage on the Japanese within, sending other forces under the Korean Generals Yi Il and Kim Ungso to attack the city from the east. The assault began in earnest on February 8, with Li Rusong personally leading repeated assaults from the southeast corner of the city. Gaining access to the city under cover of a heavy smoke screen through its west gates, the Ming troops were soon battling in the streets with Konishi Yukinaga's defenders. With other Chinese pressing to the north, south and west, Yukinaga was forced to withdraw eastward, to the Pongwollu Pavilion on the city outskirts. Li Rusong, with 20,000 mounted troops, along with a small force of Koreans, hastened to pursue, but were ambushed by a large Japanese formation. Only the timely arrival of a relief force led by his brother saved Li from capture and the destruction of his cavalry. That night, Yukinaga retreated across the frozen Taedong River, moving south towards Yongsan.

The ramifications of the defeat were major, destroying the myth of Japanese invincibility. It also "changed the way the Japanese fought the rest of the war. Until the Ming got involved the Japanese largely relied on their superior training, morale, and firearms to carry the day. The Battle of Pyongyang convinced the Japanese they could not go head to head with the Ming when the latter could bring their big guns to bear."[47]

Battle of Haengju

With the loss of Pyongyang, mounting supply problems, and facing a vitalized enemy, the Japanese commanders elected to retreat *en masse* south as far as Hanseong, effectively abandoning the four northern provinces to the allies. However, even the security of this position appeared to be in question, as the Korean General Gwon Yul was at the time threatening Hanseong from the south. Having

Above: A ghost appearing before Toyotomi Hideyoshi's nephew Kobayakawa Hideaki, who took part in the second Japanese invasion of Korea. *(Asian Art & Archaeology, Inc/Corbis)*

thwarted the campaign in Jeolla, Gwon had quickly advanced northwards from there, re-taking Suwon, and establishing himself at the Doksung fortress. Ukita Hideii sallied out from Hanseong at the head of his forces to lay siege to the fort, but withdrew, having failed to dislodge the Koreans. Kwon pursued the retreating Japanese troops sharply, inflicting heavy casualties, but on gaining the outskirts of the capital, he swung south and occupied a mountain fortress at Haengju.

Bolstered by a victory at Byeokje, Kato Kiyomasa and his 30,000-strong 2nd Division moved to dislodge the Koreans from this commanding position. Awaiting them was a small garrison army of a few thousand.

Overconfident in the numerical superiority of his force, Kato ordered the Japanese soldiers to assault directly up the steep slopes of Haengju. Gwon Yul had used the little time he had to fortify Haengju well, and rained fire on the attackers with *hwacha*,[48] muskets, and bows. Kato tried nine times to break through, but each time was driven off the slopes. After suffering some 10,000 casualties, the Japanese commander finally pulled his troops back.[49]

In late February, as he was closing quickly on Hanseong from the north— apparently believing it had been abandoned[50]—Li's scouting force of 3,000 cavalry was ambushed by a large force of Japanese at Pyokchegwan, with Li himself lucky to escape through the timely intervention of his brothers, Li Rubo and Li Rumei. The badly savaged allied force limped back to Kanseong, "rendered less aggressive for the remainder of the conflict,"[51] while the Japanese fell back on Hanseong. Although accorded great significance in some accounts, the most important outcome of this encounter was to provide evidence to doubtful Chinese commanders of the efficacy of Japanese musketry and swordplay, and the vulnerability of their own cavalry.

But despite stymieing the Koreans at Pyokchegwan, the tide of war had already turned inexorably against the Japanese. Soon, Hanseong itself had to be abandoned, after an allied raid into the Japanese rear destroyed vast stocks of their crucial rice stores.[52] Facing a possible famine among their troops, the Japanese armies quit the capital on May 9. With his food supplies cut off and his forces depleted through the depredations of poor morale, desertion, disease, and a mounting casualty list, Yukinaga had already felt compelled to sue for peace. Negotiations began in the spring of 1593, with China and Korea offering to cease hostilities if the Japanese would stage a partial withdrawal from Korea. Yukinaga had little option but to accept the terms. By the early summer, much of the Japanese army had withdrawn back across the sea. The Ming government also withdrew most of its expeditionary force.

For both China and Japan, however, this was considered a mere hiatus, and for the next four years, as negotiations aimed at resolving the differences between the belligerents continued, each maintained a strong

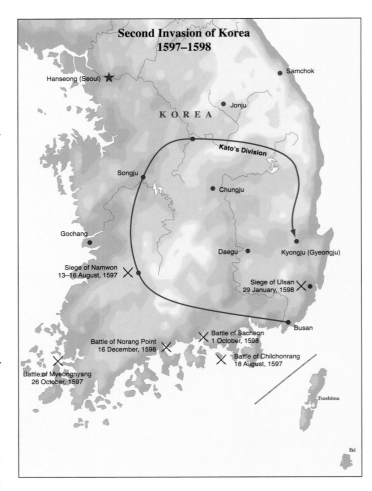

presence on the Korean peninsula. The Japanese sat tight in the series of *wajo* (coastal fortresses) they had constructed at Sosaeng'po, Yangsan, Kichang, Kimhae, Angol'po, and Kojedo, watched over warily by attendant Chinese troops. Kato Kiyomasa himself took a role in the occupation, commanding for a time a 10,000-strong garrison that was rotated through Sosaeng'po.[53]

The first attempts at resolving the dispute came in the summer of 1593, when a Chinese delegation visited Japan, remaining at Hideyoshi's court for more than a month; the next year an envoy from Hideyoshi traveled to Peking. But these and other efforts were unproductive and the peace negotiations eventually collapsed, presaging the dispatch of another invasion force to Korea in 1597.

Second Invasion (1597–1598)

The Koreans took advantage of the four-year hiatus to examine the reasons why the land army had been so conspicuously outdone in battle by the Japanese. Yu Seong-ryong, the senior minister, highlighted several key weaknesses in their defenses. He pointed to the condition of many castles, many of which were in an unfinished state and therefore easily breached, and also to the need for more cannons with which to defend them. Yu also emphasized a need to form a supplementary line of defenses right across Korea, with Hanseong in the center.

These appraisals finally convinced the Korean court of the need for reforms in the military also, and an agency was duly formed in September 1593 to implement them. Under its jurisdiction the two most important were, first, a restructuring of the army into units and companies and, second, an overhaul of the system of conscription, under which military service was made compulsory for all males, regardless of social rank.

While Korea refashioned its military, Toyotomi Hideyoshi considered how to rectify his own weaknesses. Ruminating over the failures of his first invasion, he saw that fundamental problems with the navy had to be addressed before any future effort could be mounted against the Koreans. To this end, during the long-drawn-out period of enforced peace, Hideyoshi oversaw concerted efforts to secure better weapons, and vessels to carry them, for his fleet. As he had before, he tried again to acquire ships from the Portuguese, but was again denied—the Portuguese, it seems, did not want to risk harming their lucrative trade with China.[54] However, according to his directives, the fleet was built into a more effective force, "as regards both seamanship and quality of ships."[55]

Once he was satisfied the weaknesses had been identified and remedied, Hideyoshi resolved to attack Korea again, his own declining health perhaps adding a sense of urgency to the matter. In early 1597, Hideyoshi and his generals began detail planning for a second invasion. This time the goal was not to be the conquest of China, but a seemingly more modest subjugation of Korea.

The command structure was also simplified. Instead of the nine independent (and sometimes competing) divisions committed during the earlier invasion, the invasion forces were unified into the Army of the Left (1st Division/Konishi, 4th Division/Shimazu, 8th Division/Ukita) and the Army of the Right (2nd Division/Kato, 3rd Division/Kuroda, 7th Division/Mori), consisting of about 50,000 men and 30,000, respectively.

On August 27, 1597, Japan commenced its second invasion of Korea. After a series of battles that routed the Korean navy at sea, a fleet of 700 ships transported an estimated 100,000 men to points on the southern and southwestern coast, to join the resident Japanese garrison.

Under the overall command of Kobayakawa Hideaki, the various divisions of the Army of the Left and the Army of the Right reached out "like the outstretched fingers of a hand seeking to extend its grasp around Korea."[56] The Army of the Left moved to occupy the southwest provinces, while the Army of the right moved north toward Seoul. Although the Chinese garrison tried to check the Japanese advance it was vastly outnumbered and could do little but delay the advance.[57] Once news of the invasion reached China, the imperial court in Peking quickly ordered the mobilization of 55,000 troops,[58] and appointed Yang Hao to command them. To support the land army the Chinese court also committed a naval force of 21,000.

In the first weeks of the campaign the Japanese were largely confined to Gyeongsang Province, and the action was limited to numerous short-range attacks against much larger Korean and Chinese forces. This in fact set the pattern for the entire war, as for much of the time the Japanese war machine remained grid-locked at Gyeongsang Province, unable to make progress, and largely on the defensive.

Siege of Namwon

Seeking to break the deadlock, the Japanese began planning a breakout from Gyeongsang into Jeolla Province, its southwestern neighbor, with the goal of occupying the provincial capital Jeonju. During the drive at Jeonju, the Japanese army achieved what is commonly seen as its only demonstrable success of the whole second campaign. Thirty miles to the southeast of Jeonju lay the important fortress of Namwon, the largest fortress in Jeolla Province, and an obvious target for any invader. A wall protected the city, with gun towers at each corner, and in front of this was a shallow, dry moat. However, the fortress was poorly situated on flat land dominated by high ground all around it, and was highly vulnerable to plunging fire. The Korean commanders had in fact wanted to abandon

Namwon and relocate to a nearby mountain fortress, but found themselves overruled by the Chinese General Yang Yuan, who had decided the city would be held.

The garrison at Namwon numbered 6,000 soldiers, of whom there were roughly equal numbers of Chinese and Koreans, supplemented by civilians who had come forward to defend the city.

Against this meager force Ukita Hideii (the overall commander of the Army of the Left) threw some 56,000 of his men. Meeting little resistance on the approach, the Japanese troops quickly cordoned the city. Beginning on August 13, they began attacks all around walls of the fortress, using ladders and siege towers. But after three days of fruitless efforts to scale the walls, Hidiie's troops met with a chance stroke of luck, when they found a gate that had been left open by those fleeing from within. Through this portal they were at last able to gain entry and sack the fortress. Yang Yuan and many of his troops had been among those who had fled—those that remained, soldiers and civilians alike, were put to death.

Shortly after the loss of Namwon, troops under Kato Kiyomasa captured another fortress at Hwangsoksan, a sprawling mountain complex garrisoned by thousands of soldiers under Generals Jo Jong-do and Gwak Jun.[59] These early Japanese victories stirred the Chinese commanders into action, and they subsequently moved to engage the Japanese south of Hanseong and halt their advance. In the early fall the Army of the Right (under overall command of Kato Kiyomasa) was finally halted in the mountains to the south of the capital at Chiksan.[60] This would be Kato's maximum point of advance; thereafter, with his cordon under constant attack from the Chinese and Korean forces, and awaiting resupply by sea, he had to adopt a defensive stance.

Naval operations

As in the first invasion, the Korean navy proved to be a determining factor in the outcome of the second. This time, however, the war at sea had begun badly for the Koreans. Once again they had failed to intercept the invasion fleet, and the navy was conspicuously failing elsewhere. It was true that the Japanese had improved their

naval forces, but the real reason for the malaise lay in the absence of the influential Yi Sun-sin, who was languishing in a prison. In the early stages of the invasion a dispute had arisen between Yi Sun-sin and King Seonjo over the former's refusal to obey an order, which would have him attempt to lay a trap for the invasion fleet in waters that he knew from personal experience to be hazardous for shipping. As it later transpired, King Seonjo's order was based on false intelligence supplied through a Japanese agent, but Yi Sun-sin was promptly demoted and jailed by King Seonjo, and replaced by Won Gyun as commander.

Battle of Chilchonryang

Upon his appointment, Won Gyun gathered the entire Korean fleet of more than a hundred ships outside of Yosu to search for the Japanese. Without prior preparations or planning, Won Gyun had his fleet sail towards Pusan. En route, he was warned of the presence of a large Japanese fleet off Pusan. He decided to attack immediately, to the apparent dismay of his captains. In the ensuing action off Chilchonryang, Won Gyun was surprised by a sudden attack by Japanese ships under Todo, Wakizaka, and Kato. Quickly outmaneuvered, his ships were brought within

Japanese fleet ran headlong into this unseen obstacle, and thirteen of them in the advance squadron were quickly capsized. In the confusion, the remains of the squadron were set upon and sunk, while the others beat a hasty retreat. During this action at least 133 Japanese vessels were sunk and in the aftermath the sorry remnants of the fleet were ordered back to Pusan, never again to challenge the Korean navy for command of the sea. In tandem with Chinese naval forces, Admiral Yi Sun-sin now asserted his control over waters of the Korea Strait, and effectively blockaded the western side of the Korean peninsula.

Siege of Ulsan

In the land war also, Japanese fortunes were in terminal decline, the army now firmly on its back heel. Once more it was facing a supply crisis, brought about by Yi Sun-sin's control of the shipping lanes and "aggravated by the fact that Korea had been so thoroughly devastated in the first campaign."[63] Blockaded to the west by Yi Sun-sin's fleet, the army commanders ordered a tactical retreat along a several-hundred-mile front to Korea's eastern and southern coasts, to the extensive network of coastal fortresses known as *wajo* that they had built and still controlled. Without supply ships to bring them provisions and reinforcements, for the rest of the war the isolated Japanese forces would remain firmly on the defensive, facing siege after siege before finally withdrawing.

Through the late fall of 1597, Kato Kiyomasa's Army of the Right was pushed back south from Chiksan, under the sheer weight of the allied advance, and the superior weapons in their possession.[64] Eventually, he withdrew south to Ulsan, a minor stronghold on the southeastern coast that he felt better able to defend.

With their enemy bottled up in the southeast, the allied forces now seized the opportunity to launch their first major offensive of the war. Some 44,800 troops set out from Hanseong on January 14, 1598, determined to attack Seosaengpo, and Ulsan, at that time under the command of Kato Yasumasa, Kuki Hirotaka, and Asano Nagayoshi. Short of food, water, and ammunition, and sorely outnumbered, they faced a difficult situation. By the end of the month the allies had reached the outskirts

Above: Chinese soldiers on the raid to Ulsan Castle, 1597.
(British Museum/Jo St Mart)

range of *teppo* fire and overwhelmed by Japanese boarding parties. The entire Korean fleet was lost (more than 160 of them according to a letter written by Hideyoshi[61]), save for thirteen of the *panokseons* that had been led away from the scene by a quick-thinking Korean officer. This would constitute the entire fighting force of the Korean navy for some time. The hapless Won Gyun made it to the shore only to be killed later by Japanese troops.

Battle of Myeongnyang

After the debacle in Chilchonryang, Yi Sun-sin was quickly reinstated, although he now had precious few ships with which to combat the Japanese naval forces. With only twelve ships and 200 men, on September 16 he led his fleet against a Japanese force of 300 war vessels in the Myeongnyang Strait. Here "he spread iron chains…between the east coast of Chindo Island and the coast of Cholla (Jeolla) Province—a tactic which might be compared to the harassment of an enemy by mines today."[62] Attempting to pass through the strait, the

Above: Korean and Chinese forces assault the Japanese around the port city of Pusan. *(Wikipedia via Jo St Mart)*

and were pushing through the outlying defenses. Their first assault on the citadel itself began on January 29, catching the Japanese army off guard and for the large part still encamped outside the walls. Battling fiercely, the Japanese troops pulled back inside the city walls.

On January 30 the allied force attacked and burned one of the outposts, inflicting many casualties and causing further withdrawals, before taking the inner stronghold of Tolsan. The timely arrival the following day of Kato Kiyomasa at the head of 500 troops proved to be the turning point in the siege, for despite repeated attacks the embattled defenders were able to shut up the fortress and wait for reinforcements to come.

With conditions within the castle growing increasingly dire, defeat appeared to be inevitable. The defenders, however, kept up their dogged resistance, even though some poor souls "froze to death at their posts"[65] and others "later resorted to eating paper and even mud in a desperate attempt to keep their bellies full."[66] Then, in the first week of February, came a glimmer of hope, as signs began to emerge that the allied forces, too, were running out of food. Finally, on February 8, Konishi Yukinaga arrived by sea with a large relief column. Over the next few days a stand-off developed, with movement much hampered by driving sleet.

Then, quite suddenly, the Chinese General Yang Hao fled the field, believing he was about to be outflanked.

196

The whole allied army broke ranks and followed. Seeing this, the defenders of Ulsan threw open the gates and pursued, halted only by a brave stand from the Ming Chinese commander Mao Guoqi.

Although the Siege of Ulsan was a victory of sorts for the Japanese, it only really served to prolong the war, while many Japanese commanders were now persuaded to seek an end to the conflict. For the allies the ramifications were equally serious, and nearly caused the collapse of the entire Sino-Korean alliance.

Beginning in the spring of 1598, Korean forces and a massive 100,000-strong Chinese host began efforts to retake the coastal *wajo*. In association with these operations, in May the Wanli Chinese Emperor sent a fleet under Chen Lin to conduct joint operations with the Koreans against the Japanese navy. Konishi Yukinaga, faced with these dual threats, voiced his concerns at the increasingly dire situation, and quietly began to scale down the Japanese presence on the Korean peninsula. During the summer and into the fall, those who remained were reduced to desperate defenses of the remaining strongholds, notably at Sach'on in October, which Shimazu Yoshihiro and his son Tadatsune successfully held against all odds.

The Ming army, totaling some 36,700 troops, used "a curious siege engine"[67] in the attack, "a combination of cannon and iron-tipped battering ram" that they employed to try and break down the gates of the fortress. At the height of the battle, this fearsome weapon suddenly blew up, scattering the Ming army. Yoshihiro quickly counterattacked, and pursued the Chinese back to the Nam River. All told, 30,000 of them perished, the nose-less[68] corpses being buried in a great mound that can be seen to this day.

Although the battle at Sach'on was "China's worst defeat at Japanese hands,"[69] the tide of the war had by now swung firmly against the Japanese, for they now had only tentative control of the coastal areas.

The death of Hideyoshi

On September 18, the final blow was dealt to the Japanese cause by the death of the great warlord,

Toyotomi Hideyoshi. Realizing that his great quest to conquer Asia had failed, on his deathbed Hideyoshi ordered the withdrawal of forces from Korea, lamenting before he died: "How could I have sent 100,000 soldiers overseas to become ghosts?"[70] In late October the Council of Five Elders sent word of his decree to the Japanese commanders, hastening a process that was in fact already underway.

The allies now determined to pressure the retreating Japanese through a series of final offensives. The first took the form of a three-pronged assault: the first against Kato Kiyomasa's strategic stronghold of Ulsan, another at the forces under Konishi Yukinaga at Sunch'on, and the third at Shimazu Yoshihiro's division at Sach'on. Another naval group under the joint command of Yi Sun-sin and the Chinese commander Chen Lin would meanwhile patrol the seas, and cut off the seaward escape routes.

Late in the year, the main allied force of 30,000, under the command of Ma Gui, moved on Ulsan. The advance was swift and effective, and in the face of impossible odds the Japanese torched their provisions and prepared to withdraw by sea. Victory was denied Ma, however, as his men were lured into a trap by the rearguard troops and were eventually forced to pull back, giving the Japanese the opportunity they needed to escape. Kato's men boarded their ships under cover of darkness on December 14, just as the allies were sailing to their deaths in the straits of Noryang.

Battle of Noryang Point

Meanwhile, at the westernmost Japanese fortress, Sunch'on, Konishi Yukinaga's 14,000 troops were still prevented from embarking their ships by an allied fleet led by Yi Sun-sin and Chen Lin. Konishi had attempted to negotiate passage for his troops through bribes to Chen Lin but, although Chen had been willing to accept and withdraw the entire allied fleet, Yi Sun-sin would have none of it.

Consequently, on December 15, some 20,000 Japanese troops from the *wajo* of Sach'on, Goseong, and Namhae boarded 500 ships and began to mass east of the narrow Noryang Strait, with orders to break the blockade of Sunch'on. However, Yi Sun-sin and Chen Lin were regularly appraised of Japanese movements by their network of spies, and led out a fleet to intercept the relief convoy. Early in the morning of December 16 they launched a devastating surprise attack against the Japanese fleet. Targeted by cannons and fire arrows, by dawn nearly half of the Japanese ships had been destroyed, and the survivors were withdrawing away to safety. Admiral Yi Sun-sin then led a final attack, seeking to destroy the scattered remnants of the enemy fleet. During this last action Yi Sun-sin was hit by a bullet on the left side of his chest, and died soon after.

Despite the loss of their great naval commander, the battle was a complete victory for Korea and their Chinese allies. With the battle still raging, Konishi Yukinaga quit

Sunch'on and retreated to Pusan; in the following days, all remaining Japanese fortresses were abandoned to the allies. Konishi, Shimazu, Kato and all the other Japanese generals withdrew to Japan on December 21. The last ships of the evacuation fleet sailed three days after, concluding the Japanese campaign on the Korean peninsula.

Aftermath

"To the Japanese it was the greatest and most ambitious project of one of the greatest and most ambitious men Japan has ever produced; to the Koreans it was the severest and most disastrous war the nation had ever experienced." So said the historian Geo. H. Jones, writing

NOTES
1 Kenneth M. Swope *Crouching Tigers, Secret Weapons: Military Technology Employed during the Sino-Japanese-Korean War, 1592-1598* The Journal of Military History 69: 1; p.11
2 Kenneth M. Swope *Crouching Tigers, Secret Weapons: Military Technology Employed during the Sino-Japanese-Korean War, 1592-1598* The Journal of Military History 69: 1; p.12
3 *Kenneth M. Swope Three Great Campaigns p.187-190*
4 Kenneth M. Swope *Crouching Tigers, Secret Weapons: Military Technology Employed during the Sino-Japanese-Korean War, 1592-1598* The Journal of Military History 69: 1; p.20
5 Kenneth M. Swope *Crouching Tigers, Secret Weapons: Military Technology Employed during the Sino-Japanese-Korean War, 1592-1598* The Journal of Military History 69: 1; p.11
6 Kenneth M. Swope *Crouching Tigers, Secret Weapons: Military Technology Employed during the Sino-Japanese-Korean War, 1592-1598* The Journal of Military History 69: 1; p.20
7 The chief envoy was Tahibana Yasuhiro
8 As Kenneth M. Swope points out, according to contemporary Japanese sources firearms technology was actually probably introduced by the Chinese much earlier than 1543. However, the teppo that the Japanese used bore a closer resemblance to European models an 'some argue the Japanese largely discarded earlier technologies when Portugese weapons were introduced.' *Crouching Tigers, Secret Weapons: Military Technology Employed during the Sino-Japanese-Korean War 1592-1598* The Journal of Military History 69: 1: Footnote to p.19
9 *An interesting study is* Seiho Arima *The Western Influence on Japanese Military Science, Shipbuilding, and Navigation* Monumenta Nipponica, Vol. 19, No. 3/4 (1964), pp. 352-379

10 Arthur J. Marder *From Jimmu Tenno to Perry: Sea Power in Early Japanese history* The American Historical Review 51: 1; p.19
11 Arthur J. Marder *From Jimmu Tenno to Perry: Sea Power in Early Japanese history* The American Historical Review 51: 1; p.22
12 Kenneth M. Swope *Crouching Tigers, Secret Weapons: Military Technology Employed during the Sino-Japanese-Korean War, 1592-1598* The Journal of

Military History 69: 1; p.22
13 The Jurchens were a Tungus people who inhabited the region of Manchuria (Northeast China) until the 17th century, when they became known as the Manchus.
14 Arthur Marder says of the *wako* 'The warlike spirit stimulated by the Mongol campaigns and the incessant domestic turmoil made many Japanese beliicose and restless. Many feudal lords and their retainers along the western coast took up piracy as a livelihood from the middle of the fourteenth century on.' *From Jimmu Tenno to Perry: Sea Power in Early Japanese history* The American Historical Review 51: 1; p.19
15 Until 1587, when Toyotomi Hideoshi moved to curtial their actions.
16 Cited in Marder *From Jimmu Tenno to Perry: Sea Power in Early Japanese history* The American Historical Review 51: 1; p.20
17 See Kenneth M. Swope *Crouching Tigers, Secret Weapons: Military Technology Employed during the Sino-Japanese-Korean War, 1592-1598* The Journal of Military History 69: 1; p.26-27 for a description of the type of cannon that the Koreans used.

18 It was the habit of many historians in Japan to emphasize the numerical discrepancy created by China's decision to commit troops to the war. However, modern scholarship makes it clear that the Chinese contribution cannot be measured in numbers alone,
19 Kenneth M. Swope argues that the Chinese artillery was one of the major contributory factors for the Japanese withdrawal. *See Crouching Tigers, Secret Weapons: Military Technology Employed during the Sino-Japanese-Korean War, 1592-1598 The Journal of Military History 69: 1;*
20 Stephen Turnbull Samurai Commanders 1577-1638 p.44-48
21 Kenneth M. Swope Crouching Tigers, Secret Weapons: Military Technology Employed during the Sino-Japanese-Korean War, 1592-1598 The Journal of Military History 69: 1; p. 27
22 Kenneth M. Swope Crouching Tigers, Secret Weapons: Military Technology Employed during the Sino-Japanese-Korean War, 1592-1598 The Journal of Military History 69: 1; p. 28
23 Sin had deliberately chosen selected this position as he feared his inexperienced troops would flee in battle easily. He therefore 'trapped' his forces in a triangular

area formed by the convergence of the Talchon and Han rivers.
24 Stephen Turnbull *War in Japan 1467-1615* p.68
25 Stephen Turnbull *War in Japan 1467-1615* p.68
26 Stephen Turnbull *War in Japan 1467-1615* p.68
27 Delmer M. Brown *The Impact of Firearms on Japanese Warfare 1543-1598* The Far Eastern Quarterly 7: 3; p.247
28 After the fall of Ch'ungju, King Seonjo retreated first to Pyongyang, then to Uiju, near the border of China, and finally sought refuge in China.
29 Stephen Turnbull *War in Japan 1467-1615* p.68
30 Stephen Turnbull *War in Japan 1467-1615* p.68
31 Stephen Turnbull *War in Japan 1467-1615* p.68
32 Arthur J. Marder *From Jimmu Tenno to Perry: Sea Power in Early Japanese history* The American Historical Review 51: 1; p.20
33 Kenneth M. Swope *Crouching Tigers, Secret Weapons: Military Technology Employed during the Sino-Japanese-Korean War, 1592-1598* The Journal of Military History 69: 1; p. 30
34 Admiral Won later sent a message to Admiral Yi that he had fled to Konyang after being overwhelmed by the Japanese in a fight. A messenger was sent by Admiral Yi to the nearby island of Namhae to give Yi's order for war preparations, only to find it pillaged and abandoned by its own inhabitants. As soldiers began to flee secretly, Admiral Yi ordered "to arrest the escapees" and had two of the fugitives brought back, beheaded them and had their heads exposed.
35 Admiral Yi was and still is a subject of reverence in both China and Japan. Admiral Togo, famed for his success at the Battle of Tsushima during the Russo-Japanese War, called Admiral Yi the greatest naval commander in history.[
36 Arthur J. Marder *From Jimmu Tenno to Perry: Sea Power in Early Japanese history* The American Historical Review 51: 1; p.20
37 Arthur J. *Marder From Jimmu Tenno to Perry: Sea Power in Early Japanese history The American Historical Review 51: 1; p.23*
38 Apparently devised by Yi Sun-sin himself, the turtle ship was essentially a panokseon with a roof covered in iron spikes, and possibly hexagonal iron plates (the fact that the turtle ships had iron armor is disputed. See Arthur J. *Marder From Jimmu Tenno to Perry: Sea Power in Early Japanese history The American Historical Review 51: 1; p.26*). There were 36 cannon

about the invasions more than a century ago. Even today, more than 400 years since the withdrawal, they remain a source of conflicting opinion. This colors some of the material that has been published on the wars, in Japan, China, and in Korea, which bury truth under a heap of subjectivity.

What can be stated with absolute conviction is that all three belligerents suffered heavily from the war. Japan achieved nothing at the cost of thousands of lives and large sums of national wealth. As Marder concludes, "The Seven Years' War, which had begun as the first stage of a grandiose project for conquering most of Asia, and of making Peking the capital of the Japanese Empire, had ended without territorial, financial or political gain."

Of the coalition that defeated them, Ming China had to bear much of the financial burden of defending Korea, all the while fighting a domestic war with the Manchus, and this ultimately led to the rise of the Qing Dynasty.[71] But for Korea, this conflict was more devastating than any other event in its history. In addition to the human losses, Korea suffered long-term damage to many facets of its society, culture, economy, and infrastructure, and never fully recovered from it.

ports, and also openings, above the cannons, through which the ship's crew could fire their personal arms. The ship powered by two sails and 16 oars, and was comparatively fast. The Koreans had 6 of these turtle ships throughout the entire war, and used them to penetrate deep into enemy formations, with the objective of sinking the enemy flag ship. Much as been made of the impact of this revolutionary craft. In fact it has been the habit to attribute the Korean naval superiority solely to this innovative vessel, discounting the many other contributory factors. Modern scholarship tends to play down the legend. See *Kenneth M. Swope Crouching Tigers, Secret Weapons: Military Technology Employed during the Sino-Japanese-Korean War, 1592-1598 The Journal of Military History 69: 1; p. 16-18*

39 Arthur J. Marder *From Jimmu Tenno to Perry: Sea Power in Early Japanese history* The American Historical Review 51: 1; p.27
40 Arthur J. Marder *From Jimmu Tenno to Perry: Sea Power in Early Japanese history* The American Historical Review 51: 1; p.28
41 Arthur J. Marder *From Jimmu Tenno to Perry: Sea Power in Early Japanese history* The American Historical Review 51: 1; p.28
42 Mention must be made of the Korean irregular forces, which sprang up all over occupied Korea. Hundreds of irregular units were formed in local districts throughout Korea, composed primarily of those who worked the land and led by landowners or priests. Most units were made up of a small number of men armed with swords and other light weapons. They went to work on harassing Japanese communication and supply lines and laid ambushes for Japanese army columns, avoiding direct confrontations, but at working times working in cohesion with other units with regular army units to form a formidable host against the Japanese invaders. By the end of 1592 these 'guerrillas' had forced the Japanese to abandon many towns and provinces.
43 Again the numbers are disputed, with some accounts quoting figures of as high as 70,000. This number is based on Swope's research.
44 *Kenneth M. Swope Crouching Tigers, Secret Weapons: Military Technology Employed during the Sino-Japanese-Korean War, 1592-1598 The Journal of Military History 69: 1; p. 34*

45 This remarkable weapon, best described as an elementary multiple rocket launcher, consisted of a wheeled cart on which was mounted a framework of launch 'tubes'. Into these were loaded up to 200 rockets to which were attached arrows. It was developed in Korea sometime in the 15th century.
46 The Battle of Haengju proved a great morale booster for the Korean army, after the reverses of the previous year. Together with the Siege of Jinju and Battle of Hansando it is considered one of three decisive victories won by the Koreans.
47 *Kenneth M. Swope Crouching Tigers, Secret Weapons: Military Technology Employed during the Sino-Japanese-Korean War, 1592-1598 The Journal of Military History 69: 1; p. 37*
48 This is a slight paraphrasing of *Kenneth M. Swope Crouching Tigers, Secret Weapons: Military Technology Employed during the Sino-Japanese-Korean War, 1592-1598 The Journal of Military History 69: 1; p. 38*
49 Arthur J. Marder *From Jimmu Tenno to Perry: Sea Power in Early Japanese history* The American Historical Review 51: 1; p.28
50 Stephen Turnbull *Samurai Commanders* Osprey b. 47
51 Delmer M. Brown *The Impact of Firearms on Japanese Warfare 1543-1598* The Far Eastern Quarterly 7: 3; p.252
52 Arthur J. Marder *From Jimmu Tenno to Perry: Sea Power in Early Japanese history* The American Historical Review 51: 1; p.29
53 Quoted in Kenneth M. Swope *Beyond Turtleboats: Siege Accounts From Hideyoshi's Second Invasion of Korea, 1597-1598.*
54 *Kenneth M. Swope Crouching Tigers, Secret Weapons: Military Technology Employed during the Sino-Japanese-Korean War, 1592-1598 The Journal of Military History 69: 1; p. 39*
55 At the height of the second campaign the Chinese had around 75,000 on the Korean peninsula, more than double the Korean strength of 30,000.
56 Stephen Turnbull *War in Japan 1467-1615* Osprey b. 71
57 *Kenneth M. Swope Crouching Tigers, Secret Weapons: Military Technology Employed during the Sino-Japanese-Korean War, 1592-1598 The Journal of Military History 69: 1; p. 39*
58 Delmer M. Brown *The Impact of Firearms on Japanese Warfare 1543-1598* The Far Eastern Quar-

terly 7: 3; p.252
59 Arthur J. Marder *From Jimmu Tenno to Perry: Sea Power in Early Japanese history* The American Historical Review 51: 1; p.29
60 Arthur J. Marder *From Jimmu Tenno to Perry: Sea Power in Early Japanese history* The American Historical Review 51: 1; p.29
61 *Kenneth M. Swope Crouching Tigers, Secret Weapons: Military Technology Employed during the Sino-Japanese-Korean War, 1592-1598 The Journal of Military History 69: 1; p. 39*
62 Stephen Turnbull *Samurai Commanders 1577-1638* p.22
63 Kenneth M. Swope *Beyond Turtleboats: Siege Accounts From Hideyoshi's Second Invasion of Korea, 1597-1598*
64 Stephen Turnbull *Samurai Commanders 1577-1638* p.22
65 The Japanese army took noses from the enemy dead to tally the body count .
66 Stephen Turnbull *Samurai Commanders 1577-1638* p.22
67 Quoted in Kenneth M. Swope *Crouching Tigers, Secret Weapons: Military Technology Employed during the Sino-Japanese-Korean War, 1592-1598* The Journal of Military History 69: 1; p. 40
68 Arthur J. Marder *From Jimmu Tenno to Perry: Sea Power in Early Japanese history* The American Historical Review 51: 1; p.29
69 Geo. H. Jones *The China Review, or notes & queries on the Far East* Vol. 23 No. 4 (1899)
70 Arthur J. Marder *From Jimmu Tenno to Perry: Sea Power in Early Japanese history* The American Historical Review 51: 1; p.30
71 In 1638 the Manchu defeated and conquered Ming China's traditional ally Korea with an army of 100,000 troops. Shortly after the Koreans renounced their loyalty to the Ming Dynasty. Then, in 1640, the peasantry revolted and began to form huge rebel bands. Unable to defend itself against the dual threats of the Manchu and the huge peasant revolts in the provinces, the Ming dynasty collapsed. The last Ming Emperor hanged himself in 1644.

EPILOG—THE BOSHIN WAR

Above: Following several earlier visits to Japan by U.S. Navy warships in search of a trade agreement, in 1852 Commodore Matthew Perry was initially refused permission to come ashore (under the policy of sakoku, but he threatened bombardment by the U.S. black-hulled steamships (the "black ships") unless he was allowed to present a letter from President Millard Fillmore requesting a trading treaty.
(Wikipedia via Jo St Mart)

For two-and-a-half centuries after the Battle of Sekigahara Japan was ruled by a succession of Tokugawa *shoguns*, through the omnipresent *bakufu* government. It was a period almost devoid of major conflict, during which time the *samurai* functioned not as warriors, but in bureaucratic or administrative posts. Nonetheless, it was during this time that the *samurai* ethic—obedience, moral integrity, and so forth—was refined and promulgated as the *bushido* code. Then, in the mid-1850s, growing dissatisfaction with the *shogunate* led some to challenge its authority and seek the restoration of the emperor as the absolute authority in Japan. This in turn was the catalyst for the Boshin War of 1868, in which the power of the once mighty *samurai* class and the *shogunate* was shattered forever.

Early in the Tokugawa era, Toyotomi Hideyoshi had established an official class hierarchy, by which Japanese society was rigidly stratified and strictly controlled. In time the rigid nature of this caste system was the font of considerable unrest. The *samurai* class of landowners was indubitably established at the apex of this society, followed in succession by farmers, artisans, and traders. However, this belies the fact that, in economic terms, those on the lower social strata held the greater power.

This brings us to one of the underlying causes of the Boshin War, which was a deep-rooted dissatisfaction over taxation. Taxes on the peasantry, which were paid in rice to the *samurai* landowner, were set at fixed amounts, and diminished over time due to inflation and monetary fluctuations. Thus the revenues collected by the *samurai* landowners were worth less and less over time. The merchants to whom they sold the rice benefited from this situation, stockpiling rice to maintain market value yet paying little for it.[1] This led to confrontations between *samurai*, who derived their income from the land, and wealthy farmers. In most cases these were limited, local disturbances, but in other instances, more widespread rebellions. However, none proved sufficiently divisive to threaten the established order.

Seclusion

However, in the event, the catalyst was provided by widespread discontent, not over economic distress, but the *shogunate*'s mollifying approach to foreign aggression. Soon after the establishment of the Tokugawa *shogunate*, the *bakufu* government adopted a policy of seclusion, known as *sakoku* in Japanese[2]. The motive for this seems to have been a suspicion that traders, merchants, and

Above: Matthew Perry's and other Americans' visits to Japan were ultimately a success in terms of opening up trading relations with Japan, but they were achieved initially only at the point of a gun, and many within Japan were dissatisfied with the *shogunate*'s handling of the situation. Here, U.S. Navy personnel and Japanese dignitaries are shown on the beach at Gore-Hama, July 14, 1853. *(Library of Congress)*

missionaries were seeking to subjugate Japan to European rule.[2] With the exception of some Dutch and Chinese, all foreigners—traders, merchants, and missionaries alike—faced restrictions. Many were simply expelled. The detrimental effect on trade can be imagined, and after some 200 years many within Japan were actively seeking a reform. In the event, the *sakoku* policy was ended under force.

On July 8, 1853, Commodore Matthew Perry of the U.S. Navy reached Edo (modern-day Tokyo) with four warships—the infamous *kurofune* or "black ships." Perry aimed the guns of his heavily armed ships towards the city, threatening to bring it down unless Japan open its doors to trade. With this blunt display of power, Japan reluctantly agreed to abandon its exclusionist policy and open its doors to foreign traders. As M. William Steele has written, "The opening of Japan to the West precipitated a crisis of unprecedented proportions," during which "the *bakufu* proved incapable of handling the new political and economic demands placed upon it."[3]

Many in Japan were deeply dissatisfied with the *shogunate*'s handling of this affair, leading them to question the authority of the *shogunate* and the ability of such a system of government to lead Japan through a rapid period of modernization. Things came to a head in March 1863, when the interventionist Emperor Komei issued his "order to expel barbarians." This act inspired attacks on the *shogunate* both from within and without, including the shelling of Shimonoseki by British warships.

Left: In March 1863 Emperor Komei issued an "order to expel barbarians," which encouraged attacks on all foreign shipping using the narrow waterway at Shimonoseki; here, British warships fire back. *(Wikipedia via Jo St Mart)*

In the face of these threats, Japan divided into supporters of the *shogun* and those who wished to establish a lawful, unified imperial rule in Japan, free from foreign influence. An opportunity for the imperialists to advance their cause presented itself in December 1866, when Emperor Komei, who had been a staunch supporter of the *bakufu* government, died. His successor on the throne was Emperor Meiji, and he quickly became the focus for opponents of the *shogunate* striving to bring about its demise through the restoration of imperial power.

On November 8, 1867, Emperor Meiji approved a conspiracy fronted by the Satsuma and Choshu clans to overthrow the *bakufu*. Soon thereafter, the incumbent *shogun*, Tokagawa Yoshinobu, resigned his post, effectively submitting to the authority of the emperor and bringing to an end the two-and-a-half-centuries-old Tokugawa *shogunate*. However, behind this apparent climb down was a desire to avoid open clashes until such time as he was in a position to challenge the pro-imperialists. In secret he sent word to *shogunate* loyalists to commence raising forces in Osaka, and await the moment to rise up against the new leadership.

The trigger was provided by the formal proclamation of the "Restoration of Power" (*Taisei Hokan*)[4] by the emperor on January 3, 1868. Simultaneously, he formally dissolved the *bakufu* government and announced the establishment of a new administration to replace it. Although the emperor and his advisers favored continued collaboration with the still-powerful Tokugawa family, a hard line faction led by Saigo Takamori pushed for a firmer approach, stripping the Tokugawa of their lands and purging them from positions of influence. Yoshinobu's response was to refute the legality of the proclamation, and deny its legitimacy. After acts of provocation by imperialist mobs in Edo, Yoshinobu began making preparations to advance on Kyoto from Osaka,[5] and once there to subdue the Satsuma-Choshu (Satcho) Alliance—the axis of opposition to the *shogunate*.

Battle of Toba-Fushimi

The first battle of the war was fought on January 27, when the advancing *shogunate* loyalists encountered the armies of the Choshu and Satsuma clans near Toba (located in what is now part of Minami-ku, Kyoto) and Fushimi, at the southern entrance to Kyoto. Although the 15,000-strong loyalist force enjoyed a three-to-one advantage in numbers,[6] the disparity was more than evened out by the fact that, for the most part, in weapons and composition the *shogunate* army was little changed from medieval times. By contrast, the Choshu and Satsuma had modern artillery howitzers, rifles, and even a few Gatling guns.[7]

Approaching a Satsuma checkpoint en route to Kyoto, the vanguard of the *shogunate* army sought but was denied permission to pass. The Satsuma force opened fire with their artillery and fighting quickly broke out. The following day an imperial banner appeared over the Satsuma lines, pronouncing the legitimacy of their cause in the eyes of the emperor, and hence the illegality of the *shogunate*'s actions. Confused and in disarray by this turn of events, the *shogunate* troops were attacked and routed. On February 1, Tokugawa Yoshinobu fled Osaka by ship to Edo, from where he would continue to fight the war. The following day, Osaka Castle was invested, bringing to an end the battle of Toba-Fushimi.

Tokugawa Yoshinobu's hopes of securing a foreign intervention in his favor were dashed when a delegation of ministers from concerned powers finally decided to recognize the new government. This support was secured through an agreement that harbors would be open in accordance with international treaties, and that foreigners would be protected.[8] In early March, foreign nations signed a formal agreement, the provisions of which disallowed any intervention or military assistance to either side.

Battle of Katsunuma

After their victory over the *shogunate* loyalist forces at the Battle of Toba-Fushimi, the imperial forces advanced northeast towards the Tokugawa capital of Edo.[9] Moving in three columns up the Tokaido, Nakasendo, and Hokurikudo, the 3,000-strong imperial army occupied the Tokugawa stronghold of Kofu, Yamanashi. Meanwhile, Kondo Isami, leader of the *shinsengumi* police force, had assembled a much-smaller force of 300 *samurai*

Above: At Toba-Fushimi, the *shogunate* forces took outdated weapons and tactics into battle against the more modern Chosu and Satsuma armies, and were defeated. *(Wikipedia via Jo St Mart)*

and policemen at Edo, and led this out to meet the approaching enemy. At the end of March the two armies met at Katsunuma (now a part of Koshu, Yamanashi). The heavily outnumbered *shogunal* forces were defeated. The survivors, including Kondo, attempted to flee back to Aizu via Sagami Province; Kondo was caught and beheaded at Nagareyama (Chiba).

The Battle of Katsunuma was the last significant military action in central Honshu during the Boshin War. In May Edo was surrounded, and surrendered by Katsu Kaishu, the *shogun*'s Army Minister.[10] Tokugawa Yoshinobu was placed under house arrest, and subsequently submitted to imperial rule. While some of his loyalists continued to resist, they were resoundingly defeated in the Battle of Ueno on July 4, 1868.[11]

While most of Japan now accepted the emperor's rule,[12] many former Tokugawa retainers retreated north from the capital, to Konodai, where they gathered to coordinate the resistance. In the second week of May, a force led by Otori Keisuke attempted to block the northward advance of the imperial troops by taking the strategically important castle town at Utsunomiya, on the road to Nikko and Aizu. However, within a few days the castle was retaken and, faced with defeat, Otori withdrew northward, by way of Nikko, and on to Aizu.

Aizu now became the focus for the revolt. After Yoshinobu's surrender, a core of *shogunate* supporters in the north, led by the Aizu clan, had resolved to fight on. In May they formed the *Oetsu Reppan Domei* (Northern Alliance) comprising the domains of Sendai, Yonezawa, Aizu, Shonai, and Nagaoka.[13] Together they could muster a formidable host of 50,000 troops. But this numerically strong force was badly compromised by poor equipment, and still relied on centuries-old fighting methods. Moreover, the soldiers had very few modern weapons,

Above: This 1850s *samurai* warrior still carries his swords at his belt, but the rest of his personal belongings are held on a pole over his shoulder as, in reduced circumstances, he is forced to travel to look for work. *(Hulton Archive/Getty Images)*

his Gatling guns, but was unable to prevent his castle from falling on May 19. The imperial army continued to progress north, to the limits of Aizu, where on October 6 a group of 700 *shinsengumi* men under Saito Hajime failed to stall them at the Battle of Bonari Pass. At this juncture the *Ou reppan domei* alliance fell apart, leaving Aizu without an ally and forced to stand alone. Beginning in October, imperial forces besieged Tsuruga Castle, the seat of the Aizu domain. After a month-long battle, Aizu finally capitulated on November 6.

For the few thousand men who stubbornly refused to admit defeat the position in Sendai had already become untenable. On October 12, the former *shogun*'s navy, led by Enomoto Takeaki,[17] carried the remnants of the army from Sendai to Ezo (now known as Hokkaido). Here, Enomoto announced the establishment of the Ezo Republic, and petitioned the Meiji emperor to be allowed to develop Hokkaido as a *samurai* domain, but this was refused.

In April 1869 an imperial fleet and an infantry force of 7,000 men sailed north, and in the second week of May defeated Enomoto at the Battle of Hakodate. Goryokaku Fortress, the Ezo capital, was surrounded and surrendered on May 17, and the short-lived republic thereafter was no more.

The transitions that Japan underwent in the Meiji era are beyond the scope of this book. Hilary Conroy says that "in a single generation of historical time the Japanese of the Meiji era had to face the mind-wrenching and emotion-searing realization that their past way of life, seemingly tried and true for centuries, had become hopelessly inadequate."[18]

In the brave new society that was suddenly thrust upon the Japanese, there was to be no place for the estimated two million *samurai*.[19] Under the new government the *samurai* were stripped of their domains, their stipends, and their class privileges—including the right to carry swords in public.[20] Although the new government created a western-style, conscripted army, and some *samurai* entered its ranks as officers, openings were limited. Unemployment among former *samurai* was high, leading to unrest and scattered revolt, the most

save for a couple of surreptitiously purchased Gatling guns[14] and 2,000 modern French rifles in the hands of the Nagaoka. This parlous state of affairs is laid bare by the fact that attempts were made to build cannons made of wood reinforced with roping, and the use of large stones as projectiles.

In May 1868, Yamagata Aritomo and Kuroda Kiyotaka led an attempt by the imperial army to seize Niigata harbor,[15] in Echigo, to give them a northern port for the provisioning of the campaign against the newly organized *Ou reppan domei* in Aizu.[16] In the ensuing Battle of Hokuetsu, Makino Tadakuni, the *daimyo* of Nagaoka, inflicted substantial casualties on the imperial troops with

serious of which was the short-lived Satsuma Rebellion, led by Saigo Takamori in 1877. But by this time, the *samurai* as a class were in terminal decline—never again would they hold the status that their kind had once borne. But, although the age of the *samurai* disappeared forever, their spirit lives on with subsequent generations of Japanese, whom it continues to inspire and influence to this day.

Above: In 1877, nine years after the Meiji Restoration, a major rebellion in Kyushu concentrated the opposition of conservative elements to the westernization of Japan. The traditional forces, including, for example, *samurai*, infuriated at no longer being allowed to carry swords, were defeated by the new conscript army. Thousands were executed. Here the brave new officers in their western-style uniforms accept the surrender of un-uniformed rebels. *(Asian Art & Archaeology, Inc./Corbis)*

NOTES

1 M. William Steele *Edo in 1868. The View from Below* Monumenta Nipponica, Vol. 45, No. 2 (Summer, 1990), p.130

2 M. William Steele Against the Restoration. *Katsu Kaishu's Attempt to Reinstate the Tokugawa Family* Monumenta Nipponica, Vol. 36, No. 3 (Autumn, 1981), pp. 314

3 M. William Steele *Against the Restoration. Katsu Kaishu's Attempt to Reinstate the Tokugawa Family* Monumenta Nipponica, Vol. 36, No. 3 (Autumn, 1981), pp. 313-314

4 M. William Steele *Edo in 1868. The View from Below* Monumenta Nipponica, Vol. 45, No. 2 (Summer, 1990), p.132

5 M. William Steele *Against the Restoration. Katsu Kaishu's Attempt to Reinstate the Tokugawa Family* Monumenta Nipponica, Vol. 36, No. 3 (Autumn, 1981), pp. 299

6 Harold Bolitho *The Echigo War, 1868* Monumenta Nipponica, Vol. 34, No. 3 (Autumn, 1979), p. 261

7 For the whole course of the war, foreign powers including France and Britain intervened in the war, either supplying weapons, or military expertise, and sometimes both. For more on this see Harold Bolitho *The Echigo War, 1868* Monumenta Nip-

ponica, Vol. 34, No. 3 (Autumn, 1979), pp. 259-277

8 This stirred up xenophobic sentiment and led to several attacks on foreigners. In the so-called Sakai incident on March 8, 1868, eleven French sailors were killed by Tosa *samurai*. Fifteen days later, the armed delegation of Sir Harry Parkes, the British ambassador, was attacked by samurai while riding through Kyoto.

9 M. William Steele *Against the Restoration. Katsu Kaishu's Attempt to Reinstate the Tokugawa Family* Monumenta Nipponica, Vol. 36, No. 3 (Autumn, 1981), p. 301

10 For more on this man's role in the Boshin War see M. William Steele *Against the Restoration. Katsu Kaishu's Attempt to Reinstate the Tokugawa Family* Monumenta Nipponica, Vol. 36, No. 3 (Autumn, 1981), pp. 299-316

11 M. William Steele *Against the Restoration. Katsu Kaishu's Attempt to Reinstate the Tokugawa Family* Monumenta Nipponica, Vol. 36, No. 3 (Autumn, 1981), pp. 311-313

12 For more on this see John Breen *The Imperial Oath of April 1868: Ritual, Politics, and Power in the Restoration* Monumenta Nipponica, Vol. 51, No. 4 (Winter, 1996), pp. 407-429

13 Harold Bolitho *The Echigo War, 1868* Monu-

menta Nipponica, Vol. 34, No. 3 (Autumn, 1979), p. 266

14 From the German arms dealers Edward and Henry Schnell

15 Harold Bolitho *The Echigo War, 1868* Monumenta Nipponica, Vol. 34, No. 3 (Autumn, 1979), p. 266

16 Harold Bolitho *The Echigo War, 1868* Monumenta Nipponica, Vol. 34, No. 3 (Autumn, 1979), p. 266

17 Enomoto had refused to surrender the shogunate navy after the fall of Edo. See M. William Steele *Against the Restoration. Katsu Kaishu's Attempt to Reinstate the Tokugawa Family* Monumenta Nipponica, Vol. 36, No. 3 (Autumn, 1981), pp. 305-307

18 Introduction to *Japan in Transition Thought and Action in the Meiji Era 1868-1912* Ed. Hilary Conroy, Sandra T, W Davis and Wayne Patterson Fairleigh Dickinson University Press (1985)

19 See Sakeda Masatoshi, George Akita *The Samurai Disestablished. Abei Iwane and His Stipend* Monumenta Nipponica, Vol. 41, No. 3 (Autumn, 1986), pp. 299-330

20 This became law in 1876

INDEX

Figures in **bold** indicate the illustrations; figures in *italics* indicate the references in captions and the boxed text. Subheadings are arranged in chronological order.